THE AMERICAN DREAM

ALEXANDER GREEN
NEW YORK TIMES BESTSELLING AUTHOR

THE AMERICAN DREAM

WHY IT'S STILL ALIVE…
AND HOW TO ACHIEVE IT

WILEY

Copyright © 2026 by Oxford Financial Publishing, LLC. All rights reserved.

Published by John Wiley & Sons, Inc., Hoboken, New Jersey.
Published simultaneously in Canada.

No part of this publication may be reproduced, stored in a retrieval system, or transmitted in any form or by any means, electronic, mechanical, photocopying, recording, scanning, or otherwise, except as permitted under Section 107 or 108 of the 1976 United States Copyright Act, without either the prior written permission of the Publisher, or authorization through payment of the appropriate per-copy fee to the Copyright Clearance Center, Inc., 222 Rosewood Drive, Danvers, MA 01923, (978) 750-8400, fax (978) 750-4470, or on the web at www.copyright.com. Requests to the Publisher for permission should be addressed to the Permissions Department, John Wiley & Sons, Inc., 111 River Street, Hoboken, NJ 07030, (201) 748-6011, fax (201) 748-6008, or online at http://www.wiley.com/go/permission.

The manufacturer's authorized representative according to the EU General Product Safety Regulation is Wiley-VCH GmbH, Boschstr. 12, 69469 Weinheim, Germany, e-mail: Product_Safety@wiley.com.

Trademarks: Wiley and the Wiley logo are trademarks or registered trademarks of John Wiley & Sons, Inc. and/or its affiliates in the United States and other countries and may not be used without written permission. All other trademarks are the property of their respective owners. John Wiley & Sons, Inc. is not associated with any product or vendor mentioned in this book.

Limit of Liability/Disclaimer of Warranty: While the publisher and the authors have used their best efforts in preparing this work, including a review of the content of the work, neither the publisher nor the authors make any representations or warranties with respect to the accuracy or completeness of the contents of this work and specifically disclaim all warranties, including without limitation any implied warranties of merchantability or fitness for a particular purpose. Certain AI systems have been used in the creation of this work. No warranty may be created or extended by sales representatives, written sales materials or promotional statements for this work. The fact that an organization, website, or product is referred to in this work as a citation and/or potential source of further information does not mean that the publisher and authors endorse the information or services the organization, website, or product may provide or recommendations it may make. This work is sold with the understanding that the publisher is not engaged in rendering professional services. The advice and strategies contained herein may not be suitable for your situation. You should consult with a specialist where appropriate. Further, readers should be aware that websites listed in this work may have changed or disappeared between when this work was written and when it is read. Neither the publisher nor authors shall be liable for any loss of profit or any other commercial damages, including but not limited to special, incidental, consequential, or other damages.

For general information on our other products and services or for technical support, please contact our Customer Care Department within the United States at (800) 762-2974, outside the United States at (317) 572-3993 or fax (317) 572-4002.

Wiley also publishes its books in a variety of electronic formats. Some content that appears in print may not be available in electronic formats. For more information about Wiley products, visit our web site at www.wiley.com.

Library of Congress Cataloging-in-Publication Data is Available:

ISBN 9781394361663 (Cloth)
ISBN 9781394361670 (ePub)
ISBN 9781394361687 (ePDF)

Cover Design: Hannah Green
Author Photo: Courtesy of the Author

SKY10126895_092425

This book is dedicated to Rob Fix, not just a good man but my best man.

CONTENTS

Introduction — 1

Part 1 Proof That the American Dream Is Alive and Well — 13

Chapter 1: The American Dream Defined — 15

Chapter 2: What's So Great About America — 23

Chapter 3: Things Aren't What They Used to Be . . . and That's a Good Thing — 33

Chapter 4: Time Prices and the American Dream — 37

Chapter 5: The Future Is Better Than You Imagine — 49

Chapter 6: The Founders' Ideal of Happiness — 61

Chapter 7: Why Economic Inequality Is a Bogus Issue — 69

Chapter 8: The Enemies of the American Dream — 91

Part 2 How to Achieve the American Dream — 107

Chapter 9: Why the United States Has a Record Number of Millionaires — 109

Chapter 10: How Wealth Is Created — 119

Chapter 11: The Key to the American Dream: Personal Responsibility — 127

Chapter 12: How to Make Success a Habit — 135

Chapter 13: Part of the American Dream: Home Sweet Home — 149

Chapter 14: Savings: The Seed Corn of the American Dream — 157

Chapter 15: Investing: How to Sow What You'll Reap — 169

Chapter 16: The World's Simplest Investment System — 185

Chapter 17: Staying the Course to Achieve the Dream — 201

Part 3   How to Enjoy and Preserve the American Dream — 209

Chapter 18: The Power of Optimism to Attain the American Dream — 211

Chapter 19: To Live Fully . . . Aim to "Die with Zero" — 219

Chapter 20: There Is No True Wealth Without Health — 229

Chapter 21: Paying the American Dream Forward — 245

Chapter 22: Developing an Attitude of Gratitude — 253

Acknowledgments — *263*

Index — *267*

Introduction

> To be successful at anything, the truth is you don't have to be special. You just have to be what most people aren't: consistent, determined, and willing to work for it. No shortcuts.
>
> —Quarterback Tom Brady

While I've written five previous books, I don't recall the exact moment when the inspiration to undertake each project hit me. But I certainly remember the genesis of this one.

I was sitting on my brother-in-law's front porch, reading the paper, when a short news item caught my attention. A July 2024 *Wall Street Journal*/NORC poll found that belief in the attainability of the American Dream had fallen to a record low. Only 36% of Americans believed it was still possible – that hard work leads to success and upward mobility. Nearly half said the Dream was once possible but no longer is. Seventeen percent claimed it was never real.

That astonished me – and still does. Could it be that millions of immigrants risked their lives – and often their children's lives – to come here in search of opportunities that most Americans don't even believe exist?

Apparently so. A few months earlier, an ABC News/Ipsos poll showed just 27% of Americans still believed in the Dream. Another poll from Axios in late 2023 echoed the *Journal's* findings: 36%. That's a steep decline from 2012, when – even in the aftermath of the Great Recession – 52% still believed in the Dream.

I found this so disturbing that I wrote this book-length counterargument.

The American Dream – the pursuit of a better, richer, and fuller life, regardless of where we start – is our national ethos. It shapes our identity.

What makes us uniquely American is not just the possibility of upward mobility. It is the fundamental belief that this possibility exists *for all of us*. Unlike societies built on rigid class structures or inherited privilege, America was founded on the radical notion that merit, effort, and character matter more than bloodline or social status.

The Dream says, "Your future is not predetermined by your past. Your efforts matter. Your choices have consequences. You can be the author of your own story."

The American Dream encourages innovation, risk-taking, and resilience. It provides direction when the path is unclear and hope when obstacles seem insurmountable. Belief in it turns setbacks into steppingstones and failures into learning experiences.

It places the power of change squarely in the hands of the individual, and it provides the conviction that ordinary people can turn their vision into a reality. It is not a guarantee of outcomes but of opportunity. It doesn't promise that everyone will become wealthy or famous. It promises that everyone will have the chance to improve their circumstances through their own efforts.

In communities across our nation, the evidence of its enduring power is everywhere. The veterans who use their military training to start a cybersecurity firm. The teachers whose evening classes help them become a principal. The small business owners whose food trucks become a restaurant chain. Their success stories remind us that the Dream adapts and evolves but never disappears.

The American Dream remains vital because it addresses the deepest human needs: the need for purpose, the hunger for progress, and the desire to build something lasting for future generations.

In a world increasingly divided by cynicism and despair, the American Dream stands as a beacon of possibility. It has drawn millions to our shores and has guided millions more who were born here. It is who we are as a people. It fueled America's past, unifies our present, and inspires our future.

It survives because it speaks to something eternal in the human spirit: the belief that tomorrow can be better than today, and that we have the power to make it so. That belief is part of what makes the United States exceptional.

That is what the Dream means to me. But what does it mean to those polled, especially the ones who don't believe it is attainable?

In my research, I found that conceptions of the Dream vary. Yet most fall into one of two broad categories:

- **The traditional view.** This is the classic idea: that anyone – regardless of background – can rise as far as their talents, ambition, and persistence will take them.
- **The contemporary view.** This one has a financial tilt: "I can afford to buy a home, raise a family, maintain some work-life balance, and retire comfortably."

Both views are reasonable. And both are achievable for anyone willing and able to work, save, and invest.

So why all the pessimism? I've learned it's partly a matter of perception.

Despite living in the most prosperous, free, and opportunity-rich nation in human history, many Americans – especially younger ones – have a surprisingly dim view of their country. According to a 2025 Gallup poll, a record-low 58% of US adults say they are "extremely" (41%) or "very" (17%) proud to be an American. (That's down from 90% in 2004.) Among Gen Z (born 1997–2012), that number plummets to just 47%. That's not just a generational gap. It's a crisis of confidence.

America has real challenges. But the souring of national sentiment isn't driven by facts as much as by narratives. When every institution you trust — your school, the media, even your political party — emphasizes America's sins over its successes, it's easy to internalize the message that this country is fundamentally flawed — and the Dream is no longer real.

So who's lost faith? Mainly two groups: lower-income Americans and young people. (And yes, there's quite a bit of overlap.) Many are barely staying afloat — juggling rent, bills, and basic needs. But in most cases, they simply don't know how or where to begin. That's not a moral failing. It's a knowledge gap. Most of us were never taught to budget, save, or invest — by schools or parents.

Younger folks especially need to hear this: financial stress is usually temporary. As your skills and experience grow, so will your income. Generally speaking, the older someone is the richer they are. The difference between what I earned starting out and what I earned at the peak of my career? Night and day. And my story is far from unique.

Time is the great advantage of youth. They may not have much money, but they have a lot of years ahead of them. That's critical when they start investing. Compounding is a powerful force. But it needs time to work its magic.

Older Americans, it turns out, are far more likely to believe in the American Dream — perhaps because they've seen it play out, even if imperfectly. More educated individuals tend to believe in it, too, likely because education is linked to higher income — and higher income creates more possibilities.

Black Americans are less likely than whites to believe in the Dream, which no doubt reflects our nation's long history of discrimination. Still, conditions have improved dramatically since the 1960s. And the principles I'll discuss in this book apply equally across race, gender, and class.

Democrats are more pessimistic than Republicans, perhaps because progressives focus more on perceived structural unfairness.

Interestingly, women are slightly more optimistic about the Dream than men — perhaps because men tend to equate it with career and income, while women often associate it with family, security, and fulfillment. Once again, the women appear to be on to something.

My goal with this book is to better align perceptions with reality. I wrote it for three kinds of readers:

- **Disbelievers.** They don't believe the Dream is real because they don't know what to do, aren't doing it, or don't realize they are already living it. (That last claim is provocative but stick with me.)
- **Frustrated Dreamers.** They know the Dream exists, but it feels out of reach. In the pages ahead, I'll provide them with the knowledge – and a concrete action plan – that will enable them to move forward.
- **Dream Achievers.** They've lived some version of the Dream themselves. But they worry about their kids and grandkids. Or they want to help other Americans find the path.

Why do I feel so strongly about the Dream that I felt compelled to write this book? Because this country stands on three pillars:

- The Declaration of Independence, which declares that we are a free people whose rights preexist government
- The US Constitution, which both empowers and limits government to protect those rights
- The American Dream, which is how we exercise our right to pursue happiness

Without these three pillars, the structure falters. (Without them, we are not the same nation. Not *the same people*.) The Dream isn't some sentimental slogan. It's part of our national identity – and the reason why millions throughout history risked everything to get here.

America is not perfect. It never has been. But it remains the best environment on Earth for ordinary people to build extraordinary lives.

Our markets are open. Our culture rewards effort, talent, and innovation. Our financial system allows for investing, borrowing, and wealth creation. Our freedoms protect dissent, belief, expression, and movement.

Where else do people from every continent still line up — literally and figuratively — for a chance to participate? The United States doesn't promise equal outcomes. It promises an opportunity to rise. That is the foundation of the American Dream.

You might be wondering, "Who are *you* to insist that the Dream is alive — and tell others how to achieve it?" It's a fair question.

Over the last four decades, I've dedicated my career to showing Americans how to reach their most important financial goals. I worked as a registered investment advisor, research analyst, and portfolio manager for the first 16 years. And for the past 24, I've been the Chief Investment Strategist of The Oxford Club, a group of more than 160,000 individuals in the United States and around the world who share a common goal: achieving and maintaining financial independence.

(These Members understand that wealth is not about having a lot of money. It's about choosing how you want to live your life.)

Along the way, I wrote *The Gone Fishin' Portfolio*, a *New York Times* bestseller on financial freedom. (The updated 2023 edition includes a new foreword by longtime subscriber Bill O'Reilly.) I've also written three essay collections about living a richer life: *The Secret of Shelter Island*, *Beyond Wealth*, and *An Embarrassment of Riches*.

In many ways, I feel I've lived the Dream. I have two amazing parents who are still healthy and living independently at 95 and 96. I have a loving partner of 34 years (my wife, Karen), and two adult children — Hannah and David — who are living happy, productive lives. I have close friends, good health, and plenty of interests. I enjoy my work — and my colleagues. That's why I haven't retired, even though I could have long ago. I'm wealthy — not just in assets, but in the things that matter.

You might look at this summary and counter that I haven't *achieved* the Dream so much as just been incredibly fortunate. And I won't disagree. Even if I had always made the best choices — and I certainly didn't — things could have turned out very differently with my marriage, my kids, my career, or my health. Life really *isn't* fair. Some people have better luck than others. And, as we'll see, that pertains not just to the outcome of our choices but to the circumstances — and even the era — we are born into.

While both good and bad luck have an unquantifiable effect on everyone's life, my saving and investment experience bears an uncanny resemblance to that of tens of millions of other high-net-worth individuals. And not because we all came from favorable circumstances.

I was born — with no great genetic gifts — into a solidly middle-class family. I was not a great student. I did not go to private schools. (As a kid, I didn't even *know anyone* who attended a private school.) I did not study at an elite university. I did not earn any scholarships, academic honors, or advanced degrees. I had no family connections, no mentor, and no professional network. I have never started a company, run a company, or held a management position *ever*. I was in my mid-40s before I earned my first salary. (Until then, I worked only straight commission jobs, also known as the "no deals, no meals" program.) I have never paid anyone for career advice, investment advice, or tax advice. And I have never received a dime of inheritance from anyone.

Yet I became a multimillionaire while still a young man — and continue to compound my wealth. My point is not to brag. (Indeed, there is nothing on this list — aside from the financial freedom I obtained — that is the least bit laudatory.) I just want readers to understand that my net worth did not accrue because I'm an exceptional person or came from exceptional circumstances. It happened because the principles of wealth creation work. I adhered to them. And the good news is they're available to everyone.

Achieving some level of economic security is essential to living your dreams. But here's the hard truth: most Americans are not on track. A recent LendingClub survey found that 62% of Americans live paycheck to paycheck, including 44% of those earning over $100,000. Thirty-seven percent couldn't cover a $400 emergency. Twenty-one percent have no savings. And for Americans aged 55–64, the median retirement savings is just $6,400. (Twenty-seven percent have none.)

This isn't hopeless — but it is urgent. If you got yourself into a tough financial situation, you can get yourself out. But the first step is *believing in the Dream* itself.

A negative mindset has many consequences, none of them good. It makes us reluctant to strive to improve our circumstances, resulting in financial stagnation and disappointment. It discourages entrepreneurship and job changes, further reducing opportunities for economic advancement. It leads to widespread frustration, particularly if we feel excluded from upward mobility.

This perceived lack of upward mobility, in turn, discourages hard work, innovation, and investment in education or skills development. It creates resentment, especially among those without college degrees or access to high-paying jobs. It leads to pessimism, stress, and mental health challenges. It creates disillusionment and even lowers birth rates, as many Americans feel that they cannot afford children.

If you don't believe attaining your dreams is realistic, why strive or sacrifice to achieve them? In the end, cynical thoughts become a self-fulfilling prophecy. What a terrible – and unnecessary – way to go through life, without hope, without optimism, without ambition. Especially since this view is unwarranted.

The *Wall Street Journal* poll defined the Dream as "If you work hard, you'll get ahead." Yet hard work alone isn't enough. You could labor hard for 30 years or more, but if you never save or invest, it's unlikely you'll live the Dream. What it takes is financial discipline, smart risk-taking, and a plan. We'll discuss all these things here. And, as you'll see, you can start small.

Other factors have reduced belief in the Dream in recent years. Inflation hit hard. Wages stagnated while stocks and housing soared – benefiting asset owners but hurting renters and non-investors. A third of Americans don't own a home. And over 40% don't own stocks. To them, a booming real estate market or S&P 500 means nothing.

Real median earnings for full-time workers declined 1.6% in 2023, while those with only a high school diploma saw an even steeper drop of 3.3%.

In short, Americans dealt with stagnant incomes, higher interest rates, and sticker shock on essentials like food, gas, and utilities. No wonder so many were sour on the economy – and the Dream – especially those on the low end of the economic ladder who can least afford price increases.

But let's zoom out. Since 1960, inflation-adjusted incomes have more than doubled. And today's income buys a dizzying array of high-quality goods and services.

However, income alone isn't wealth. If you earn six figures and spend six figures, you're just standing still. Wealth consists of assets that can generate passive income. Assets are what give you freedom – to weather setbacks, deal with emergencies, and retire on your own terms.

Americans everywhere can take responsibility for their financial future by following a battle-tested plan that allows them to save, invest, and compound their money until it provides complete financial security. How much that takes will depend on a household's chosen lifestyle. But, in the pages ahead, I'll reveal what I call "the world's simplest investment system," one that you can use straight away.

No one can live the Dream with constant financial stress. You may want to teach elementary school, do social work, serve in the Navy, or become a jazz singer. But every lifestyle requires a cash flow, so money will always be part of the equation.

You've heard that the best things in life are free. That money can't buy happiness. That it won't win you true love or genuine friendship. These things are true. But they're not the whole story. You can't reach your potential or live life to the fullest if you spend your days worrying about money.

Money is independence. It liberates you from want, from work that is drudgery, from relationships that confine you. No one is truly free who is a slave to their job, creditors, circumstances, or overhead.

Money determines the kind of house you live in and the neighborhood your kids grow up in. If you're sick, it can mean the difference between a good doctor and an amazing doctor. If you need an attorney, it's the difference between using an ambulance chaser and getting the best legal representation money can buy.

Wealth is the great equalizer. It doesn't matter if you're a man or a woman, Black or white, young or old, gay or straight, handsome or homely, educated or not. If you have money, you have power – in the best sense.

Wealth is freedom, security, and peace of mind. It allows you to do and be what you want, to support worthy causes and help those closest to you. It enables you to follow your dreams, to spend your life the way *you* choose.

Money gives you dignity. It gives you freedom. It gives you choices. Money matters. You have a right – and, I'd argue, a responsibility – to achieve some level of financial independence.

This book will help you do that.

In Part 1, I'll prove the Dream is alive.
In Part 2, I'll show you exactly how to achieve it.
In Part 3, I'll address the obstacles you're likely to face – and discuss some important things that money can't buy.

Achieving the American Dream is simple. But that doesn't mean it's easy. (If it were, everyone would be living it.) Yet the path is straightforward. And if you enjoy a good challenge, I hope you'll embrace it.

There are two main points I want to emphasize in this book. The first is that you cannot achieve your dreams if you don't sincerely believe it's possible. Unfortunately, a lot of Americans have adopted a catastrophizing mentality that sees all our problems as endemic: Our country's ideals are a sham. Society is a cesspool of injustice. Climate change is unstoppable. Racism is forever. And the American Dream is a fiction. Newcomers from around the world just haven't gotten the message.

It takes a long time – perhaps a lifetime – to develop this maladaptive mindset and no writer can overcome it with a few anecdotes. It takes a sustained argument, which you'll find throughout the book. Believing that depressing cultural narrative destroys your sense of agency. It makes it harder to live ambitiously. It also happens to be dead wrong. So I'll take aim at those who promote it to achieve their own ends.

My other main point is in our modern society – heck, in any society – it is not possible to live your dreams and at the same time be "bad at money." You probably didn't receive the financial education you deserved. But you can't let that hold you back.

You need to learn money like a language – and I'll share the most important principles in the chapters ahead.

My goal with this book is to provide a universal blueprint that anyone can use – and build on – to achieve financial freedom and live the life of their dreams. Is it the only way? Certainly not. But it is a widely proven way – and available to everyone, regardless of their starting point.

A final note . . . when friends and business colleagues discovered I was writing this book, many of them offered advice. Most of it – indeed all of it – was quite good. However, many made suggestions about how the country needs to change – or how institutions need to be reformed – to make it easier for Americans to succeed. I didn't disagree with these suggestions. But this book isn't about public policy. It's isn't about what Congress should do. It's about what *you* should do.

You can't reform the public education system. Or rewrite your state's occupational licensing laws. But you can write your own story. The question here is not "How should the nation change?" but "What can I change, starting today, to achieve my most important goals?"

My objective is straightforward: to help you live the American Dream . . . however *you define it.*

PART 1

Proof That the American Dream Is Alive and Well

CHAPTER 1
The American Dream Defined

Create the highest, grandest vision possible for your life, because you become what you believe.

—Entrepreneur Oprah Winfrey

What proof do we have that the American Dream still exists – and what's the most reliable way to achieve it?

After spending four decades researching, writing, and speaking on this subject, I know that the Dream is real. Millions of Americans are living proof of it. Whether you're just starting out, trying to get back on track, or looking to help others, I want to help guide you forward.

When I talk to skeptics, I hear similar arguments. Many are battling tough circumstances. But they've also absorbed the media's relentlessly negative narrative, echoed by Hollywood and parts of academia.

It goes like this: America is irredeemably racist, sexist, and unjust. The economy is rigged. The middle class is shrinking. Wages haven't kept up with inflation. Violent crime is surging. Pollution is worsening. Climate change is making the planet uninhabitable. And our free-market system — the supposed root of it all — allows a fortunate few to get rich while everyone else gets poorer.

That description is not just wide of the mark. It's a *Matrix*-like distortion of reality.

It has less to do with reality and more to do with ideology, selective reporting, and an education system that prioritizes grievance over gratitude.

Let's start with the environment. Young people routinely say climate change will render the planet uninhabitable within their lifetimes. But as Bjorn Lomborg, president of the Copenhagen Consensus Center, has consistently shown, this alarmist narrative isn't backed by data. Yes, the climate is changing — but the human race is not facing extinction. In fact, climate-related deaths have *plummeted* over the last century, even as global temperatures have modestly increased.

Why? Because of economic growth, technological innovation, and improved infrastructure. Wealthier societies are better equipped to deal with extreme weather. If we truly care about the environment, the best strategy isn't panic — it's progress.

Michael Shellenberger, a former environmental activist and *Time* magazine "Hero of the Environment," makes a similar case. In *Apocalypse Never*, he points out that the modern environmental movement has abandoned science in favor of fear. Nuclear power, for example, is the safest and most reliable form of low-carbon energy, yet many activists oppose it.

The pessimism doesn't stop with climate. Many young Americans believe that systemic racism is more entrenched than ever. Yet Heather Mac Donald, a fellow at the Manhattan Institute, cites mountains of data that show the American legal system, police forces, and public institutions are not engaged in widespread discrimination.

Yes, disparities exist. But disparities are not the same as discrimination. As Thomas Sowell has argued for decades, unequal outcomes are not necessarily evidence of unequal treatment. Cultures, choices, and incentives matter.

Sowell, in particular, cuts through much of today's intellectual fog. A Stanford economist and author of more than 30 books, he has consistently warned about the dangers of historical ignorance and ideological bias.

His work reminds us that wealth is not the default condition of mankind — poverty is. America didn't "fail" because not everyone is rich. It *succeeded* by lifting more people out of poverty than any other nation in history. The average American today lives better than royalty did a century ago.

If we want a generation that believes in the future, we need to start telling the truth about the present. Because despair is paralyzing.

For example, ask the average American about violent crime today, and they'll likely tell you that it is spiraling out of control. But that perception simply doesn't match reality.

According to the FBI's Uniform Crime Reporting data, violent crime in the US has fallen sharply over the last three decades. The national violent crime rate peaked in 1991 at 758 incidents per 100,000 people. By 2023, that rate had dropped to just 380 per 100,000 — a 50% decline. Murder, robbery, rape, and aggravated assault are all significantly lower than they were in the early 1990s.

Even recent headlines about surging crime rates during the pandemic have been misleading. Yes, homicides rose in 2020 and 2021, driven by COVID-era disruptions, economic stress, and reduced policing. But the 2023 data shows a major reversal. Homicides fell by 12% nationwide — the largest single-year drop in American history. Robbery and burglary also declined.

So why do so many people think things are getting worse? Two reasons: media and memory.

The news cycle thrives on fear. A single high-profile crime — especially one caught on video — can dominate headlines for days and give the impression that violence is rampant. Social media amplifies this effect, creating a constant stream of shocking clips with no context about long-term trends.

Meanwhile, personal memory is short. Most Americans don't remember — or weren't alive during — the true crime waves of the 1970s, 1980s, and early 1990s, when cities like New York, Los Angeles, and Chicago saw double or triple the number of homicides they see today. Those were the years when people really were afraid to walk alone at night.

Today, Americans are safer than they've been in generations. But you wouldn't know it from the coverage – or the political rhetoric. Violent crime is in a long-term cycle of decline. That's not an opinion. It's a fact.

Turning to the economy, real wages stagnated during the early 2020s due to high inflation. But the tight labor market and rising asset values have since driven household net worth and income to record levels. According to the US Census Bureau, median household income reached a record $80,810 in 2023, up from $77,540 the year before.

Many believe the middle class is shrinking because Americans are getting poorer. In fact, the opposite is true: more are moving into higher income brackets. As of 2023, about 39% of US households earned $100,000 or more – the highest ever recorded. According to Pew Research, the share of Americans in upper-income households nearly doubled from 11% in 1971 to 19% in 2021.

Globalization and automation have made certain low-skill jobs obsolete. But the solution isn't to protect unskilled labor – it's to encourage skill building. In a knowledge-based economy, education and specialization are the surest paths to upward mobility.

Yes, the highly educated are building wealth faster. But the gains aren't limited to the top. Real incomes have more than tripled since the 1960s. And each income quintile has risen, just at different rates.

Still, even among educated Americans, there's a surprising pessimism about mobility. I saw it firsthand in a debate I had a few years ago with Dr. Gregory Clark, a Cambridge- and Harvard-educated economist, at FreedomFest in Las Vegas.

The debate proposition? "The American Dream Is Over for Most Americans."

It was an Oxford-style debate. We polled the audience before we began to see where they stood. Then we polled them again at the end – following a robust Q&A session – to see if they were moved one way or the other by our arguments.

Before the discussion, the audience – like the broader public – was split. Yet Dr. Clark presented an austere view. He argued that birth circumstances and luck determine destiny, that mobility in the United States is no better than in "socialized" nations like Sweden or even autocracies like China. He claimed, "The American Dream is a complete myth."

His core metric? Intergenerational income correlation – how closely children's earnings match their parents'. If the number is 1, there's no mobility. If it's 0, children's outcomes are completely untethered from their parents'. His claim: the United States sits near the middle of the pack, no better than European welfare states or even preindustrial societies. He insisted that "the idea of the American Dream just doesn't hold. It's an *illusion*."

Yet his comparison was deeply flawed. China, despite economic reforms, remains authoritarian. Advancement often depends on loyalty to the communist regime. In preindustrial England, wealth was typically inherited or seized. To suggest America – where talent, grit, and risk-taking drive opportunity – is no different strains credibility.

Let's look at global context. According to the World Bank, a $60,000 annual income places you in the top 1% of earners worldwide. In 2023, nearly two-thirds of US households earned more than that. Americans often complain about domestic inequality, while ignoring how affluent the average American is by global standards.

According to the OECD, the average net-adjusted disposable income per capita in the United States is 68% higher than the OECD average. That means American households have significantly more spending power than those in other wealthy nations.

According to the 2025 "UBS Global Wealth Report," global wealth rose by 4.6% in 2024. Yet it wasn't evenly distributed across regions. In the continuation of a long-term trend, Americans aren't just getting richer – they're doing it faster, smarter, and in greater numbers than anywhere else on the planet.

More than 379,000 Americans became millionaires in 2024. That's over 1,000 a day. The United States now has 23.8 million millionaires, nearly 40% of the global total. (Mainland China is a distant second with 6.3 million millionaires. And that's a nation of over 1.4 billion people.)

It's not just American hedge fund managers and tech founders getting rich. UBS hailed the rise of "everyday millionaires," individuals with $1 to $5 million in investable assets. That's a powerful testament to long-term opportunity.

However, at the end of our debate, Dr. Clark concluded: "There is no American Dream. And there is no special place in the world that American liberty represents."

When it was my turn, I presented evidence to the contrary, much of which I'll share in Chapter 2. We rank among the top nations in economic freedom. We are a meritocracy. Advancement is driven by effort, not patronage. Failure isn't fatal here. It's seen as part of progress.

Clark claimed that social mobility is weak. But in fact, most Americans climb the income ladder as they age and gain skills. Workers move from entry-level jobs to mid-tier roles to higher-paying ones. That's economic mobility in action.

Economists Phil Gramm, Robert Ekelund, and John Early wrote a superb book called *The Myth of American Inequality*. It examines how government data often undercounts income by ignoring taxes, transfers, and benefits.

Using Census, Treasury, and Pew data, they show the following:

- Real incomes have risen across most time periods.
- All income groups have gained over time – especially those who work, learn, and persist.
- Intergenerational mobility is high, with nearly 90% of adult success determined by effort, not inheritance.
- A full 93% of children born into the bottom income quintile surpass their parents.

Their conclusion? "Economic mobility is alive, powerful, and widespread in America today."

Many haven't yet reached financial independence. But the opportunity exists. The path is there.

I'm no professional debater. Yet after my debate with Dr. Clark, not one hand went up in favor of the resolution that the American Dream is over. The organizer, Mark Skousen, called it the first unanimous wipeout in over 20 years of debates at FreedomFest.

Not everyone is thriving, of course. Some face daunting obstacles. Others are stuck due to bad circumstances, poor decisions, or a lack of knowledge. But millions have overcome far worse to achieve far more.

The American Dream is real. But it is not guaranteed. It is not an entitlement. You don't collect your Dream at some government office.

It is an aspiration . . . an achievement . . . a journey. Something you build with discipline, resilience, and purpose. But it all starts with believing in the possibility.

In the next chapter, we'll look at what sets America apart – and talk about how you can use this knowledge as a springboard to achieving your own dreams.

CHAPTER 2
What's So Great About America

> America. It is the only place where miracles not only happen, but where they happen all the time.
>
> —Novelist Thomas Wolfe

One reason many Americans doubt the Dream is that they've lost faith in the country itself.

They've been inundated by academics, journalists, and pundits who frame the United States as a deeply flawed nation – one in decline, unworthy of admiration. This narrative has gained traction, particularly among younger Americans. Yet this national self-loathing seems uniquely American.

A few years ago, I took a tour of Italy – my favorite country outside the United States – with friends and colleagues. We visited Milan, Verona, Lake Como, Venice, and many lovely farms and vineyards in the Tuscan countryside. Along the way, we learned a great deal about that country's historic past.

At lunch with our guide in Milan, I said, "You've told us a lot about the incredible achievements of the Roman empire, about how Latin became the West's foundational language, about your country's amazing Renaissance writers, painters, sculptors, poets, and composers, and about your unique and beautiful culture today."

She nodded her head and thanked me.

"But let me ask . . . do some Italians argue that these achievements don't really represent your country? That what *truly* defines Italy is that the Roman empire subdued and enslaved other peoples, that your nation was the birthplace of fascism under Mussolini, and that you were an ally of Adolph Hitler in World War II?"

She cocked her head in disbelief. "Of course not," she said. "We all know those things. But why would anyone argue that they *define* us?"

"Exactly," I said. "Now let me tell you what's been happening in the United States."

I explained how a steady drumbeat of criticism from certain corners of education and media has convinced many Americans that we are a shameful, unjust nation – that our past sins outweigh our present achievements, and that the American Dream is over.

Even the founders have been vilified. Statues of Washington, Jefferson, and Lincoln have been torn down. Some claim these men were nothing more than white supremacists with retrograde views.

Of course, slavery, conquest, and male domination existed in every civilization for thousands of years. That doesn't excuse them. But insisting that historical figures "really should have known better" ignores the fact that we are all *people of our time*.

Politics is the art of the possible. If our revolution in 1776 had to include equal rights for slaves, Native Americans, and women, it couldn't have happened. Even white men without property were denied the vote.

It took many decades, a war between the states, women's suffrage, civil rights, and gay rights to build a more inclusive society and begin to fulfill the American ideal of liberty and equality.

It's easy to look back and see what the founders got wrong. But they got some monumental things right. They laid the groundwork for the most inclusive, dynamic, and powerful nation the world has ever seen.

Fireworks fill the skies each Fourth of July because our nation's birth was *revolutionary* – not in the sense of replacing one set of rulers with another but in placing political authority in the hands of the people.

Our Declaration of Independence is a timeless statement of inherent rights, the true purposes of government and the limits of political authority. Our core beliefs are enshrined in the Constitution and Bill of Rights, the longest-serving foundation of liberty in history.

Reflect on just a few things that make the United States an exceptional nation:

- Americans are just 4.3% of the world's population, yet we create almost a quarter of its annual economic output.
- Our economy is no. 1 by a huge margin. It is larger than nos. 2 and 3 – China and Japan – combined.
- We are the world leader in technological innovation. The telephone, television, airplane, and internet were all invented here. So were blood transfusions, heart transplants, and countless vaccines.
- If we are no different from other Western democracies, why were transformative companies like Apple, Google, Facebook, Amazon, Microsoft, Twitter, Netflix, Snapchat, Instagram, PayPal, Tesla, Uber, Moderna, and Nvidia – to name just a few – all founded here?
- The United States accounts for 22% of the patents in force abroad, up from 19% in 2004. That's more than any other nation.
- Our space probes and orbiting telescopes explore and explain the cosmos. We put astronauts on the moon more than half a century ago. And recent launches by SpaceX and Blue Origin demonstrate the technological prowess of our private sector.

- The US dollar is the world's reserve currency. (This "exorbitant privilege" lowers our borrowing costs, reduces exchange-rate risk, and increases access to capital.)
- The American military is the primary defender of the free world. (See World War I and World War II for details.)
- American agriculture is the envy of the world. Our farmers now grow five times as much corn as they did in the 1930s – on 20% less land. The yield per acre has grown sixfold in the past 70 years.
- For decades, experts warned us that we had to end "our addiction to foreign oil." Yet thanks to new technologies – like hydraulic fracturing and horizontal drilling – we are not just the world's leading oil producer but a net exporter.
- The United States is home to 8 of the world's top 10 universities, according to the latest QS World University Rankings.
- American workers are the most productive in the world, consistently ranking at the top in output per hour worked.
- American entrepreneurship is unmatched. The United States ranks among the easiest places in the world to start and scale a business – just ask any immigrant founder of a billion-dollar startup.
- The United States is first in pharmaceutical innovation, accounting for more than half of all new drugs introduced globally over the past decade. Americans have access to more treatments than any country in the world.
- The United States also leads the world in science, engineering, entertainment, and the arts.
- Since 1950, about 40% of all Nobel Prize laureates have been Americans. That accounts for more winners than the next five countries combined.
- No nation has produced more Olympic champions.
- No nation attracts more immigrants, more students, or more foreign investment capital.
- Americans adopt more foreign-born children each year than any other nation.
- And Americans are the most charitable people on Earth, both in the aggregate and per capita. The Giving USA Foundation recently reported that US charitable donations climbed 6.3% to a record $592.5 billion in 2024.

How did our small republican experiment transform and dominate global culture and the world economy? Geography played a big role. Buffered by two oceans and a rugged frontier, we had plenty of cheap land and vast natural resources. (But then so did countries like Russia and Brazil.)

We have opened our arms to tens of millions of immigrants who dreamed of a better life and helped to build this country. In the process, we have developed an astounding capacity for tolerance.

The mainstream media's meta-narrative – that we are a racist, sexist, homophobic nation – is not based in fact. Yes, there is a gulf between the median household income and net worth of Black and white households in the United States. But that disparity is not due solely to racism. Other factors include family formation, quality of schools, educational attainment, homeownership, savings rates, and levels of equity ownership. (I'll discuss this in greater detail in Chapter 9.)

Rates of interracial marriage have risen sharply. Nearly one in five newlyweds in 2022 were interethnic, according to Pew Research.

As of 2025, the mayors of America's three largest cities are Black. Two Supreme Court justices are Black. The racial makeup of Congress roughly mirrors the nation as a whole. And the United States remains the only majority-white nation to elect a Black president. Not just once but twice.

The average woman in the United States makes less than the average man, true. But that is not de facto evidence of discrimination. Studies reveal that after accounting for vocation, specialization, education, experience, and hours worked, the difference between what men and women earn is negligible. It is against federal law to pay a woman less than a man – or a Black person less than a white person – for the same work. (And we have no shortage of tort attorneys.)

The vast majority of Americans support same-sex marriage. And gay couples have average higher median household incomes than heterosexual ones – due in part to higher workforce participation and lower child-rearing costs.

I'm not suggesting that other nations don't have proud histories, unique traditions, or beautiful cultures. I'm delighted when I get a chance to visit South Africa, Australia, or Argentina, not to mention cities like Paris or Rome. There's a lot to love about day-to-day life in other countries.

However, people around the world don't talk about the French Dream or the Chinese Dream. Only one nation is universally recognized as the Land of Opportunity. That's because America cultivates, celebrates, and rewards the habits that make men and women successful. Anyone with ambition and grit can move up the economic ladder. Everyone has a chance to improve their lot, regardless of circumstances.

Jamie Dimon, CEO of JPMorgan Chase, put it this way in the *Wall Street Journal*:

> *The U.S. has the best universities, hospitals and businesses on the planet, and our people are the most entrepreneurial and innovative in the world, from the factory floor to the executive suite. We have by far the widest, deepest and most transparent capital markets, and a citizenry with an unparalleled work ethic and "can do" attitude.*

American ingenuity, technology, and capital markets have created dramatic improvements in communications, transportation, manufacturing, computing, retailing, food production, construction, health care, finance, pharmaceuticals, robotics, sensors, artificial intelligence, genetics, 3D printing, and dozens of other industries. These have benefited citizens not just here but all over the world.

Britain's *Economist* magazine recently published a report on American economic performance over the last three decades. It concluded that the US economy isn't just dominant. That dominance is *accelerating*.

In 1990, the US economy accounted for 40% of the gross domestic product of the G7 nations. By 2022, it accounted for 58%. In 1990, American income per person was 24% higher than the income per person in Western Europe. Today it is about 30% higher.

The productivity rate since 2010 of US workers is double that of the euro zone, Canada, and Britain. And US-led artificial intelligence innovation will widen the productivity chasm even more.

The United States has a number of structural advantages. High taxes and overregulation of labor and business formation in other countries have been detrimental to long-term growth.

Plus, US financial markets are the only ones big enough to absorb global capital flows. Other countries would need to build liquid, scalable equity, and debt markets to attract global capital the way we do.

That's not likely to happen anytime soon. Nvidia is larger than the entire London Stock Exchange. Apple is bigger than the Paris Stock Exchange. Amazon is bigger than the German Stock Exchange. Meta is bigger than the Nordic Stock Exchange. And Microsoft is bigger than the Swiss Stock Exchange.

The United States accounts for 64% of the global equity market capitalization and 41% of global fixed income. Approximately 58% of foreign exchange reserves are in dollars. And every business day, over half of all international transactions are settled in dollars.

The amount of seed and venture capital to fund innovations isn't available elsewhere. (That's why the future is invented here.) And more than 60% of US households own equities in their brokerage or retirement accounts, an investment level unmatched in other markets.

That means Americans don't just have higher incomes and lower taxes. They also have greater wealth. No country has more millionaires than the United States. The Federal Reserve reported in 2022 that 12.4% of American households have a net worth of $1 million or more. If you include home equity, the percentage is close to 18%.

According to Statista, the average financial wealth per US adult is $580,000. The average financial wealth per European adult is less than $94,000. (And the Census Bureau recently reported that American poverty recently hit an all-time low.)

Our economic recovery from the COVID-19 pandemic was the strongest of any major economy. The American stock market has generated the world's highest returns over the last three decades. If you had invested $10,000 in the S&P 500 in 1990, you would have had $251,000 at the end of 2024. If you had invested $10,000 instead in a global equity index that excludes US stocks, you would have about $48,000 over the same period.

In short, Americans earn more income, have greater assets, and enjoy higher investment returns. That's because the American brand of capitalism is tilted toward dynamism, with freer markets and smaller welfare states.

As you can see, the notion that America is an exceptional nation is not, as some would argue, just a crude strain of patriotism. Our country embodies timeless ideals, an optimistic attitude, and an enthusiastic endorsement of the pursuit of happiness.

Yes, we've made mistakes along the way and face no shortage of problems and challenges today. But the birth of the United States ranks among *the greatest events* in world history.

Is it all perfect? No. But the system works – and continues to lift people up.

Some will hear these facts and concede that the country is in better shape than generally acknowledged. Yet they'll still insist that we live in a horrible world at a terrible time – and it won't be long before we're all circling the drain.

(Many young people believe the outlook is so dire that they are forgoing having children. That can be a big mistake, even when money is tight. Babies are worth it even when raising them is hard, which is most of the time. Don't let finances stop you from starting a family. Trust me, the money will take care of itself.)

It's not hard to see why so many Americans are pessimistic. Turn on the news and you'll hear stories of war, terrorism, crime, disease, natural disasters, corruption, domestic violence, poverty, economic inequality, nuclear proliferation, environmental degradation, and political dysfunction in Washington.

Polls show Americans believe the American Dream is fading, our children face limited opportunities, and the country – if not civilization itself – is decidedly on the wrong track. Yet this dour perspective – one recycled 24/7 by the national media – is a gross distortion of the world we live in.

The problems mentioned are real. But they don't define the state of the nation. That's why I like to share what broadcaster Paul Harvey used to call "the rest of the story."

Why is this important? Let me give you an analogy.

Imagine that I showed a roomful of grade-school students a video compilation of a former basketball player. In clip after clip, he can't do anything right. He shoots air balls, blows layups, misses rebounds, drops passes, clanks free throws, double-dribbles, and steps out of bounds.

When the film is over, I tell my young audience, "This player's name is Michael Jordan. What do you think of him?" Most – knowing nothing more about him – would reply, "Jeez, he's terrible."

Everyone else – and especially basketball fans over a certain age – would lose their minds. Not because Michael Jordan never shot air balls, dropped passes, or clanked free throws. He did . . . many times. But the video – though made up entirely of real incidents – is a gross distortion of the man's abilities and career. In short, I selected *real events* to create a *false impression*.

The national media – through its prism of negativity – does the same every day. The news is a highly nonrandom sample – run 24/7 – of the worst things that happened each day in a world of more than eight billion people. Meanwhile, good news gets ignored or pushed aside.

For example, every day, 137,000 people around the globe escape extreme poverty. (This has been the trend for more than 30 years now.) Life spans are getting longer. Living standards are improving. Literacy rates are increasing. Educational attainment has never been greater. IQs – believe it or not – are rising. More people than ever have health insurance. More patients are surviving cancer and heart disease. (According to the American Cancer Society, cancer deaths have dropped 34% over the past two decades. That translates to 4.5 million deaths avoided, thanks to fewer smokers, better treatments – including groundbreaking immunotherapy – and early detection.) Terrible diseases like malaria, sleeping sickness, and hepatitis C are being reduced or eliminated. Jihadi terrorist attacks – an obsession 20 years ago – are sharply lower. Median US household incomes and net worth recently hit record levels.

Things are getting better for most people in most places in most ways. That does not mean that everything is getting better for everyone everywhere in every way. That wouldn't be progress. That would be a miracle.

But we in the United States today work shorter hours, have more purchasing power, enjoy goods and services in almost limitless supply, and have more leisure time than ever before.

Yes, we live in a world with crime, war, poverty, and other serious problems. Yet the media makes no attempt to paint a faithful depiction of the lives most of us lead. Its business model is to deliver your attention to advertisers. And they know consumers have a bias toward negative news. So it's drip . . . drip . . . drip . . . drip . . . drip . . . all day, every day.

Most Americans don't know that wars between nations, civil wars, terrorist incidents, violent crime, domestic violence, child abuse, and even abortions are all down.

If you want a thorough examination of this phenomenon, I encourage you to read *The Better Angels of Our Nature: Why Violence Has Declined* by Steven Pinker.

Upon learning that violence is in a long-term cycle of decline, some shrug and say that may be true, yet people have rarely treated each other so poorly. Pinker provides some much-needed perspective:

> *Cruelty as entertainment, human sacrifice to indulge superstition, slavery as a labor-saving device, conquest as the mission statement of government, genocide as a means of acquiring real estate, torture and mutilation as routine punishment, the death penalty for misdemeanors and differences of opinion, assassination as the mechanism of political succession, rape as the spoils of war, pogroms as outlets for frustration, homicide as the major form of conflict resolution – all were unexceptionable features of life for most of human history. But, today, they are rare to nonexistent in the West, far less common elsewhere than they used to be, concealed when they do occur, and widely condemned when they are brought to light.*

Despite the ongoing conflicts in some parts of the world, life today is far safer and more peaceful than it was throughout most of human history.

Some will concede that the United States is exceptional in many ways. And, yes, we live in a more peaceful and affluent world. But in the past, they'll insist, the American Dream was far more affordable.

In Chapters 3 and 4, I'll explain exactly why that common belief simply doesn't hold up.

CHAPTER 3

Things Aren't What They Used to Be... and That's a Good Thing

> Nothing is more responsible for the good old days than a bad memory.
>
> —Franklin Pierce Adams

There is a widespread misconception in this country that things were far better for most Americans back in "the good old days." A Gallup poll asked, "Overall, do you think life in America today is better, worse, or about the same as it was 50 years ago for people like you?" Nearly 6 out of 10 Americans (58%) responded that life was better 50 years ago.

That response shows just how poorly history is taught in our public schools. Especially when you consider that at least 58% of Americans are either female, Black, or gay. Things were not better for "people like them" a half-century ago.

There is also a strong belief that life was easier for middle-class Americans in the second half of the 20th century because life was more affordable. Yet this view is based more on nostalgia than on a sober analysis of the facts.

Many Americans – especially those from older generations – look back at the 1950s and 1960s as a golden era when one income could support a household, homes were cheap, and college was affordable.

While it's always tempting to romanticize the past, the idea that Americans in the mid-20th century had a better lifestyle than Americans today just doesn't stand up to scrutiny.

For starters, Americans were far poorer in 1960 than they are today. Yes, economic growth was faster in the postwar era. But poverty rates were higher, particularly among minorities and rural populations. (And for those who fall through the cracks today, our social safety net is broader and more robust than it was then.)

It's true that one income could support a household back then – but that income was modest, and luxuries were few. In 1960, median household income was about $5,600, or roughly $57,000 in today's dollars. That income covered food, housing, medical care, transportation, education, and everything else.

Today, median household income is over $80,800 (US Census Bureau, 2024) – a 42% real increase from 1960. And while costs for some things have risen, most essential goods and services have become vastly more affordable when adjusted for time worked, as I'll discuss in Chapter 4.

People also have far more flexibility in how they earn today. Remote work, freelancing, and side hustles allow millions of Americans to create multiple income streams and manage their own schedules – unheard of in the mid-20th century.

Communication in the 1950s and 1960s was limited to landline phones, snail mail, and three network television stations. No internet. No smartphones. No email. No GPS. No videoconferencing. No global connectivity.

Homes built in the 1960s were roughly 25% smaller, and square footage per person was about a third of what it is today. Modern homes are not only larger – they're better built, better insulated, and filled with appliances and technologies that didn't exist a generation ago.

In 1960, the average home had no dishwasher, no central air conditioning, and likely just one black-and-white TV. Today's homes are packed with conveniences: computers, tablets, multiple smart TVs, washers, dryers, microwaves, and HVAC systems that keep us cool in the summer and warm in the winter.

Back then, only about 60% of American households owned a car – and the cars they did have were far less safe, less reliable, and less efficient. Today, there are about 290 million registered vehicles in the United States – more cars than licensed drivers.

Medical technology in the 1960s was crude by modern standards. Antibiotics were still relatively new. There were no MRIs, CT scans, or minimally invasive surgeries. Childhood diseases that are now largely preventable – including measles and polio – were far more common. Cancer detection and treatment were far less effective. Heart surgery was risky and rare.

Life expectancy in 1960 was 69.8 years. Today, it's just under 79 years, even after the dip from COVID-19. Infant mortality has dropped by over 80%. Most diseases that were deadly or debilitating in 1960 are now manageable – or preventable.

A common lament is that the United States has a lower life expectancy despite spending more on health care than other developed countries. But America also has more chronic disease and drug addiction, which have more to do with poor lifestyle choices than failures in our health care system. US cancer survival rates are higher than in most developed countries because Americans have access to more treatments than any country in the world.

College is more expensive today. But it's also more accessible. In 1960, only 45% of high school graduates enrolled in college. Today, that number is closer to 60%, and a far higher percentage of Americans complete some form of postsecondary education. Grants, scholarships, online degrees, and community college programs have expanded access dramatically.

More Americans than ever before attend college, start businesses, travel internationally, and pursue lifelong learning. The ability to switch careers, reinvent yourself, or learn new skills online was unimaginable in the 1960s.

Jobs back then were often repetitive, physically exhausting, and offered little upward mobility. The modern job market isn't perfect, but it provides far more opportunity for flexibility, growth, and fulfillment.

And for many Americans – especially women, people of color, and gays – the so-called golden age of the 1950s and 1960s was anything but. Women were expected to stay home. Legal segregation was the law in much of the country. Gay Americans had to hide their identities at the risk of arrest, assault, or worse.

The idealized "American family" was not just a cultural archetype – it was a narrow, exclusive vision that left out millions.

Today, Americans have far more personal freedom. More legal protections. More opportunity to define family and career on their own terms. That's progress.

While some elements of mid-century life may seem simpler, they came at the cost of comfort, freedom, and opportunity. Yes, our lives today are more complex. But we have more choices, better tools, and greater control over our destinies.

We have more liberty. More equality. More representation. More access to technology, travel, health care, education, information, and global markets than any generation in history.

We are safer, healthier, and, in most measurable ways, richer. In short, the American Dream hasn't disappeared. It's evolved. It's no longer about owning a home with a white picket fence. It's about building a life that aligns with your values – whether that means starting a business, working remotely, traveling the world, raising a family, or retiring early.

The Dream today is more diverse. More flexible. And more achievable.

Romanticizing the past may feel comforting. But when we look at the facts – past and present – today's society offers a better chance than ever to live a fulfilling, empowered life.

And isn't that what the American Dream is all about?

CHAPTER 4

Time Prices and the American Dream

> The real voyage of discovery consists not in seeking new landscapes, but in having new eyes.
>
> —Marcel Proust

The facts I've laid out so far demonstrate that life has gotten far better – not worse – for most Americans. Yet some readers will insist they are not living the Dream for a different reason: things have become increasingly unaffordable.

It's a common belief. And understandable. Prices are more visible than wages. When you see the sticker on a car, the total on your grocery receipt, or the amount on your rent check, it's easy to think, "I'm falling behind."

Yet most Americans aren't.

Some might feel exasperated to hear this. After all, they've *seen* the Consumer Price Index (CPI) go up. They've *paid* increasingly higher prices over the years. And they are irritated to hear that most things have become *more* affordable.

Yet – contradictory as it sounds – it is possible for goods to simultaneously become more expensive and more affordable. This paradox exists because while we buy things with money, we pay for them with time, in hours and minutes of work.

To measure affordability, we need to compare the price of goods and services to hourly compensation (wages and benefits). The resulting ratio is called the *time price*.

A time price is the length of time the average worker labors to afford something. Prices are expressed in dollars and cents. But time prices are expressed in hours and minutes.

We can transform any money price into a time price by dividing the money price by hourly income. For example, if a pizza costs $20 and you earn $20 an hour, then the pizza costs 60 minutes of your time. If, a year later, the price increases to $22 but your income has increased to $24 an hour, the time price is now 55 minutes.

It's more expensive in dollars, but cheaper in time. Which is more meaningful? In our daily lives, time is our most limited and nonrenewable resource. That's why time prices matter. And they reveal something stunning: *most things have become dramatically more affordable over time.*

Understand this key point: the CPI tells us if something has become more expensive. But the time price tells us if it has become more affordable.

Time prices are an excellent way to measure increases or decreases in our abundance over time for three reasons:

- Time prices cannot understate or overstate inflation since prevailing prices and wages are used at every point on the timeline.
- Time prices are independent of currency fluctuations. (They can be measured in euros, yen, or any other currency.)
- Time prices provide a standardized way of measuring changes in well-being.

In their eye-opening book, *Superabundance*, authors Marian L. Tupy and Gale L. Pooley measured the costs of 50 commodities between 1980 and 2020. They didn't just find that the time prices of some of them went down. The time prices of *all of them* went down.

In fact, the average time price decline of those 50 commodities – including oil, natural gas, wheat, cotton, soybeans, beef, corn, pork, and sugar – was a whopping 75.2%. Put differently, a blue-collar worker had to work 75% less to afford the same amount of these things.

Unless we're at the gas pump or the grocery store, however, we don't usually buy commodities. We buy finished goods. Yet the time price decline in these was just as dramatic. And in many cases, more so.

Over the same 40-year period, the time price of a utensil set declined 51%, a dishwasher declined 62%, a washer declined 65%, men's clothing declined 72%, a bicycle declined 74%, a vacuum declined 83%, and a food processor declined 86%. This isn't cherry-picking. It's across the board (see Figure 4.1).

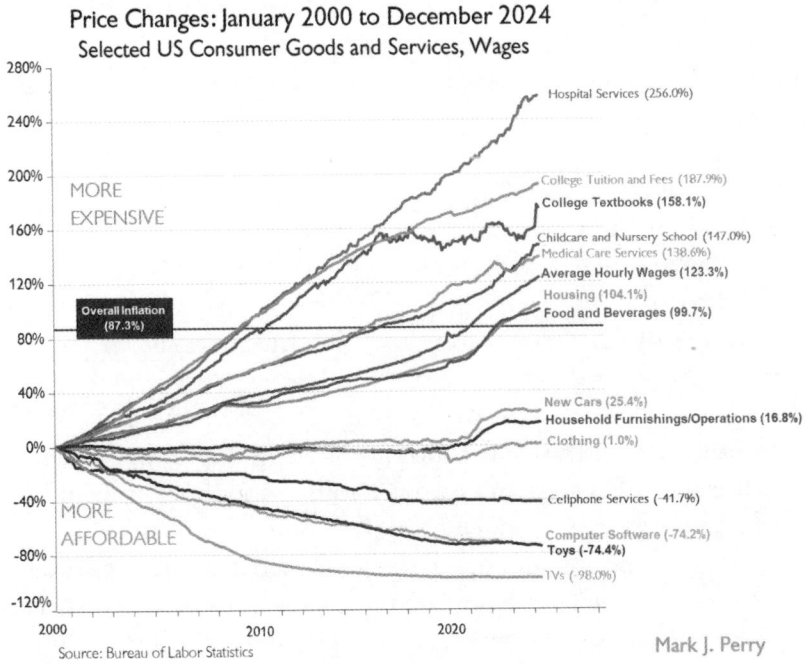

FIGURE 4.1 Chart of the century

Source: https://humanprogress.org/time-pricing-and-mark-perrys-chart-of-the-century/

And that's just for blue-collar workers. White-collar workers — especially those with a college degree — saw time prices drop even more dramatically because their incomes are higher and rose faster.

THE BIG ONE: HOUSING

Housing always feels expensive — because it is. But even here, time prices tell a surprising story. Let's compare 1980 with 2020.

In 1980:
- Median home price: $64,600
- 30-year fixed mortgage rate: 13.74%
- Monthly mortgage payment: $752.15
- Average home size: 1,595 sq. ft.
- Blue-collar hourly wage: $9.12
- Hours of labor per month to cover the mortgage payment: 82.5 hours

In 2020:
- Median home price: $336,900
- 30-year fixed rate: 3.11%
- Monthly mortgage payment: $1,440.45
- Average home size: 2,261 sq. ft.
- Blue-collar wage: $32.54
- Hours of labor per month to cover the mortgage payment: 44.3 hours

In other words, the *time* it took to buy a home dropped nearly 50% over these 40 years. And on a per-square-foot basis, time prices dropped even more — down 62%.

Over time, houses got more affordable in real, time-adjusted terms — even as they got larger, better built, and more feature-rich.

Today's houses have higher quality construction, are more energy efficient, contain numerous home appliances, and almost always include modern features like central heat and air and granite countertops.

It shocks many Americans to learn that between 1980 and 2020, homes became larger, higher quality, and *much more affordable* to the average American.

Yes, since 2021, home prices and interest rates have risen sharply, reversing some of those gains. But that's a short-term shock, not a long-term trend. And even now, interest rate strategies (like seller financing and assumable mortgages) can help buyers reduce borrowing costs. We'll discuss these in Chapter 10. It's often said that real estate is about location, location, location. But housing affordability is more often about financing, financing, financing.

It's impossible, of course, to measure the 40-year time price decline in things like laptops, smartphones, and flat-panel TVs because none of these were even imagined in 1980.

Other price declines are hard to measure as well. For example, how do you compare the average cost of a book in 1980 to the more than 10 million that are free to download today from Google's digital library?

Nobody thinks about the cost of a long-distance phone call today. But growing up, I did. In college, I could only afford to call from my school in South Carolina to my home in Virginia at night when AT&T offered lower rates. Today I routinely have FaceTime calls with friends overseas at no cost.

Over the last 50 years, music listeners have gone from vinyl records to 8-track tapes to cassettes to CDs to MP3 files to streaming. Today you can listen to almost any song, anywhere, at any time for next to free.

Other products are not free but considerably more affordable when measured in hours worked. In 1924, for example, a new Ford Model T sold for $260. Sounds great until you realize that the average blue-collar worker earned 51 cents an hour in wages and benefits. In 2024, a new Nissan Versa cost $16,290. Blue-collar workers earned about $36.50 an hour. The time price has declined by 12.5%. And the Versa compares quite favorably to the Model T in power, comfort, safety, durability, convenience, and reliability.

In 1971, a pair of soft contact lenses cost $65 and a fitting by an eye doctor ran about $550, putting the total cost at $615. Unskilled workers earned about $2 an hour. Today an eye exam is around $120, and lenses start at $200, putting the cost at $320. Unskilled workers earn around $16.51. In other words, the time price has declined 84%.

In 1970, the price for a roundtrip airline ticket from New York to London was $550. Blue-collar workers earned $3.93 an hour at the time. (In my family, the folks who spent so lavishly were viewed as members of the "jet set.") Today, the same flight has dropped to about $467 and blue-collar workers earn about $36.15. The time price has decreased 91%.

In 1972, you could book a seven-day cruise from Miami to the Caribbean for $240. Blue-collar workers earned about $4.59 an hour at the time. Today, you can book a seven-day cruise out of Port Canaveral for $549. For blue-collar workers who earn $36.15 an hour, the price has dropped more than 70%.

Natural diamonds take more than a billion years to form. But scientists can now produce one in a little over two hours. The resulting plunge in prices is bad news for the DeBeers diamond monopoly. But it's great news for jewelry buyers, especially when measured in hours worked.

Apple introduced the Macintosh in 1984 at a retail price of $2,495. Unskilled workers earned about $5 an hour at the time. Today a new iMac sells for $1,299 and unskilled workers earn about $16.51 an hour. The time price has decreased by 84.2%. And the difference between a 2025 Mac and the 1984 Mac is like comparing a Lamborghini with a skateboard.

That's time price abundance.

Not all categories saw time price declines. Health care, college tuition, and childcare – heavily regulated, heavily subsidized, and labor-intensive – have outpaced inflation. These markets don't benefit from the "economics of knowledge," where producing multiple copies of a prototype costs less and less.

But even in those areas, alternatives are emerging:

- Online education is dramatically cheaper and more flexible than traditional degrees.
- AI in health care is improving diagnostics, streamlining care, and lowering costs.

- Many elective procedures (Lasik, cosmetic surgery, dental implants) have dropped in price significantly — because they're outside the insurance system and thus more exposed to market forces.

We saw the biggest spike in inflation in 40 years during the Biden Administration, thanks to massive deficit spending, near-zero interest rates, and the temporary shutdown of the global supply chain. Yet time prices still came down by the end of 2024, extending the long-term trend.

Between 2000 and 2024, the CPI rose 82.2%. But hourly earnings for blue-collar workers rose 115.1% — outpacing inflation by more than 40%. That means an hour of work buys 18.1% more goods and services in 2024 than it did in 2000.

That's progress. Just not the kind that the media bothers to cover.

Unlike money, time can't be counterfeited or inflated. There is perfect equality here. We all get 60 minutes in an hour and 24 hours in a day. Our time is truly our most precious resource, the only one that cannot be recycled, stored, duplicated, or recovered. When time prices decrease — as they have for decades now — an hour of time buys more products and services.

It's often said that "time is money." But it's just as accurate to say that "money is time." And while people often compare what they make with someone earning more, they rarely stop to realize how much more they can buy today compared with what they could buy in the past for the same hours worked.

Time prices are the one unimpeachable standard to compare abundance from one era to another. And their fall is not due to an increase in material resources. It is due to the expansion of knowledge, which enables us to use resources more creatively and effectively.

This is a powerful phenomenon, yet one that is not commonly understood. Being able to afford more while working less is further evidence that most Americans are living the Dream *without realizing it*.

Most of us take the long-term improvement in our standard of living for granted. Indeed, there is a common misconception that increasing progress and prosperity have been the norm for as long as human beings have been around. Yet history reveals that this is decidedly *not the case*.

Imagine, for example, that the Roman statesman Cicero was magically able to time travel and visit Thomas Jefferson at Monticello more than 1,800 years later. Cicero would arrive at the coast of Virginia the same way Jefferson would have made the trip to Italy. He would ride a horse to the nearest port and trust his fate to a windblown ship. When Cicero arrived at Monticello months later, things would look quite familiar. Jefferson's home was heated by fire in the winter, and the doors and windows were left wide open in the summer, the same as in ancient Rome. Jefferson read by candlelight, drew his water from a well, ate mostly what he raised, used an outhouse, and owned slaves, just like Romans did 18 centuries earlier.

Cicero would learn that four of Jefferson's six children did not survive early childhood. Nothing new there. This was sadly the case for most of human history. (Jefferson's wife died at age 33 of complications from giving birth to their sixth child.) Except for a few notable innovations – like the printing press, gunpowder, and the compass – life in 1800 was hardly distinguishable from life almost 2,000 years earlier.

Since then, however, there has been an explosion in human progress and prosperity. Economic historian Deirdre McCloskey calls it the Great Enrichment, a period of exponential wealth creation that started more than 200 years ago and is still accelerating.

This is plainly visible in the quality of your transportation, the speed of your communications, your many laborsaving devices, and the huge variety of goods, services, and outright luxuries available to you at the click of a button.

Thomas Jefferson did not have electricity, cars, trains, airplanes, radio, television, cameras and video recorders, smartphones, computers, lasers, batteries, the World Wide Web, antibiotics, vaccines, pacemakers, artificial hearts, MRI scans, gene therapies, and countless other lifesaving and life-enhancing innovations.

Now fast-forward to today. Tupy and Pooley analyzed the time prices of hundreds of commodities, goods, and services spanning two centuries and found that resources became not scarcer but more abundant as the population grew.

Even though the nominal cost increased greatly, how long you'd need to work to buy it *decreased*. Time prices are an excellent way to measure increases in human well-being over time. Especially when measured in decades, wages rise faster than prices, allowing Americans to buy more while working less. This is a big part of the American Dream by anyone's definition.

And it flies in the face of virtually everything the mainstream media tells us about the modern economy. George Mason University economics professor Donald Boudreaux writes that the authors of *Superabundance* "bust the myth of middle-class stagnation to smithereens." *Skeptic* magazine publisher Michael Shermer calls the book a "fact-filled reminder of how good our lives are compared to ages past." And Nobel Prize–winning economist Angus Deaton says it provides "hope that the doom-mongers will be wrong about the future, just as they always have been wrong about the past."

What is most responsible for this exponential increase in abundance? Two things: freedom and people. Freedom is crucial because it allows people to create and profit from their innovations. (That's why goods and services have *not* become cheaper for the average consumer in Cuba, Venezuela, North Korea, and other unfree nations.)

But this phenomenon is not about freedom alone. It's also about more people. *A lot more people*. People generate knowledge. Knowledge multiplies output. And freedom lets people share, trade, and profit from their discoveries.

The freer a society, the greater its time price gains. The more people it empowers, the richer its outcomes. Scarcity didn't win. Innovation did.

We have increased food supply, for instance, by increasing yields from existing fields. We've increased our agricultural efficiency so much that less than 2% of the US population farms at all.

After more than a century of intensive fossil fuel use, we have more known deposits of oil and gas than ever before. (And we've surveyed only a tiny portion of the planet.) Overpopulation is not a threat. On the contrary, limiting population growth limits brainpower. Yet generations of schoolchildren have been taught that population growth makes resources scarcer.

Indeed, academia and the media repeatedly warn us that we are consuming the planet's natural resources at an alarming rate . . . and that they will soon be gone. Not true. Resource abundance is growing faster than the world population.

Our economy has reached such a level of efficiency and sophistication that we are producing an increasing amount of goods and services while using ever-fewer resources. For example, from 2014 to 2024 US real gross domestic product grew by 27.6%. But, over the same period, energy consumption decreased by 1.3%.

Western countries have learned how to get the most energy with the least emission of greenhouse gases. As we climbed the energy ladder from wood to coal to oil to gas, the ratio of carbon to hydrogen in our energy sources fell steadily. As a result, fewer American cities are now shrouded in a smoggy haze.

Our distant ancestors spent most of their waking hours hunting and gathering food to live. Yet the typical American today earns their food in a matter of minutes. And we are spoiled for choice.

For example, there are 768 varieties of breakfast cereal available at Walmart. Even a worker earning minimum wage can buy most of them for less than 30 minutes of labor. We have more goods and services available – and work fewer hours to afford them – than any previous generation.

The world today is incomparably richer than it was in decades past. Yet the doomsayers are unable to see it – or don't want to. Instead, they continually warn us that the end is nigh. As a result, many Americans are unable to enjoy the countless advantages of modern life because they believe it is on the verge of ending – and there is nothing they can do about it.

As Matt Ridley notes in his book *The Rational Optimist*:

> *In my own adult lifetime, I have listened to the implacable predictions of growing poverty, coming famines, expanding deserts, imminent plagues, impending water wars, inevitable oil exhaustion, mineral shortages, falling sperm counts, thinning ozone, acidifying*

rain, nuclear winters, mad-cow epidemics, Y2K computer bugs, killer bees, sex-change fish, global warming, ocean acidification, and even asteroid impacts that would presently bring this happy interlude to a terrible end. I cannot recall a time when one or other of these scares was not solemnly espoused by sober, distinguished and serious elites and hysterically echoed by the media.

Don't buy it. Especially the claims about "overpopulation." The most important resource in today's world is not oil or natural gas or some rare earth mineral. It's people. By applying their intelligence and creativity, individual men and women make other resources more abundant.

Additional people don't just create additional demand. (Although that also promotes growth and prosperity.) They represent an additional supply of ideas, knowledge, and productive work.

We shouldn't underestimate the power of this. Or what time prices tell us. When you spend less time laboring to feed and clothe your family, put a roof over your head, keep the lights on, and pay your bills, you are gaining the ultimate wealth: more time to do what you really want.

This is not just prosperity. It's *superabundance*. And another reason to acknowledge that the American Dream is alive and well – for those with eyes to see it.

CHAPTER 5

The Future Is Better Than You Imagine

> Opportunity is missed by most people because it is dressed in overalls and looks like work.
>
> —Thomas Edison

There's a reason the American Dream has persisted — despite recessions, inflation, political division, and cultural upheaval. It works — just not equally and automatically.

It works for people who understand the underlying principles. For those who are willing to take personal responsibility. For those who understand how to create value, make good choices, and commit to long-term action. If there's a magic formula, that's it.

The American Dream works because it's built on a timeless truth: **in a free society, outcomes are not guaranteed — but opportunities are.** That distinction is critical.

But if the Dream is real, why do so many people feel it's out of reach?

Here are the biggest roadblocks:

- **Pessimism.** If you believe it's not possible, you won't even try. That mindset kills more dreams than failure ever could.
- **Debt.** Living beyond your means traps you in a cycle of anxiety and stagnation.
- **Lack of skills.** In a modern economy, unskilled labor pays less and is easier to replace.
- **Procrastination.** Time is your greatest asset. Wasting your 20s or 30s financially compounds your struggle.
- **Entitlement.** Believing you deserve success – without work, risk, or patience – sets you up for disappointment.

None of these issues are permanent. All can be fixed. But only if you recognize them – and choose to make a change. The biggest obstacle to living the Dream is not rich people, the state of the economy, or "the system." It's what's going on between your ears.

We are unbelievably fortunate to have been born in an exceptional country at the greatest moment in history to be alive.

In some countries, there's no upside because there's no ownership, no incentive, and no freedom to rise. But in America – and in other free nations – you can change your circumstances. You can reinvent yourself. You can learn a skill. Start a business. Move to a better job market. Change careers at 40. Build wealth from nothing. That's the Dream.

Yet many Americans no longer believe it. Not because they've tried and failed – but because they've *heard* it's not possible. That success is about luck or privilege or exploitation.

In other words, they've been lied to. They've been told – by Dr. Gregory Clark and others – that your starting point determines your outcome. That your parents' income defines your ceiling. That your gender or race or ZIP code dictates your economic fate. That capitalism is zero-sum. That someone else's wealth means less for you. That wealth is stolen or hoarded, not created. That rich people exploit, rather than innovate. That financial success is shameful, or even immoral. None of that holds up to scrutiny. The Dream still works – and we have the data to prove it.

For decades now – in both my investment columns and books – I've countered the mainstream media's negative narrative. And in 2018, I gained a powerful ally: Steven Pinker. He is a Harvard psychologist, bestselling author, and one of the world's most influential thinkers, according to *Time* magazine. His book, *Enlightenment Now*, is a tour de force. Using comprehensive evidence – not to mention 75 mind-blowing graphs – he demolishes the cynical attitude that pervades today's public discourse by revealing how our lives are becoming not worse as many feel, but longer, healthier, safer, freer, less violent, and more prosperous. Not just in the United States but in most countries around the globe.

Multiple data points – from human life spans to living standards to incidents of war and violent crime – reveal that long-term trends in human health and welfare are strongly positive.

What is responsible for this moral and material progress? The short answer is Enlightenment ideals of rational thinking, science, and humanism. Using extensive data, Pinker highlights increased life expectancy, reduced child mortality, declining global poverty, decreasing rates of violence and war deaths, gains in gender equality and civil rights, and even rising levels of happiness globally.

While acknowledging ongoing challenges like carbon emissions and the threat of nuclear proliferation, he emphasizes that these are solvable problems if Enlightenment principles are upheld.

In the West, they have already vanquished a host of enemies, including religious fundamentalism, authoritarianism, tribalism, nationalism, Marxism, and – more recently – postmodernism.

Pinker rightly notes that "none of us are as happy as we ought to be, given how amazing our world has become." The number and variety of ways the world is getting better are astonishing. He notes, as an example, that Americans today are 37 times less likely to be killed by lightning than in 1900. How is this even possible? Thank better weather forecasting, doppler radar, improved electrical engineering, greater safety awareness, and – for those unfortunate enough to be struck by lightning – higher-quality emergency care.

Life is safer in almost every other way, too. Over the past century, Americans have become 59% less likely to fall to their deaths, 90% less likely to drown, 92% less likely to die by fire, 92% less likely to be asphyxiated, 95% less likely to be killed on the job, 96% less likely to be killed in an auto accident, and 99% less likely to die in a plane crash.

Other trends are also strongly positive. Divorce rates are down. Domestic violence is down. Child abuse is down. Even maladies that had gone up in recent years – like suicide rates and opioid deaths – have come down recently.

Americans work 22 fewer hours per week than they did in the late 19th century and lose 43 fewer hours to housework. That means we have more time to do the things we really want to do.

Few books literally change your perspective of the world. *Enlightenment Now* does. Bill Gates – an avid reader as well as one of the world's richest men – calls it "the greatest story that no one knows."

Incidentally, you might imagine that when the book came out, readers were delighted to learn about all the ways that life is improving. Instead, the book provoked a fierce blowback from many.

Not because critics disproved his numbers or poked holes in Pinker's logic. On the contrary, they conceded that his book is packed with solid statistics, clear graphs, and credible sourcing. The real problem was that it was seen as an ideological threat.

In some circles, progress isn't just overlooked – it's unwelcome. If life is getting longer, safer, richer, and freer for most people – as it most certainly is – then capitalism, democracy, and incremental reform are working. That implication undermines movements built on the premise that the system is completely broken.

Pinker himself puts it bluntly: some intellectuals "hate progress." And especially intellectuals who call themselves progressives. Why? Because acknowledging improvement undercuts the urgency of their social reforms. And it removes the moral high ground that comes from portraying the world as a burning building. For some, that shift is simply too much to bear.

This nation and the world are in far better shape than most realize – or admit.

That's because our ancestors replaced tradition, dogma, and authority with reason, debate, and institutions of truth-seeking. Adopting an evidence-based worldview won't just make you more upbeat and better informed, it will make you far more successful in business and investing. And, therefore, more likely to achieve the American Dream.

We owe a tremendous amount of our success to the Scientific Revolution and the Industrial Revolution, as well as democratic institutions like free and fair elections, property rights, and the rule of law.

But we shouldn't overlook the beneficial effects of capitalism. It is the greatest wealth creator – and antipoverty program – ever devised. It enabled the industrialization and innovation that has slashed poverty, fed billions, emancipated women, educated children, and created widespread prosperity.

We count on corporations – large and small – to provide us with virtually all our wants and needs . . . the cars we drive, the planes we catch, the clothes we wear, the homes we live in, the medicines that heal us, and the computers and smartphones that make our lives so much easier and more productive.

Investing in these companies not only fuels innovation and efficiency but also enables us to reach our financial goals. Yet I regularly talk to men and women who don't own equities, largely due to profound (and unjustified) antibusiness attitudes. Many can hardly utter the phrase "corporate profits" without a bit of spittle flying from their lips.

They are down on capitalism. Especially young people, the same folks who are the most pessimistic about achieving the American Dream. Gallup data from 2019 found that about 50% of young adults view socialism positively, a rate that has remained steady since 2010. At the same time, positive views of capitalism among young adults has declined.

Why? Many say they don't want to pay for college. They don't want to pay for health insurance, either. And retirement? Most are too young to have given it much thought. But some polls show they view retirement as their employers' or the government's responsibility. These "free" goods and services may sound good in theory, especially if you're young and unaware how the world works. But these folks might look south to see how cradle-to-grave socialism has panned out in the workers' paradise of Venezuela.

Or take energy . . . . Abundant, affordable, and reliable energy is vital to human flourishing. It powered the industrialization that slashed poverty, fed billions, improved education, and helped liberate women from traditional roles. Yet I regularly hear folks claim that the Earth is running out of oil and gas and that our fossil-fueled civilization is "unsustainable."

If we are running out of oil and gas, why are they both cheaper than they were several years ago? (These critics seem unaware that technological innovations like horizontal drilling and hydraulic fracturing have greatly increased the supply.) As for the environmental impact, there is good news on this front, too, despite hysterical claims in the mainstream media. Seaborne oil transport has become vastly safer. (The annual number of oil spills is down from more than a 100 in 1973 to 10 in 2024.) And this is true, even though vastly more oil is shipped today.

Thanks to habitat protection and conservation efforts, many species – including eagles, manatees, condors, pandas, rhinos, and tigers – have been pulled back from the brink of extinction. (Some species remain in a precarious state but, according to ecologist Stuart Pimm, the overall rate of extinctions has been reduced by 75%.)

As Pinker writes in *Enlightenment Now*, "The world's progress can be tracked in a report card called the Environmental Performance Index, a composite of indicators of the quality of air, water, forests, fisheries, farms and natural habitats. Out of 180 countries that have been tracked for a decade or more, all but two show an improvement."

Many ecologists insist that environmental protection requires smaller populations, slower economic growth, and lower living standards. It turns out that just the opposite is true. The wealthiest countries have the cleanest environments. And as the poor ones get wealthier, they get cleaner, too. That's reason to celebrate.

Given these positive facts, some will concede that not only the United States but even the world is in better shape than is commonly recognized. Yet they still insist that we face a nightmarish future.

I invite them to read a book by British physicist David Deutsch. It was one I'd had on my shelf for over a decade – and had never gotten around to reading. Yet I kept coming across other writers who referred to it as "groundbreaking," "dazzling," and "the most optimistic book ever written." When I finally picked it up, I couldn't put it down. In *The Beginning of Infinity: Explanations That Transform the World,* Deutsch explains why human progress is not only accelerating but *potentially boundless.*

Reading it will not only make you more grateful. It will make you much better informed. The infinity that Deutsch refers to in the title is knowledge, which he explains is limitless. Few would disagree with this statement. But most don't understand the implication: *knowledge creates wealth.*

For example, for untold centuries all the energy we needed – in the form of oil and natural gas – was available right beneath our feet, below the surface of the Earth. But we didn't know how to discover it, drill for it, extract it, refine it, or use it.

That's partly because we lacked the tools – machines, electric lights, and so on – that the energy could power to make our lives better. (The Scientific and Industrial Revolutions hadn't happened yet.) Today, however, the situation is very different. Scientists and engineers invent, develop, and use elements, compounds, materials, and processes in unprecedented ways.

For example, building today's logic chips can require more than 1,500 manufacturing steps. Historically, performance gains in microchips were accomplished by shrinking the individual components, until, eventually, chipmakers bumped up against a hard limit on how tiny the elements on a chip can become.

Yet tech manufacturers today can deliver ever faster and more capable computers and smartphones thanks to profound discoveries *at the atomic level.*

Everything, from the food you eat, to the clothes you wear, to the buildings you live and work in, is due to the specialized knowledge of scientists, engineers, farmers, manufacturers, miners, extractors, builders, refiners, transporters, bankers, insurers, venture capitalists, and others who – coordinated by commercial and financial markets – trade products, services, and specialized skills for money.

It isn't that our distant ancestors wouldn't have enjoyed progress. They would have loved longer, safer, easier lives. But they couldn't imagine it. And they didn't experience it. Prior to the Scientific Revolution, discoveries such as fire, stone tools, agriculture, and navigation happened so rarely that it appeared that the world essentially never improved.

Over the last 200 years, knowledge has exploded, leading to a standard of living that was inconceivable throughout most of our history. And this progress – like the expansion of the universe itself – is *accelerating*. In the not-too-distant future, we will have transportation, communications, medical treatments, health care, goods and services, and *investment opportunities* that cannot be appreciated today. As Deutsch points out in *The Beginning of Infinity*, "Everything that is not forbidden by the laws of nature is achievable, given the right knowledge."

Think about that statement for a moment. Every possible advance that could benefit you and the rest of humanity is either (1) impossible because it is forbidden by the laws of physics or (2) achievable given the right knowledge. And "the right knowledge" is increasing at an unprecedented rate.

Forty-five years ago, you didn't have a personal computer. Thirty years ago, you didn't have an internet connection. Twenty years ago, you didn't have a smartphone. Fifteen years ago, you didn't have electric cars, voice recognition technology, cloud computing, 3D printing, augmented reality, 5G, mRNA vaccines, or the Internet of Things. Five years ago, you didn't have ChatGPT, Perplexity, or other generative artificial intelligence (AI) platforms.

AI will soon send human progress into overdrive. It is in the process of turning human resources into superhuman resources. Consider that AI never eats, sleeps, or takes vacations or even a bathroom break. It is a partner that never tires, never runs out of ideas, never takes your requests personally, and finishes projects faster than you can delegate them to another human being.

In a recent *Wall Street Journal* editorial, Marc Benioff, the chairman and CEO of Salesforce, noted that he had been part of many waves in technology – from cloud computing, to mobile, social media, and AI. But he insists that nothing compares to the transformation that is happening now.

There is a revolution happening in AI-driven digital labor. Autonomous intelligent agents act on their own, collaborate, and continuously learn and improve. Organizations of any size can now scale beyond human limits. This means that despite shrinking labor pools, productivity – the engine of economic expansion – may hit 3% growth.

As Benioff writes,

> *AI agents can do tasks at an unprecedented scale and speed – reaching long-underserved parts of the world. Education agents can create bespoke learning plans for students. Urban planning agents can analyze traffic, energy and housing data to design smarter cities. Health agents can track disease outbreaks, optimize vaccine distribution and connect patients with care.*

People are not prepared for all the positive change that will take place. That's because humans are biologically programmed to think in linear terms since our ancestors operated in a world that was slow and incremental. However, today's world is driven by exponential change, where technologies double in power or efficiency approximately every 18 months. This shift creates rapid innovation.

Author Peter Diamandis, a renowned entrepreneur, talks about "the six Ds of exponential growth":

- **Digitization.** Technologies become digital, enabling them to scale rapidly.
- **Deception.** Early growth appears slow and insignificant, making it easy to overlook.
- **Disruption.** Once the technology reaches critical mass, it disrupts existing industries.
- **Demonetization.** Costs plummet as the technology becomes more efficient. (For example, sensors costing millions in the 1960s now cost just $1.)
- **Dematerialization.** Physical products are replaced with digital alternatives. (For example, smartphones replace cameras, video recorders, CD players, and GPS devices.)
- **Democratization.** As costs decline, the technology becomes widely accessible for everyone.

Moreover, these exponential technologies do not develop in isolation but converge to amplify their impact. For example, AI, robotics, 3D printing, and virtual reality are combining to revolutionize fields like transportation, manufacturing, and education. This convergence accelerates innovation and creates new paradigms for problem-solving.

Nowhere will this have a bigger impact than health care. In the past, it was rudimentary. For example, in 1927 Calvin Coolidge was president. His 16-year-old son Cal Jr. developed a blister playing tennis without socks at the White House. It became infected. Five days later, he died. Why? Because there was nothing that the best doctors in the country could do for the son of the most powerful man in the world before the advent of antibiotics.

There has been tremendous positive change in health care over the past century. Not just for powerful people – and their families – but for everyday Americans. And now exponential technologies are set to transform the world of medicine.

In a *Wall Street Journal* interview, Dr. Lloyd Minor, dean of the Stanford University School of Medicine, said,

> *The drug discovery process is on the cusp of being transformed in ways that will dramatically improve the number of therapies that get to patients . . . we'll see a lot of new medicines coming out – and medicines more specific to a disease and an individual rather than medicines that are generic in terms of treatment of everyone who has this disorder.*

Novel drugs and medical devices are already extending and improving our lives. But Dr. Minor concludes that AI is "a transformative moment in human history," creating the most radical and "most positive transformation in health since the introduction of antibiotics."

It's not just medicine, of course. Exponential technologies are making our communications faster, our transportation safer, and our working and recreational lives easier. Our quality of life is improving. And so is global prosperity.

AI can already help you with researching, writing, strategizing, analyzing, planning, brainstorming, summarizing, communicating, or helping with any task that could use massive data processing and critical thinking skills to augment human intelligence.

AI can create graphic art, edit copy, boost research, or even translate your spoken videos into any foreign language. Most businesses appeal to customers by providing a product or service that is better, faster, or cheaper. However, businesses face something called the *service trilemma*. If a product is good and fast, it's not likely to be cheap. If it's cheap and fast, it's not likely to be good. And if it's good and cheap, it's not likely to be fast.

Yet AI will revolutionize business by making products and services better and cheaper while delivering them faster. AI is pushing the boundaries of how computers – and the machines they operate – can make our lives better and easier.

How? It offers the skills and algorithms to process information and reach conclusions from big data incredibly quickly. It helps computers perform many humanlike tasks, such as data collection and entry, invoice generation, email responses to customer queries, and software testing. This frees workers to focus on tasks that do require human abilities.

The world now creates more than 2.5 quintillion bytes of data each day. AI is the only way to effectively process and use all this information. (Already, more than 35% of companies use some form of AI in their business.) AI enables computers, robots, and other connected devices to mimic the perception, learning, problem-solving, and decision-making of the human mind.

This enables machines to perform specific tasks with increasing accuracy and without human intervention. Applications are now used for speech recognition, language processing, virus and spam prevention, autopilot technology, image recognition, real-time recommendations, even automated stock trading.

Anything that can be achieved by human intelligence can be sped up and enhanced by AI. People will have better outcomes across virtually every domain of human activity, including comprehension, creativity, conflict resolution, health, and longevity.

Productivity – doing more with less – will accelerate dramatically, driving economic growth, creating new ideas, new jobs, and whole new industries.

AI will augment human intelligence to solve problems better and faster than ever before. That means the progress we've already discussed will not only continue but speed up, making us richer and more productive.

By understanding these mechanisms – and cultivating an exponential mindset – individuals and organizations can better capitalize on the transformative potential of emerging technologies.

Renowned futurist Ray Kurzweil often describes a future of rapid, transformational change driven by exponential technology growth. His optimistic outlook is based on what he calls the *law of accelerating returns*. Technological progress builds on itself, creating a positive feedback loop that accelerates innovation across various fields.

For example, he argues that exponential advances in various fields will lead to 100% of electricity generation by renewables within 10 years, successful treatments for 95% of deaths by major diseases, and a dramatic slowing of the aging process.

Far-fetched? A lot of Kurzweil's past predictions seemed so. Yet he has repeatedly beaten the oddsmakers, with many of his forecasts coming true.

It is undeniable that technology has greatly improved our world for the better, that the advances are difficult if not impossible to foresee, and that the future could be far more wonderful that many expect.

If so, it will enable more Americans to experience the Dream . . . and faster than ever before.

CHAPTER 6

The Founders' Ideal of Happiness

> I hope I shall possess firmness and virtue enough to maintain what I consider the most enviable of all titles, the character of an honest man.
>
> —George Washington

When someone learns about all the ways modern life is getting better – medical breakthroughs, rising living standards, increasing purchasing power – they often respond with, "Well then, why are Americans so unhappy?"

The short answer is – they're not.

The perception that Americans are deeply unhappy is mostly fueled by headlines about declining rankings in global happiness indexes. But when you examine the actual data, the story is far more optimistic than it appears at first glance.

Yes, in the 2025 *World Happiness Report*, the United States dropped to 24th place, the lowest it's been in years. But that's still ahead of most of the world. And when you factor in other metrics – gross domestic product (GDP) per capita, social support, generosity – Americans rank quite well. In fact, the United States ranks fourth globally in GDP per capita at $76,276. That level of prosperity contributes significantly to our material well-being and life satisfaction.

We also rank 12th in social support, meaning most Americans feel they have someone to count on. And we're 16th in generosity, showing a widespread willingness to help others – financially and otherwise. That matters a lot. Because social support is a key indicator of real-life contentment.

Economic prosperity, while not everything, remains a critical foundation for happiness. Yet many of the issues causing discontent today – especially among the young – aren't financial at all. They're social and psychological. Studies show higher rates of depression and anxiety linked not to income, but to excessive social media use, digital comparison, and online tribalism. But here's the empowering truth: those behaviors are within our control. My mantra is "log off and live." Not all day, of course, but more of the day. Because the less time you spend comparing your life to other people's curated highlight reels, the better off you are.

Political polarization also drags down our collective mood. However, I'd rather live in a country where people argue loudly than one where they're not allowed to argue at all. (Try publicly disagreeing with the government in Russia, Iran, or China and see what happens.) For all its dysfunction, our political system still protects free speech. And that's no small thing.

The Declaration of Independence proclaims that we all have a natural right to pursue happiness. Yet the founders had a very different understanding of happiness than we do today.

To us, happiness often means pleasure, fun, or feeling good in the moment. To them, it meant something deeper and more enduring. They were steeped in the works of classical thinkers – Epictetus, Seneca, Cicero, Marcus Aurelius – and Enlightenment philosophers like Locke, Hume, and Montesquieu. These people didn't define happiness as a surge of dopamine. They defined it as the attainment of virtue.

Their inspiration came from books like *Plutarch's Lives*, which compared heroic figures from Greek and Roman history to teach moral lessons. They studied the *Golden Verses of Pythagoras*, which urged moderation in all things: speech, appetite, ambition, and behavior. And they were well-versed in *Cicero's Tusculan Disputations*, a collection of philosophical dialogues on how to rise above suffering and master one's emotions.

To the founders, happiness was not about the right to feel good – it was about the right to live well. That meant cultivating character. Practicing discipline. Living intentionally. It was a lifelong process and a moral journey – a daily challenge to improve oneself in thought, word, and deed. They didn't conflate happiness with wealth or possessions. In fact, they warned against it. True happiness, they believed, comes from self-improvement and service to others. That's the Stoic view: control what you can and accept what you cannot.

The founders viewed life as a struggle between reason and passion. The goal is to strengthen the intellect, moderate harmful emotions, and achieve a measure of self-control that is the key to happiness. They viewed this as a kind of spiritual practice. It didn't involve yoga or meditation, but rather an intense focus on battling their own shortcomings.

And they had plenty. These men were made not of marble but of flesh and blood. George Washington struggled with his temper his whole life. John Adams was vain and irritable. Thomas Jefferson was a spendthrift who could never balance his books and died deeply in debt. Benjamin Franklin was a prideful eccentric with a penchant for what he called "air baths," sitting naked in front of an open window for extended periods. Alexander Hamilton was arrogant and vengeful (which led to his fatal duel with Aaron Burr).

They recognized their flaws. And worked to overcome them. Because they believed that personal self-government was the essential precursor to political self-government.

This is why Franklin's quip outside Independence Hall still resonates. When asked, "What kind of government have you given us?" he replied, "A republic – if you can keep it."

That *if* speaks volumes. A republic requires vigilance. Virtue. Wisdom. It demands a citizenry willing to think critically, act responsibly, and delay gratification. Without those traits, freedom erodes. And the lessons of ancient Rome loom large.

The founders saw that when citizens surrendered their personal discipline in favor of bread and circuses, liberty vanished. That's why they designed a system filled with checks and balances – mirroring the same need for internal checks within each of us.

It's the reason we have three branches of the federal government, two branches of the legislature, the presidential veto, the veto override, super-majorities, judicial review, and so on. The president can check the impulsive passions of Congress with a veto, just as the Senate can cool the passions of the more democratic House. And the Supreme Court can counter both branches by ruling their actions unconstitutional.

The goal of each of these institutional checks is to slow down deliberation so that the government can act wisely . . . the same way individuals can slow down and check their worst impulses through virtuous self-mastery.

The founders realized there are no perfect people. As Madison declared, "If men were angels, no government would be necessary. If angels were to govern men, neither external nor internal controls on government would be necessary."

This kind of Stoic wisdom fell out of fashion in the 1960s with the Woodstock ethos: "If it feels good, do it." It continued into the 1970s (dubbed the "Me Decade") and the materialistic 1980s. Even today's mantra – "You do you" – encourages everyone to follow their own personal bliss. Unfortunately, this intense focus on the pursuit of pleasure has had the opposite effect, with rising rates of depression and anxiety.

To the founders, the pursuit of happiness had a deeper and nobler meaning than it does today. For them, happiness was the result of living a good life. That required the cultivation of virtuous qualities: integrity, courage, equanimity, resolution, industry, frugality, and humility, among others. They viewed the pursuit of happiness not as the liberty to do whatever feels good in the moment, but as the freedom to make wise choices that help us develop our character and talents throughout our lives.

Take delayed gratification, for instance. In 1972, Stanford researchers conducted the now-famous marshmallow experiment. Young children were offered one marshmallow immediately or two if they could wait 15 minutes. Years later, those who waited fared better – not just in school, but in life.

The takeaway? Self-control predicts long-term success.

So does industry. Jefferson wrote to his daughter Martha in 1787, "Determine never to be idle. It is wonderful how much may be done, if we are always doing." He believed that a busy, engaged mind was a happy one. And science backs him up: purpose and productivity are strongly correlated with emotional well-being.

But the founders didn't think of leisure as mindless entertainment. To them, it meant time away from commerce to pursue learning, reflection, and growth. Jefferson's daily schedule included reading, writing, and long walks. Washington rose early, worked hard, and read voraciously.

The contemporary focus on self-gratification rather than self-improvement can lead to a sort of narcissistic preoccupation rather than happiness. Yet the same virtues that the founders insisted lead to a happier life are the very ones that make the attainment of the American Dream easier.

Here's what I mean: industry, thrift, courage, and temperance are essential to achieving our most important financial goals. This becomes apparent when we investigate how individuals accumulate wealth over a lifetime.

I recognized as a youngster that we all start with nothing and make our way in the world *by serving others*. Some young people will stop me there and disagree. A friend's son told his father on college graduation, "I refuse to work for *the man*." (However, playing the guitar in a coffee shop didn't create the life he dreamed of, either.) "The man" is a synonym for someone – or, more particularly, some business – that is competing to satisfy customers. A lot of kids miss that these days. Ask them what teachers do, and they'll say, "educate kids." Ask them what doctors do, and they'll say, "heal the sick." Ask them what businesspeople do, and they'll say, "make money."

But teachers and doctors make money. Everyone gets paid for their work. So, they haven't really said anything about what businesspeople do. Here's a better explanation: they offer to make our lives better. We all depend on businesses to provide us with life's essentials — food, clothing, shelter, utilities, health care, and so on — as well as all the discretionary items that we want but don't need.

How is helping people solve their problems — or offering some product or service they want or need — "selling out"? It seems to me that the less virtuous path is thinking about myself and what I want rather than other people and what *they* want.

Everyone survives by serving others, often in more ways than one. For example, I provide articles and columns that my publisher needs. In doing so, I provide investment advice for my subscribers. That, in turn, provides my family with income. It's a win-win-win.

Personal industry is the first virtue. Work generates income. Working hard — and upgrading your skill set — creates more income. And more hours, more workdays, a side hustle, and/or a second job creates more income still.

The next virtue is frugality. Not deprivation — discipline. Most people don't struggle financially because they earn too little. They struggle because they spend too much. Like me, I'm sure you've known adults who earn a good living and still blow through everything they make each year. They are undisciplined spenders who simply must have the big house, the fancy car, the designer clothes, the impressive trips, and so on.

If you can afford these things and still save, great. But if you can't, it may be time to make some serious adjustments. And no one is in a better position to know where to cut back than the individual doing the spending.

Once someone has demonstrated industry and frugality, the next virtue is courage. If you keep your money in super-safe investments like Treasury bills, certificates of deposit, and money market funds, you will earn a low return, one that may not even keep up with inflation. That means you need to have the courage to buy real estate and/or stocks, even though no one can guarantee that your investments will be profitable.

Real estate tends to appreciate over time. But it generally requires a substantial mortgage and ongoing costs, like maintenance, repairs, property taxes, homeowner's insurance, and so on. Nothing has beaten the long-term return of a diversified portfolio of stocks.

The key is smart risk-taking. Not gambling. Not speculation. But educated, deliberate investing.

Diversification reduces your risk. Owning three profitable businesses is less risky than owning one profitable business. And owning 30 stocks – or 300 – is a lot less risky than owning one or two.

History shows that if you have the courage to move beyond ultraconservative investments and take intelligent risks, your returns will be far higher and your progress toward your most important financial goals far quicker.

Then comes the need for still another virtue: temperance. As the money compounds in value, many investors find the temptation to spend it irresistible. They decide they simply must have life's luxuries. I won't argue against these things. I've enjoyed plenty of them myself. However, I will argue that they should be worked into the household budget or saved for separately.

Why? Because if you see your growing retirement portfolio as a big pot of money that can be raided when an opportunity arises, there is a strong probability that's exactly what will happen. And that comfortable retirement? It will be a lot less comfortable – or a lot further off.

In short, the people who created this country built a moral structure on money. They emphasized hard work, temperance, and frugality. Their stoic legacy inhibited luxury and self-indulgence. Over the past 40 years, however, those social norms have been undermined. Debt and living for the moment have been strengthened. Character and restraint have been replaced by signaling and spending. And it has put a lot of Americans behind the eight ball financially.

It doesn't have to be this way. And for an increasing number of us, it can't be this way. No one needs to be a paragon. But the founders were on to something. Virtuous living is its own reward. A powerful side effect is that it also leads to increasing material rewards. Industry, frugality, courage, and temperance build character. But they will also help you build your net worth. And economic security is a big part of living the American Dream.

CHAPTER 7

Why Economic Inequality Is a Bogus Issue

> Everyone talks about inequality of outcome. But no one talks about inequality of effort.
>
> —Retired builder Braxton Green

Having read this far, you realize that by virtually every objective measure Americans today are better off than ever. Our standard of living has never been higher. Our life expectancy has doubled over the past century. We have never had faster communications, larger homes, safer cars, more laborsaving devices, more effective medicines, easier long-distance travel, more modern conveniences, or greater entertainment choices at our fingertips. And, thanks to soaring asset values, US household net worth is near record highs. We should count our blessings.

Yet, as I discussed earlier, many academics and journalists would prefer that we adopt *their worldview* — one rooted not in gratitude but in grievance. And they have what they believe is the perfect issue to make us feel angry, bitter, and demoralized: economic inequality.

When the founders signed the Declaration of Independence — which proclaims that "all men are created equal" — none of them believed that people are born with equal abilities and ambitions or that government could or should seek to engineer equal outcomes in Americans' efforts to succeed. Indeed, inequality has been pervasive since the very beginnings of recorded history. As historians Will and Ariel Durant pointed out, "Freedom and equality are sworn and everlasting enemies, and when one prevails the other dies."

Fortunately, Americans have chosen freedom. And that's a good thing since in societies where governments proclaim the goal of income equality, both poverty and inequality are more widespread than in societies promising freedom and opportunity.

Economic inequality is a bogus issue for four reasons. The first is that economic equality only exists in societies where everyone is poor. And no one wants that. The second is that income inequality — despite media claims to the contrary — is not getting worse. The third is that — unlike poverty — economic inequality is irrelevant to your personal well-being. And fourth, upward mobility based on merit — while creating unequal outcomes — benefits us all.

As Phil Gramm and Donald J. Boudreaux write in *The Triumph of Economic Freedom*,

> *As a whole the people are much better off in nations that choose freedom. Income inequality is grossly overstated in the official statistics of the United States because the Census Bureau chooses not to count two-thirds of all transfer payments paid to the recipients, while it fails to treat taxes paid as income lost to the taxpayers. When these corrections are made, the measure of income inequality is reduced by three-quarters. Counting all transfer payments and taxes, income inequality in America is lower today than it was in 1947.*

It's true that income and wealth distribution in the United States is unequal. But that's largely due to differences in aptitudes, household nurturing, ambition, persistence and, of course, luck. Not because someone engineered things that way.

Instead of recognizing rising prosperity across the board, redistributionists want you to compare your income and lifestyle to that of America's wealthiest individuals – so that even if you are safe, comfortable, and moving ahead, you can still feel that you've been shortchanged.

However, the facts suggest that for most Americans life has improved dramatically. Here's just one example: in 1950, American families spent 53% of their disposable income on food, clothing, and shelter – the basics. By 1970, it was down to 44%. Today, it's about 32%, according to US Bureau of Labor Statistics data.

And those figures don't even capture the vast improvement in quality.

Forty years ago, a basic television had a 25-inch screen, grainy resolution, and poor reception. Today, even a modestly priced flat-screen delivers 4K ultra-HD and streams thousands of on-demand programs.

Cars didn't come with heated seats, touch screens, backup cameras, and surround-sound speakers. Most vehicles easily last 150,000 to 200,000 miles – a huge leap from the past.

Even the homes we live in are bigger and better. The median square footage of new single-family homes in 2023 was 2,217 square feet, up from 1,500 square feet in 1973, despite smaller household sizes.

The cultural narrative encourages you to ignore this. Although we are living so much better than our recent ancestors, you can look up at those in the top 100th of 1% and feel bitter instead.

For example, Bill Gates has a 66,000-square-foot mansion that overlooks Lake Washington. Warren Buffett zips around the country in his private jet, a Bombardier Challenger 6,000. Oracle founder Larry Ellison has a 453-foot yacht with 82 rooms, a private cinema, and an extensive wine cellar.

But ask yourself: when Tiger Woods dines at a steakhouse, does he get a better cut of meat than you do? Does Oprah Winfrey have an iPhone that is faster than yours? Does Elon Musk have superior Wi-Fi?

Of course not. Once your basic needs are met and your lifestyle is secure, the returns from more wealth are mostly marginal.

Perhaps we need a bit of perspective. In the not-too-distant past, most American men earned a living doing hard, backbreaking work in farming, forestry, mining, or construction. We built things by hand. We blazed trails, forded rivers, crossed mountain ranges, and built our own homes and barns.

Almost nobody does those things anymore. Our lives are sedentary. Health experts have to remind us to walk, swim, stretch, and "exercise our cores." Nobody told your grandparents to exercise their cores. They were too busy trying to survive.

Maybe it takes a humorist to wake us up. In a *Wall Street Journal* column, Dave Barry wrote, "My mom, like my dad, and millions of other members of the Greatest Generation, had to contend with real adversity: the Great Depression, the Dust Bowl, hunger, poverty, disease, World War II, extremely low-fi 78 rpm records and telephones that – incredible as it sounds today – *could not even shoot video.*"

It's true the rich have gotten richer – but the rest of us have, too. Standards of living across all income levels have improved. Even America's poor are better off than the vast majority of people around the world today – and practically everyone in human history.

Most Americans below the poverty line now live in climate-controlled homes, have access to running water, internet, smartphones, flat-screen TVs, and often at least one automobile. They also live in larger accommodations than the average European.

Adjusted for inflation, household spending per person among the lowest-income fifth of Americans is comparable to median households in the early 1970s.

Historically, being poor meant having to struggle to get enough calories to survive. Today we have the opposite problem. Obesity has created a health-care crisis among the poor, since it is highly correlated with heart disease, diabetes, stroke, dementia, and even some forms of cancer. That's not good. But it's better than hunger and starvation.

The poor today can access unprecedented educational resources for free. Khan Academy, Coursera, YouTube, even full MIT and

Harvard courses are available online. If you want to learn about investing, AI, coding, or real estate, you're just a few clicks away.

They can also video chat with friends and family across the country and around the world. The wealthiest industrialists of the Gilded Age – men like Rockefeller and Carnegie – couldn't dream of the knowledge and communication tools now available to anyone with a smartphone.

And yet . . . many people in this country still feel miserable. Why? Because they're comparing themselves upward – constantly. Not to their parents. Not to global or historical averages. But to the richest people in the nation.

As former vice president Spiro Agnew noted, they're influenced by the "nattering nabobs of negativism" – pundits, columnists, and podcasters who amplify grievance and ignore progress.

Let me be clear: poverty and social mobility are real issues. We should support efforts to lift the bottom and make opportunity as widely available as possible. But economic inequality? The fact that Jeff Bezos and Elon Musk have more money than the rest of us? That's a problem people create in their heads.

It's built on a myth – that wealth is static and finite. Many are upset about this issue because they believe we live in a world where the only way one person has more is if someone else has less. This is a misconception. And a story from my childhood helps explain why.

I grew up in a middle-class household in the Shenandoah Valley of Virginia. My family belonged to a modest club with a swimming pool. At the end of each summer, the club held a pool party, one where a particular event drove us kids into a frenzy. The pool manager would take a large bucket of coins – mostly pennies and nickels but also some dimes and a few quarters – and toss them out into the pool.

The kids would take a minute to line up along the edge, gazing eagerly at the glittering coins below. Then he blew a whistle. We all dove in and scooped up as many coins as we could, obviously trying to pick up the dimes and quarters first. The big kids – who were stronger and could hold their breath longer – would always grab the most. That left less for us smaller kids. And there was nothing we could do about it.

Believe it or not, there are millions of educated adults who think this is essentially how our modern economy works. They suppose that a fixed amount of money exists and we're all in a mad scramble – often referred to as "the rat race" – to scoop up as much as possible, with the strongest or greediest taking the most. If Steph Curry and Taylor Swift have more – as they most certainly do – that means the rest of us necessarily have less, just like the smaller kids at the pool. And that's not fair!

These folks subscribe to the lump-sum fallacy, the idea that wealth – like those coins in the pool – exists in a fixed quantity. Yet this is completely wrong. Wealth isn't just distributed (or redistributed). It is created. It grows over time. If this weren't true, national gross domestic product (GDP), household incomes, and household net worth – in inflation-adjusted figures – would not keep increasing.

US GDP has grown from $1 trillion in 1947 to over $27 trillion in 2024, adjusted for inflation. That's not redistribution – that's wealth creation.

Let me use a different analogy: if I have a large vegetable garden, it doesn't prevent you from planting one of your own. If I have six children, that doesn't stop you from having your own kids. If Elon Musk has a fortune, that doesn't stop you – or anyone else – from building a fortune of your own.

Yet it's a safe bet that most Americans – and, sadly, most American journalists – don't understand this. The *Washington Post* recently ran an article about the problem of the "wealth gap." It lamented the fact that most of the country's wealth is in the hands of a relatively small percentage of the population.

Here's how *Post* writer Christopher Ingraham put it:

> Let's imagine that there are just 100 people in the United States. The richest guy (and, yes, he's probably a guy) owns more than one-third of the total wealth in this country. He's got a third of all the property, a third of the stock market and a third of anything else that can be owned. Not bad.
>
> The next-richest four people together own 28 percent of all the stuff. The next five people together own 14 percent of all the things, and the next 10 own 12 percent.

> We've accounted for just 20 percent of the people but nearly 90 percent of the total wealth. You can probably tell where this is going.
>
> By the time we reach the bottom 40 percent of Americans, guess what? We've run out of stuff. Sorry guys, you get nothing.

This is so ignorant it's hard not to laugh. Ingraham truly believes that if you are someone who has worked, saved, invested, and now has significant assets, you have somehow deprived others. Thanks to your wealth accumulation, the country has "run out of stuff" (whatever that means) – and ordinary folks "get nothing." The editorial staff at the *Post* thought this made enough sense to run it.

The piece is totally misleading. Wealth isn't taken. It's created by meeting human needs.

Let's use a real-world example, examining one of the best-known celebrities in the nation: Oprah Winfrey. Oprah rose from poverty and a challenging childhood in rural Mississippi to become a highly influential media personality. Along the way, she became one of the richest women in the world with a net worth of more than $3 billion. She got there by offering tremendous value. Oprah produced content that millions of people willingly consumed. They watched her show, bought her books, tuned into her interviews, and trusted her recommendations. She built a media empire as a result.

I would like Christopher Ingraham – or anyone else for that matter – to explain how Oprah getting rich somehow deprived wealth and opportunity to the rest of us. How would her prodigious income and net worth have somehow fallen into our pockets if she hadn't earned it? How did her success deprive *anyone* of being economically successful themselves?

It didn't happen. She earned her fortune by serving a huge audience. Along the way, she provided jobs, launched careers, and gave away millions to charity. The same logic applies to most high achievers. Whether it's Bezos, Jobs, Walton, or Musk – they got rich by solving problems and creating value, not by stealing wealth from others.

Funny how when you stop talking about "millionaires and billionaires" and start thinking about how wealth is created – by meeting people's wants and needs – this reality becomes clear.

Some will concede that the ultrarich earned and deserve their prodigious wealth. But they're angry for another reason: they don't pay their "fair share" of taxes. Yet that's also untrue. The US tax code is highly progressive. And the share of taxes paid by the affluent is much higher than their share of income.

According to the latest IRS data:

- The top 1% of income earners paid 40.4% of all federal income taxes in 2022.
- The top 10% paid 72%.
- Meanwhile, the bottom 50% paid just 3%.

That last number overstates the reality — because tens of millions of Americans receive refundable tax credits, meaning they pay negative income taxes. Meanwhile, the people most often criticized for "hoarding" wealth are the ones funding most government services.

Some insist that we should have an annual wealth tax that hits the rich and benefits the poor and underclass. Wouldn't that be a good way to help more people live the American Dream?

No. It wouldn't. Aside from the morality of the government taking wealth from those who earned it and giving it to those who didn't, wealth taxes are questionable constitutionally, economically harmful, and historically shortsighted. They are a textbook case of good intentions producing bad results.

Let's start with the basics. The US Constitution was deliberately written to restrict the federal government's taxing power. And the Supreme Court has been clear: only realized income qualifies for taxation. In *Eisner v. Macomber* (1920), the Court drew a bright line: unrealized gains are not income.

Any effort to call an increase in net worth "income" runs smack into that precedent. And it's not just semantics.

Redefining wealth accumulation as taxable income presents three inescapable problems:

- **Valuation.** How do you fairly assess the taxable value of illiquid assets like family businesses or private equity holdings?

You can't. The process becomes arbitrary and subjective, opening the door to legal disputes and bureaucratic overreach.
- **Double taxation.** Capital gains and estate taxes already apply to appreciated assets. A wealth tax would pile on an additional layer, making long-term investment less attractive and punishing wealth creation.
- **Retroactivity.** Trying to tax past asset appreciation as if it were current income violates the Fifth Amendment's protection against government takings without just compensation.

However, confiscatory taxes don't just run afoul of the Constitution; they also fail the basic test of sound economics.

Global experiments with wealth taxes have all followed the same playbook – and the results are consistently destructive.

- **Capital flight and investment declines.** Spain's 3% wealth tax led to a 20% exodus of millionaire capital within 18 months. Norway lost $3.4 billion in taxable wealth after a modest 1% increase. And France? Ten thousand millionaires left the country between 2002 and 2012 before the tax was ultimately scrapped.
- **Market distortion and illiquidity.** When people are forced to sell assets just to pay the tax bill, valuations get distorted. Investors turn to tax shelters instead of growth-focused ventures. And when assets are valuable but illiquid, taxpayers face liquidity crises.
- **Broad economic damage.** A 2% wealth tax in the United States would shrink GDP by more than 6% and eliminate over one million jobs within a decade. Wages would fall, capital investment would dry up, and the middle class – despite being "exempt" – would see an 8% drop in income.

It's not just theory. In Spain, inequality didn't budge under the wealth tax, but the economy shrank 4.3% annually. That's not redistribution. That's destruction. We've seen this pattern before. The federal income tax was introduced in 1913 as a "modest" levy on the richest 1%, with rates starting at 1% and peaking at 7%. Fast-forward to 2022: the top 1% still pays more than 40% of all income taxes, yet middle-class households now face the following:

- Marginal rates over 22% on income above $89,450
- Payroll taxes of 15.3%, capped only for Social Security
- Nearly 10% in additional state and local taxes in high-tax states

How did that happen? Three mechanisms:

- **Bracket creep.** Inflation quietly pushes taxpayers into higher brackets.
- **Base broadening.** Deductions get eliminated (as in 1986), making more income taxable.
- **Rate normalization.** "Temporary" tax hikes (like those during World War II) become permanent.

The income tax started as a tax on the wealthy. It's now a system that hits the middle class harder than colonial taxes ever did relative to income. Is it not likely that the same thing would happen with a wealth tax, hitting first billionaires, then millionaires, then the rest of us?

Confiscatory taxes don't make the system fairer. They make it less efficient and more punitive. And wealth taxes aren't just unsound policy – they are a violation of the property rights on which this country was built.

Rather than chasing wealth taxes that are unconstitutional and economically counterproductive, Congress should do what it rarely does: simplify the existing tax code, broaden the base through economic growth, and keep America competitive in global capital markets.

The Constitution's limits on direct taxation weren't written by accident. They reflect a deep understanding that prosperity is driven by protecting individual rights – not punishing success. That's the real way to build a stronger, freer, and more prosperous America.

Groups like Oxfam ignore this. Oxfam describes itself as "a global organization that fights inequality to end poverty and injustice." Each year, it issues alarmist reports warning of "extreme inequality," pointing out that billionaires control more wealth than half the world's population. Their message: the rich are getting richer, and that's inherently unfair. It proposes annual wealth taxes of 2% on millionaires, 3% on multimillionaires, and 5% on billionaires.

As I've explained, that would be counterproductive. But there's an even bigger issue here. Global economic inequality is falling, not rising. According to a recent UBS/Credit Suisse Global Wealth Report – the very one that Oxfam used to reach its conclusions – most inequality indicators are at their lowest levels in a century. The global Gini coefficient measuring inequality has fallen from 92 to 88 since 2000. The top 1% of income earners saw their global share drop 9.2% over this period. Global poverty is now at its lowest level ever recorded: 8.6%, down from 29% in 2000.

The data clearly shows that global inequality is narrowing. More people are entering the middle class. Poverty is shrinking. Living standards are rising. Yet Oxfam – and others – are obsessed with redistribution. Like many people and organizations, Oxfam doesn't understand how the global economy works. It believes that wealth and poverty is a zero-sum game, that the only way one person gets more income – or greater wealth – is by taking it from or denying it to others.

If the world economy were a pizza, this would be true. A hungry person who took two slices would leave fewer slices for everyone else. But that's not how the economy works. The economy is more like a pizza oven. We bake more pies all the time. And anyone willing to contribute can share in the wealth.

It's simply not true that successful people reduce opportunities for the rest of us. If you got a raise last year, it doesn't mean that someone else got a pay cut. If your portfolio earned a big return, it doesn't mean someone else lost money.

The real shame of Oxfam – and other organizations that exaggerate the problem of economic inequality – is that they always blame "the rich" instead of encouraging the non-rich to get educated, develop skills, and embody the personal characteristics (like reliability and persistence) that will enable them to rise economically.

Yes, some folks will lag due to no fault of their own. Some are born with a low IQ (a big detriment in a knowledge-based economy). Some may have physical, mental, or emotional limitations. Others may have simply had tragic circumstances or a terrible run of luck.

But Oxfam dislikes wealth more than it hates poverty. So its proposed solutions are never about empowering men and women to create real change in their lives. Instead, it's always about higher taxes and more redistribution. Yet history shows that these policies lessen opportunities for those at the bottom of the income ladder, making it harder for them to succeed.

To fix the income inequality that matters most to you – your own household's – the key is not to focus on what other people have. It's to ask a few hard questions to the face in the mirror.

Have I done enough to increase my value to my current or prospective employer? Have I managed my monthly wages and expenses well? Have I saved regularly? Have I invested those savings wisely? Have I left my investments alone to compound – Warren Buffett calls it "a snowball rolling downhill" – so that they create ever greater wealth?

These are the questions that can lead to powerful, life-changing habits – and true financial independence. Being resentful and envious of those who have more? That doesn't achieve anything. Envy has been called the worst of the seven deadly sins because unlike greed, lust, gluttony, sloth, pride, and wrath it doesn't provide even a moment's relief or pleasure.

If you don't have enough money to live your version of the American Dream, what should you do? I've spent the last four decades studying how people get rich in America – and why so many don't. A good summary of what I've learned over this period can be found in *The Millionaire Next Door* by Thomas Stanley – and *The Next Millionaire Next Door*, a collaboration with his daughter Dr. Sarah Stanley Fallaw.

They discovered that wealthy households follow a remarkably similar formula. They optimize their education or marketable skills, maximize their incomes, live within their means, save regularly, invest prudently, and let their money compound over a long period of time, generally decades.

Virtually everyone who is nearing retirement age today who isn't financially independent has made one or more of the following mistakes:

- They didn't work enough.
- They worked but didn't save.
- They saved but didn't invest.
- They invested but not wisely.
- They invested wisely but couldn't resist spending their capital rather than letting it compound.

Some people don't like this analysis. Not because it doesn't align with the real world, but because it does. And that means taking responsibility for your own economic well-being.

Before some readers accuse me of being uncaring or hardhearted, let's recall that we're not talking about poverty here. Unlike economic inequality, poverty is a real problem. Some folks – not most but some – find it impossible to earn a living wage and save. I support a social welfare network for those whose mental or physical disabilities – or tragic circumstances – make it impossible for them to rise. For the rest of us, the path to financial success is straightforward.

Let's talk about the economic inequality that matters most: what your income is and what it could be.

Essentially, your earned income is decided by nine factors:

- Your educational attainment
- Your chosen profession
- Your years of experience
- Your hours worked
- Your work ethic
- Your social skills
- Your competence and proficiency at what you do
- Your ability to cooperate with, inspire, and lead your coworkers
- And your ambition to rise in the organization

If you want to earn more, the choice is clear: make yourself indispensable to someone. Yes, certain people are born with greater genetic gifts than others. You and I were not born with the looks of Brad Pitt, the physique of LeBron James, or the intellect of Isaac Newton. Too bad for us.

Some are dealt better hands. They are born to more supportive parents or into more affluent households. (Although I'd take the former over the latter any day.) But it's up to each of us to play whatever hand we're dealt as skillfully as possible.

From an economic standpoint, that means maximizing your education and marketable skills; showing competence, reliability, and integrity at work; and doing whatever you can to rise in the organization. (Or else seek better alternatives elsewhere.)

Complaining that "capitalism is broken," "the system is rigged," and "life isn't fair" will not increase your income or net worth one iota. It is, however, guaranteed to make you unhappy.

Warren Buffett – someone who knows a thing or two about wealth accumulation – wrote about economic inequality in an Op-Ed piece in the *Wall Street Journal*:

> *"The poor are most definitely not poor because the rich are rich. Nor are the rich undeserving. Most of them have contributed brilliant innovations or managerial expertise to America's wellbeing. We all live far better because of Henry Ford, Steve Jobs, Sam Walton and the like."*

You probably don't have the skills or the access to capital that these geniuses had. But that isn't necessary. There are simple steps you can take to ensure your own financial independence. We'll discuss those in Chapters 14 through 17.

Social scientists and other academics often claim that wealth disparity in this country is due not to differences in education, skill, hard work, persistence, and calculated risk-taking but merely to "luck."

They make this argument to persuade others to accept their remedy: radically higher taxes and greater income redistribution. To counter those who prefer to keep most of what they earn, the media labels them greedy, selfish, uncaring . . . and, of course, "lucky." How much does luck or good fortune really have to do with it? You be the judge.

According to the US Census Bureau, three-quarters of households in the top income quintile have two workers. Less than 5% of those in the bottom quintile do. For every hour worked by a bottom-quintile household, a rich household works five. Is it *lucky* that one household works five times more than another – or is there a better, alternative explanation?

That's not just luck. That's effort.

Bruce Grocott, a Labour party member of the House of Lords, once said, "I have long been of the opinion that if work were such a splendid thing, the rich would have kept more of it for themselves." Wake up, Bruce. According to the Census Bureau, workers in the top 5% average 57.7 hours a week. That's not lounging around. That's grinding.

A study published recently by the National Bureau of Economic Research – using a rich vein of survey data tracking individuals as far back as 1979 – found that the more people work over their lifetimes, the more they earn. (No surprise there.) But a major determinant of total lifetime hours worked is individual choice. Some prefer to work more. Some prioritize other activities.

The study found that those who work more earn more because they accumulate more skills during the extra time on the job. The overlapping effect of more hours and greater skills acquisition account for a hefty share of overall differences in lifetime earnings. The truth disturbs some, but income inequality is often a matter of choice rather than intractable economic or social forces.

Of course, it requires more than just long hours to achieve financial independence. You also need to save, invest, and compound. Most of us work, but too many don't save.

Those who are unable to work deserve our empathy. But that cannot possibly describe most of us. As I pointed out previously, the US Census Bureau estimates that the median household income was $80,610 in this country in 2023.

Let's imagine that you and I are two hypothetical families earning exactly the median income. Then watch how quickly our behavior changes our economic circumstances.

I'm a spendthrift. I blow every penny I make each year. You, however, are more prudent. You regularly save 3% of your monthly income – $190 a month – through a Roth IRA. Let's further stipulate that you invest it in a plain-vanilla S&P 500 Index fund that generates nothing more or less than its average long-term return of about 10%.

After the first decade, with dividends reinvested, you have $36,830. I have zero. As you can see, things are already unequal.

In 20 years, you have $131,865. (Finding $400 for an emergency is not a problem.) I have nothing. In 30 years, you have $378,361. (I still have nada.) And in 40 years, you have more than $1 million. Plus, it's tax-free. (Let's remember you were smart enough to invest in a Roth IRA where distributions are tax-free.)

Senator Bernie Sanders will stand at the podium and condemn you for your greed. (As if living within your means, deferring gratification, saving, and investing is selfish behavior.) But he will ask me – who saved nothing and therefore has nothing – for my vote, so that he can fix the maldistribution of wealth in this country.

Of course, you may not have 30 or 40 years to save and invest. In that case, you need to earn more, save more, or earn a higher rate of return . . . or all three. If you saved 10% of your income rather than 3% and invested in the higher-returning Russell 2000 index of small-cap stocks, for example, you would have $141,305 in 10 years and $580,176 in 20 years. You would be a millionaire in less than 25 years. Amp up the savings or the returns even more and you'll be there quicker still.

In short, it's your behavior rather than luck, fortune, or "the breaks" that ultimately determines your financial well-being. What can you do – specifically – to accelerate your wealth accumulation?

- Upgrade your education or marketable skills to maximize your income.
- Live beneath your means. (When your outgo exceeds your income, your upkeep becomes your downfall.)
- Save as much as you reasonably can, while still living a balanced life. (Saving all your money for retirement is like saving all your sex for old age. It doesn't make a lot of sense.)
- Invest those savings in the world's highest returning asset: a diversified portfolio of high-quality stocks.

- Minimize your investment costs.
- Tax manage your portfolio – as with a Roth IRA or other qualified retirement plan – to avoid the prying hands of the IRS.
- Let your money compound as long as possible.
- And try to stay married. (Not always possible, in some cases, but a divorce settlement will do far more damage to your net worth than a bear market.)

Is this realistically achievable? Indeed, it is. As a former money manager, I watched hundreds of clients do just that. They weren't lucky. They had a plan. They stuck to it. And they reaped the rewards. With time and discipline, you can, too.

What about the great disparity between Black and white incomes and household net wealth? Even after the Civil Rights Acts of the 1960s outlawed explicit discrimination, informal barriers persisted for decades. So yes, the legacy of racism has affected wealth accumulation.

While much remains to be done, I'd like to believe that Martin Luther King Jr. would be pleased with the progress the nation has made over the last 65 years.

The Civil Rights Act of 1964 and the Voting Rights Act of 1965 were landmark pieces of legislation that outlawed racial discrimination. Since the passage of the 1968 Fair Housing Act, racial segregation in housing has fallen by 30%. The number of African American elected officials at various levels of government has increased significantly since the 1960s.

There have been significant advances in education and employment opportunity for African Americans. There is far more financial inclusion, with greatly improved access to banking, investments, and homeownership. There is a growing Black middle class, and the number of Black-owned businesses has increased dramatically.

African Americans have made major contributions to American culture, music, sports, entertainment, literature, and art. More African Americans than ever are attending college and pursuing higher education. And there are clear signs that racism has declined.

When I was born, for example, interracial marriage was forbidden in over 30 US states. But in 1967, the Supreme Court in *Loving v. Virginia* made interracial marriage legal in all 50 states.

There has been economic improvement as well. Over the past 50 years, according to a recent study by the Pew Research Center, the proportion of Black Americans who are high income (more than $156,000 a year) has risen from 5% to 12%.

(And Indian Americans are the highest earners in the country with a median household income of $145,000 in 2022. That's hard to square with the notion that we routinely discriminate against "people of color.")

Fewer Black Americans are poor than 50 years ago, and more than twice as many are rich. Yet Black poverty remains disproportionate. And so does household net worth. At the end of 2022, white households had a median net worth of $250,400, while Black households had a median net worth of just $27,100.

Is this due primarily to racism, as social justice advocates maintain? Racism certainly exists in some quarters today. But not every disparity can be attributed to discrimination. In American sports, for example, Blacks are overrepresented in professional football and basketball. Whites are overrepresented in professional hockey and tennis. Hispanics are overrepresented in Major League Baseball.

Geographic and cultural differences – that lead to differences in abilities – provide a better explanation for this than racial discrimination.

White households on average have much greater wealth in this country than Black households. Yet Asian households have the highest median net worth of all: $320,900. Are white Americans really discriminating in favor of Asian Americans? Perhaps there is a better explanation.

For example, earned income – and ultimately net worth – is highly correlated with education. Asian American households, on average, have greater educational attainment than white households. And white households, on average, have higher levels of educational attainment than Black households.

Studies show that better-educated individuals of any race have higher incomes. For example, 2020 census data shows more than nine million Black Americans with higher incomes than the median incomes of white Americans.

There are also counties in Appalachia where the median household income of white Americans is thousands of dollars less than the median household income of Black Americans.

Aside from formal education, there is the matter of basic financial knowledge. According to the 2023 Personal Finance Index report from the TIAA Institute and the Global Financial Literacy Excellence Center, American adults have a "generally poor" level of financial literacy.

Polls show that only about a third of adults have a high financial knowledge – as shown by their ability to answer five questions about topics like compound interest, inflation, and risk. The percentages are much lower for Black and Hispanic adults.

High school financial instruction overwhelmingly lowers loan delinquencies, improves credit scores, and reduces the use of expensive services like payday lending. Yet, according to the Center for Financial Literacy at Champlain College, just seven states – Alabama, Iowa, Mississippi, Missouri, Tennessee, Utah, and Virginia – require high school students to take a semester-long personal finance course. And five states have no personal finance requirements whatsoever.

Aside from differences in education and financial literacy, some of us are born into affluent families – with all the advantages that entails. Families are the primary transmitters of social capital. Some children are taught the advantages of industriousness, self-reliance, personal responsibility, and the deferral of gratification. Others are not.

Personal striving also plays a role in determining who thrives. Economic inequality between individuals can often be the result of differences in aptitude, effort, resourcefulness, and persistence.

Household formation also plays a role. For example, white, female-headed, single-parent families have had a poverty rate more than double the poverty rate of Black married-couple families in every year from 1994 to 2020, the latest year for which data is currently available.

The data shows that Black married couples in which both husband and wife are college educated earn more than white married couples where both husband and wife are college educated.

It also shows that Black immigrants earn more than native-born Black Americans – and are less likely to live in poverty. It's hard to believe that white Americans discriminate more against native-born Black Americans than Black immigrants.

None of this refutes the notion that employer biases can be responsible for disparities in income and, ultimately, household wealth. Serious wealth accumulation is a process that takes decades.

Yet when I think back to the 1980s and 1990s, I recall countless business meetings where – unless lunch was being served – every face in the room was white. That certainly wasn't because there weren't any African Americans qualified to sit at the table. Even after formal discrimination ended in the United States, informal discrimination endured for many years.

Black people in America suffered through 250 years of slavery plus another 150 years during which they were denied equal opportunities. They were forced to attend separate but unequal schools. They were routinely passed over for jobs and promotions. They were subject to redlining, which confined them to the poorest neighborhoods in town. They were denied personal loans and mortgages, even when their incomes and credit scores were adequate.

It's not possible to quantify exactly how much these factors from years past affect the median net worth of Black households today. But any fair-minded individual would concede that the effects were subtractive for long-term wealth creation.

Circumstances have improved for most Black Americans over the years. Government programs have played a role. But then so has the private sector. In the pursuit of profits, businesspeople hire the most qualified people they can find for every position. Passing over better-qualified candidates because of their skin color is not a smart business move. Especially since those individuals can take their talents to a competitor.

Other factors also affect wealth accumulation. It's not just a matter of how much we make. It's how we budget. How we spend.

How we borrow. Whether we insure. How we save. How we invest. And whether we own our homes – and build equity – or rent.

In short, race alone doesn't explain wealth disparities. Education, marriage, household structure, savings behavior, financial literacy, and work hours also matter – a lot.

And here's the good news. Whether a person is Black, white, brown, or purple, the rules of wealth creation are the same. Studies show that the wealthiest Americans stay in school as long as they can, earn as much as they can, save as much as they can, invest as smartly as they can, and leave their money untouched – so it can compound in value – as long as they can.

These are the basic principles of wealth creation, available to strivers of every race, gender, creed, and orientation. They are the essential steps in achieving financial independence – and living the American Dream.

CHAPTER 8

The Enemies of the American Dream

> Some ideas are so stupid that only intellectuals believe them.
> —Novelist George Orwell

By now you realize why America is truly an exceptional nation. You recognize that our standard of living has never been higher. You understand that for decades US wages have risen faster than prices, making most things more affordable, not less so. And you see that the nation's richest people do nothing to limit others' opportunity to rise, making economic inequality a bogus issue.

So who has convinced so many US citizens that the American Dream is dead?

It's a group of powerful influencers that I call *the enemies of the American Dream*.

The effect of these people is both pervasive and dangerous. They damage the hopes and ambitions of millions. For some, the harm is unintentional. Others do it deliberately – because they have a cause to promote, a candidate to elect, or a product to sell.

Regardless of intent, the impact is the same. These voices make it far less likely that you'll achieve your most important financial goals. That's why I call out their arguments for what they are: mental clutter that poisons your outlook, weakens your motivation, and obscures the fact that the American Dream is still alive and attainable.

Let's take a closer look at these dream killers.

ENEMY OF THE DREAM NO. 1: U.S. PUBLIC EDUCATION

According to national assessments, the reading and math skills of American students are not only stagnant, they're getting worse.

In 2024, 67% of eighth graders scored at or below the basic reading level, the worst performance since the National Assessment of Educational Progress (NAEP) began testing in 1992. Only 60% of fourth graders reached the same threshold. Many assume these results stem from the pandemic – and that certainly didn't help – but the declines predate COVID-19 and are seen across all regions, school types, and demographics.

The *Wall Street Journal* noted, "Worsening reading skills have potentially wide-ranging consequences. Test scores have been linked to the economic success of both the nation and individuals. Students with limited reading skills are less likely to graduate from high school."

That also means they are less likely to work a higher-paying job. Perhaps we should change that well-known bumper sticker from "If you can read this, thank a teacher" to "If you haven't achieved the Dream, thank a teacher."

Not only are reading skills down but so are math skills. Polls show that Americans graduate from high school lacking even the most basic financial literacy.

High school graduates today are often financially illiterate. Many can't calculate compound interest, don't understand how IRAs or 401(k)s work, and can't compare fixed-rate versus adjustable-rate mortgages. And many of their teachers don't understand these things, either.

Equally concerning is the shift in how history is taught in public schools. Many educators have moved away from the traditional narrative of American exceptionalism, which emphasized the nation's many achievements – our progress, innovation, and resilience – and instead emphasize slavery, the subjugation of Native Americans, colonialism, racial discrimination, and social inequality. They have mistaken part of the story for the main thread.

During COVID-19 lockdowns, many parents saw firsthand what their children were being taught – and were alarmed. In some cases, students were being told that the United States is an inherently flawed and fundamentally unjust society where the average citizen is shut out of opportunity.

I remember when my son David came home from middle school and told me his math teacher had told the class the American Dream doesn't exist. She called it "the American Pipe Dream."

David – having heard me champion the opposite viewpoint for years – objected, loudly. So loudly, in fact, that his teacher invited me to speak to the class. I accepted and gave a 35-minute presentation, complete with data, graphs, and historical context – much of the same information I've presented in this book.

Afterward, there was no discussion. No Q&A. Just a polite thank-you and an escort to the door.

I have no doubt his teacher genuinely believed what she told her students. And she has the right to her opinion. But I pulled my son out of that school (for that and other reasons). What still puzzles me is why she felt the need to share her pessimism with her class. I guess she felt she was only speaking "her truth."

But that view isn't supported by facts. And it wasn't preparing her students to believe in their own potential.

ENEMY OF THE DREAM NO. 2: MAINSTREAM MEDIA

Yes, I'm back with public enemy no. 2. As I've noted throughout, a strong negativity bias runs through the nation's news coverage. Positive developments are often glossed over — or ignored completely — while bad news is repeated endlessly, often stripped of context and presented in the most alarming way possible.

That's why, regardless of the party in power or the actual economic data, polls have consistently shown that most Americans believe the country is on the wrong track.

(This has remained fairly consistent through expansions and recessions and under both Democratic and Republican administrations.)

A 2022 analysis by the American Psychological Association found that over 90% of news headlines are negative, with stories increasingly designed to provoke emotions like fear, anger, and disgust.

Why is media coverage so negative? Because that's where the money is. Media companies prosper based on the size of their audience. And since human beings are hardwired to be on a continual lookout for potential threats and dangers, the media piles them on . . . real, potential, and imagined.

It's not that the things the media reports aren't true. It's that facts are regularly taken out of context and delivered without a counterbalancing perspective. Mitigating factors make a story less sensational. And the less sensational a piece is, the less likely it is to be viewed, heard, liked, or shared.

Part of this is just the nature of the news. Bad things happen quickly. Good things generally take time. It takes a long time to put up a building but only a few seconds to blow one up. (And the latter makes better television.)

Plane crashes always make the news and car crashes almost never do, even though car crashes kill far more people than plane crashes each year. As a result, many people have a fear of flying. But almost no one has a fear of driving. This creates misperception of risk. Some folks fly with white knuckles from New York to Los Angeles and then heave a sigh of relief as they pull onto the San Diego freeway. Statistically, that makes no sense.

Heavy consumers of news often become glum. They are also more likely to experience anxiety, depressed moods, or a feeling of learned helplessness. No wonder trust in the media is near an all-time low.

People who don't follow the news are called *uninformed*. But those who follow it closely are often *misinformed*.

If you're looking for a solution, let me suggest 1,440 Daily Digest. It's a free, daily email newsletter that delivers concise, fact-based summaries of the most important news stories across various topics, including politics, business, science, sports, and entertainment. Its aim is to provide unbiased, digestible information to readers who want to stay informed without the influence of sensationalism or political agendas.

ENEMY OF THE DREAM NO. 3: SOCIAL MEDIA

The rise of social media has transformed the way Americans interact, consume news, and perceive the world. While these platforms offer opportunities for connection and information sharing, a growing body of evidence reveals that social media contributes to heightened pessimism among Americans.

According to a 2020 Pew Research Center survey, 64% of Americans believe that social media has a mostly negative effect on the way things are going in the country. Only 10% see a mostly positive effect.

The main reasons cited include the spread of misinformation, exposure to hate and harassment, and the amplification of conflict and extremism.

While the mainstream media is overly negative, social media is even worse. With no reputation to protect, no integrity to uphold, and no credibility to safeguard, "stuff" from various sources circulates based on algorithms that have nothing to do with truthfulness. It's the negativity bias of cable news and supermarket tabloids – on steroids.

Several mechanisms inherent to social media platforms contribute to this. News articles with negative language are more likely to be shared on social media. This incentivizes the production and dissemination of negative content, shaping the tone of discourse and exposing users to a disproportionate amount of negative information.

Social media CEOs – like all CEOs – want to maximize revenue. To maximize revenue, they maximize engagement. To maximize engagement, they maximize outrage. In short, the algorithms choose outrage because that generates the most revenue.

A significant share of Americans – about one in three – worry that social media does more harm than good to their mental health. Nearly half believes it hurts society at large. Some – like author and neuroscientist Sam Harris – believe the misinformation and negativity bias on social media has gotten so bad that he fears the country may become "ungovernable."

Even in my own field – investment publishing – there are people who take bad news, twist it into apocalyptic predictions, and then sell you a newsletter to "protect your wealth." Why? Because it sells, year in and year out.

Their usual claim is that you are going to lose *everything* you've worked for your whole life unless you take Joe Blow's Get-Rich-Tomorrow investment letter and learn how to protect yourself from the coming currency collapse, stock market crash, economic Armageddon, or Greater Depression that lies dead ahead.

Most of these guys – and they do tend to be men, not women – have been saying much the same thing not just for years but decades. The reasons get a regular freshening to reflect the latest scary headlines . . . but their dystopian conclusions remain the same. Why? Because *fear sells*. Or, as one perma-bear editor told me over dinner one night, "My job is selling gloom and doom to grumpy old men."

In other words, if you've reached a certain age . . . and you have a pessimistic outlook . . . and you've bought a subscription to some guru who believes the US economy and financial markets are finally going down for the count. . . you might be getting played like a Stradivarius. And this makes it *far less likely* that your financial goals will be met.

ENEMY OF THE DREAM NO. 4: PUBLIC INTELLECTUALS

Public intellectuals are also perennial doom-mongers. Let's consider their motivations – and their impact on your dreams.

In intellectual circles, pessimism is equated with moral seriousness. Journalists believe that by accentuating the negative they are acting as watchdogs, muckrakers, and whistleblowers. Intellectuals know that they can attain instant gravitas by pointing to an unsolved problem and arguing that it is a symptom of a sick society.

Pessimism for this group is also a form of upstaging. Intellectual elites compete for prestige and influence. Complaining about our modern society makes them feel superior to businesspeople, politicians, and, of course, the great unwashed.

They sincerely believe that they are equipped with the knowledge and authority to direct the rest of us. (This was especially apparent during the COVID-19 pandemic.) They don't believe that we can make good decisions for ourselves. So – as our moral and intellectual betters – they presume to tell us what to think and what to do.

People with extraordinary mental abilities – scientists, researchers, engineers, and others – are responsible for many of the great advances in medicine, science, and technology that have benefited us all. But few of these folks are *public intellectuals*.

Economist Thomas Sowell defines that group as people whose final output is not products or services but *ideas*. He's referring to theorists, critics, and ideologues whose only validation process is the approval of their peers, people in academia, or the press who think *just like they do*. This conveniently insulates them from the consequences of their ideas when they fail in the real world.

In his bestselling 1968 book *The Population Bomb*, for example, environmentalist Paul Ehrlich said, "the battle to feed all of humanity is over. In the 1970s the world will undergo famines – hundreds of millions of people are going to starve to death in spite of any cash programs embarked upon now."

Looking back more than half a century later, we know that some people in poor countries succumbed to malnutrition. But the mass famine that Ehrlich predicted was spectacularly wrong. In fact, many countries were stuck with unsold agricultural surpluses and populations struggling with obesity. Professor Ehrlich stuck to his doomsaying as the years went by. But his scary predictions about mass starvation never came to pass.

The surprising thing is that he not only continues to receive widespread acclaim from journalists and academics but also honors and grants from prestigious institutions. He even won a MacArthur Fellowship, widely known as the "genius grant."

Ehrlich is hardly an exception. In the early 20th century, astronomer and mathematician Simon Newcomb, known for his work on celestial mechanics, said, "Flight by machines heavier than air is unpractical and insignificant, if not utterly impossible." In the 1920s, British economist John Maynard Keynes predicted that deflation, rather than inflation, would be the dominant problem of the future. Nobel Prize–winner Paul Krugman wrote in 1998, "By 2005 or so, it will become clear that the Internet's impact on the economy has been no greater than the fax machine's."

This pessimism about humanity's ability to advance and solve problems is not just restricted to economics and technology. Many intellectuals openly attack the very idea of a meritocracy, where advancement is based on ability and talent rather than class or privilege.

Take one of the nation's most widely known intellectuals, Noam Chomsky, for example. Chomsky, who openly championed Hugo Chavez's rise to power in Venezuela before his economic mismanagement and political repression caused a humanitarian catastrophe, wrote a book titled *Requiem for the American Dream*.

Knowing Chomsky's socialist ideals, I resisted reading it initially. But I felt that I had to give a fair hearing to intellectuals who deny the existence of the Dream. It would be an understatement to say I found the book unpersuasive. From the beginning, I felt like I was hearing the ravings of an overserved patron at the end of the bar. By the end, I was reminded of the gag headline featured in an episode of *The Simpsons*: "Old Man Yells at Cloud."

Chomsky believes the American Dream is dead because workers don't control the means of production. Instead, the top executives – who answer to the board of directors and, ultimately, the shareholders (who include millions of mom-and-pop investors) – are in charge.

What Chomsky proposes – putting the workers in charge of the nation's major corporations – has never been adopted by any country in the world at any time in history. And for good reason. To believe the workers – who didn't start the company, have no experience running it, and stand to lose nothing (since they own nothing) if it fails – is completely unrealistic. Apparently, this is no obstacle to intellectuals, most of whom have never worked in the private sector and live in castles in the air.

Of the American Dream, Chomsky says, "It's all collapsed." And the culprit, in his view, is rich people. He finds it deplorable that the constitution prevents the majority of Americans from organizing and ultimately confiscating the property of the economically successful.

He is down on the United States generally, referring to it as "a settler-colonial society, the most brutal form of imperialism." It never occurs to Chomsky that there is not one acre of livable land on Earth that is occupied by people who didn't, or whose ancestors didn't, take it by force. Since time immemorial, humans have seized land from prior settlers. Even tribes in North America took "native land" from other tribes in the centuries before Europeans arrived. (The exception was the first humans who crossed the land bridge from Siberia and entered the Americas more than 20,000 years ago.)

Like many progressives, Chomsky divides the world into oppressors and the oppressed. He argues for sharply higher taxes, greater redistribution, and whatever confiscation is necessary to take wealth from the people who earned it and turn it over to those who didn't. In the name of fairness, equality, and social justice, of course.

This idea appeals to many. But it hasn't created prosperity anywhere it's been tried. Thanks to Hugo Chavez's policies and legacy, for example, Venezuela has experienced one of the largest mass migrations in modern history. In 2024 alone, an estimated 7.7 million Venezuelans fled the country due to severe economic deprivation and political repression. Those who remained have resorted to extreme measures, including scavenging for food from dumpsters.

It would be comforting to think that public intellectuals like Paul Ehrlich, Paul Krugman, and Noam Chomsky are outliers. Sadly, they are not. Economist Thomas Sowell has written extensively about the effect of intellectuals' ideas on society. They often promote ideas that sound noble in theory but fail to work in practice.

These ideas always focus on *systemic* explanations for social problems, which fosters a sense of helplessness and dependency, two qualities that do nothing to help anyone achieve the American Dream.

Many intellectuals operate in a realm detached from reality, where their ideas are judged by how they sound, not by their results. They promote ideas such as victimhood and oppression to explain economic inequalities. This can't help but have a dispiriting effect on those who adopt them.

Their pessimism isn't just naïve. It's toxic. Rather than highlighting the values that drive success – such as hard work, perseverance, thrift, risk-taking, and personal responsibility – their narratives blame *external forces*. By downplaying personal agency, they convince young people that they are powerless to change their circumstances.

This is clear in their discussions about capitalism, a system they describe as inherently exploitative and unfair. The reality? Capitalism, despite its flaws, has lifted millions out of poverty and created unprecedented opportunities for upward mobility. The disparagement of capitalism – and the promotion of socialism – have contributed to a culture of dependency, where individuals are encouraged to look to the government for solutions rather than relying on their own initiative.

The influence of public intellectuals in shaping public discourse can hardly be overstated. Most Americans don't listen to them directly. But their ideas and opinions are reflected in the work of journalists and editorialists who admire them and who have a tremendous impact on public discourse. Together, they discourage personal responsibility, foster a sense of helplessness, and undermine the values that have allowed hundreds of millions to achieve their most important goals.

The problem? Pessimists *sound like* they're trying to help you, warn you, or protect you. Optimists, however, sound like boosters, cheerleaders, or Pollyannas who view the world through rose-colored glasses. In reality, optimism – aside from its clear benefits in business and investing – is essential to living a longer, healthier life (as I'll discuss in Chapter 18).

ENEMY OF THE DREAM NO. 5: POLITICIANS

Other apostles of pessimism include politicians on both sides of the aisle. They bear a lot of blame for the general feeling of despair about the state of the nation. And I say that as a lifelong political junkie. I don't write much about politics in my weekly columns – and for a good reason. I write for a publisher. The publisher's goal is to attract readers, make them satisfied customers, and benefit from their continued patronage and referrals.

However, talking politics does not make most Americans happy. It makes them angry. In fact, politics in this country has morphed into a kind of secular religion. Partisans routinely talk not about better policies and worse policies or even right policies and wrong policies but of *good and evil*. Left-wing and right-wing political ideologues have even built communities of like-minded brethren, a catechism of sacred beliefs, a well-populated demonology, and an utter confidence in the righteousness of their cause.

In today's hyper-partisan atmosphere – it makes no sense to inflame or offend some percentage of your customers by wading unnecessarily into political waters. The key word here, however, is *unnecessarily*.

As chief investment strategist of The Oxford Club, my mission is to give investment advice that works. That means at times I need to speak my mind about how pending or approved legislation will affect the economy, inflation, interest rates, or the stock and bond markets. Yet whenever I opine about how some new government policy or proposal will affect financial markets, I get a blizzard of emails from subscribers telling me they "didn't pay good money" to hear me spout off about politics. This includes subscribers to our free e-letters, so they must feel strongly about it.

However, I feel a responsibility to let readers know which companies are likely to be positively affected by new laws and regulations – and which are likely to end up on the short end of the stick. It would be wrong to have insights into these matters and not share them with subscribers. My objective – always – is to influence readers' investment approach, not their political views. Yet it is hard to avoid stepping on toes.

I'm only talking about politics now because it's vital that investors understand how politicians – and especially *political campaigns* – undermine the pursuit of their investment goals and negatively influence their view of the nation. Most voters – or at least most partisans – believe that politics is about principles . . . and platforms . . . and policies. And it is, partly. But for the politicians, it's mainly about something else: winning.

Politics is about gaining, holding, and wielding *power*. It's a battle of ideas. And this *really is* a zero-sum game. In every election, someone is going to win. And someone is going to lose. The stakes are tremendous. Our lives, our economy, and our country are enormously affected by the policies that are discussed, debated, and signed into law in Washington.

Politics is war. And, as we're told from an early age, everything is fair in love and war. For example, incumbents claim credit for everything positive that happened on their watch, no matter how tenuous the connection.

Yes, an administration's policies can provide a headwind – making it more difficult for Americans to succeed – or a tailwind, making it easier to succeed. But there is no lever in the Oval Office that controls inflation, interest rates, commodity prices – especially the price of gasoline – economic growth, business developments, scientific innovation, geopolitics, the performance of the financial markets, and the average temperature of the Earth.

Incumbents or their intended successors will also claim that every negative development during their term in office was caused by circumstances beyond their control – or, better still, by the other party – no matter how clear and direct the connection to the incumbents' actions and policies.

The first step in a political campaign is to define the opposition in the most unflattering light possible. Deride their character. Undermine their experience. Highlight their past mistakes. Point out their "flip-flops" on the issues. Warn voters about their real or perceived shortcomings and their dangerous intentions. And be sure to insist that this is the most important election of our lifetime. (Just like the last one.)

Some of the brickbats – especially the ones based on past votes and current proposals – are fair game and well deserved. But a lot of today's politics is nothing more than fearmongering about the dystopian future we will all face if the other party gets elected.

These pronouncements – echoed endlessly by the media – cannot help but make Americans depressed and nervous.

Political messages these days are rarely uplifting. And aside from the impact on our national psyche, investors get scared. They flee volatile but high-returning stocks for the safety of lower-returning cash. And they usually end up regretting it.

Political polarization, tribalism (red team versus blue team), and extreme partisanship are real and damaging. They leave the public misinformed and inflame passions in ways that can be destructive.

There have always been strong opinions on both sides. But the extreme negativity is largely new. During the 1984 election, Ronald Reagan ran a television commercial with the famous opening line, "It's morning again in America." In his speech accepting the Republican nomination in 1988, his successor George H. W. Bush compared America – with its many clubs and volunteer organizations – to "a thousand points of light in a broad and peaceful sky."

In 2016, when addressing the United Nations, President Barack Obama said, "Now is the best time in history to be alive. It's never been healthier. It's never been wealthier. It's never been better educated. It's never been less violent. It's never been more tolerant."

I agreed with all these remarks.

But compare those quotes with more recent political discourse. When running for office in 2015, Donald Trump said, "Sadly, the American Dream is dead." Eleven months later, Senator Bernie Sanders – who was running for the Democratic nomination for president – agreed, saying "For many, the American Dream has become a nightmare."

Likewise, when Trump made "Make America Great Again" his campaign slogan in 2016, Democrats could have parried that the United States has always been a great nation. But, no, New York Governor Mario Cuomo responded, "We're not gonna make America great again. It never was that great."

What accounts for this dramatic change in tone? It's not the state of the country. Nor is it just partisan rivalry. In my view, it's largely due to the rise of populism on both the left and right, which pits "the people" against a "corrupt elite."

Populists like to identify some other group as the source of our problems: migrants, foreign countries, overseas competitors, rich people, the opposing party, or, of course, the elites themselves, who always seem to benefit from the status quo.

The problem with populism – and its doom-and-gloom economic narrative – is that it often leads to policies that make things worse, not better. Yet in 2024, despite the volleys that went back and forth between Donald Trump and Kamala Harris, there was surprising agreement between them on populist issues.

Both stated that the United States is no longer an upwardly mobile society. Both claimed that our standard of living is at risk. Both believe that the game is rigged, making it harder for the average household to rise. And both, of course, claimed they were uniquely qualified to fix our problems.

Yet their assessment is wrong. Social mobility in this country is strong. Median income and household net wealth are at all-time highs. Unemployment recently hovered near a 50-year low lately. Our standard of living has never been greater. And it has rarely been easier for workers – and particularly investors – to get ahead, if they know how.

Most Americans don't realize these facts for several reasons. Public schools don't teach them. The mainstream media doesn't cover them. Intellectuals scoff at the very idea of progress. And much of social media is a cesspool of hysteria, half-baked ideas, and outright misinformation.

Ideas matter. A lot. But there is rarely good money to be made – or votes to be won – educating people that the nation is in better shape than most people realize. However, there is a great deal of money to be made by investors who realize the truth: that most Americans today are living far better than prior generations.

This does not mean that we don't have real problems in this country, including high prices, failing schools, declining workplace participation rates, towns and communities hurt by globalization, a high percentage of "deaths of despair," and economic displacement caused by new technologies.

There are always plenty of challenges and much uncertainty. Yet objective people should at least be able to agree on where we stand in relation to where we've been. All it takes is a look at current and historical data, without the political spin. And that data clearly shows that the trend is our friend. Americans need to understand the general direction of things so that they can capitalize on the positive trends and avoid the negative ones.

In short, those who would like to achieve the American Dream have a formidable list of enemies: our mediocre public education system, the negativity bias of the mainstream media, the hysteria and misinformation of social media, the dystopian views of public intellectuals, and the hyperbole and fearmongering of political campaigns.

Many would say these entities need reigning in or outright reform. But, as I mentioned at the start, this is not a book about public policy. It's about *personal policy*. It's about what *you can do* – given our flawed public institutions – to reach your most important goals and live your best life.

A big step in that direction is tuning out the voices of pessimism and despair. And listening instead to the voices of optimism and empowerment.

How to Achieve the American Dream

CHAPTER 9

Why the United States Has a Record Number of Millionaires

Our lives are the sum of the choices we make.

—Author Albert Camus

Ask your average American how most millionaires became wealthy, and you will hear several common responses. They inherited their money. Or they started a business. Or they earned big six- or seven-figure incomes. Or they were just "fortunate." These answers aren't entirely wrong – just mostly. Because none of them explain how *most* American millionaires actually got there.

Consider the 2025 Credit Suisse Global Wealth Report. It is the most comprehensive and up-to-date resource of its kind, analyzing the household wealth of 5.4 billion people around the globe. Over the years, the report has shown a multi-decade trend of rising wealth – and an increasing number of millionaire households.

It's not a straight line, though. For instance, during the market downturn in 2022, the number of millionaires globally dropped by 3.5 million. US millionaires declined by about 1.8 million – a sharp but temporary dip. Yet even after that reset, the long-term trajectory remains upward.

The report will surprise the many Americans who believe they know something about how millionaires become rich.

Let's start with a few basic facts from this report and others:

- The United States holds just 4% of the world's population. Yet it holds 35% of the world's total wealth.
- More than 379,000 Americans became new millionaires in 2024 – over 1,000 a day – bringing the US share to nearly 40% of the world's millionaires.
- The number of Americans with net assets between $1 million and $5 million has quadrupled since 2000.
- More than 24 million Americans have a net worth of $1 million or more. That's approximately 18% of all US households.
- The United States has more millionaires than the next five countries combined: China, Japan, Germany, the United Kingdom, and France.
- Seventy-nine percent of millionaires did not receive any inheritance from their family or relatives. (And only 3% received an inheritance of $1 million or more.)
- Eight out of 10 millionaires come from low-income families.
- The majority of millionaires did not become wealthy due to six-figure earnings. Only 31% had a $100,000 income at some time in their careers. A full one-third never did.
- How did they get there? Ninety-three percent of millionaires surveyed by Ramsey Solutions say they became rich through hard work, consistent saving, smart investing. and avoiding debt. (Basic but effective.)
- The vast majority did not start businesses. Most invested in equities and real estate.
- Contrary to the myth, 91.5% own just one property: their primary residence.

Here are a few more interesting facts. The median household net wealth in the United States in 2022 was $176,500. And while a million dollars is a substantial sum of money, it is not enough to make you a "one-percenter." You need a minimum net worth of $13.7 million to get into the top 1% of Americans by wealth. (Although you only need about $871,000 to be in the top 1% globally.) Most Americans feel that you need more than a million dollars to be "rich."

The 2024 Charles Schwab Modern Wealth Survey found that Americans view a net worth of $2.5 million as the minimum to be considered wealthy. A net worth of $778,000 is required to feel "financially comfortable."

Sounds tough? As I've said from the beginning, anyone with average intelligence can become wealthy. The principles of wealth creation are easily understood. That doesn't mean that most Americans are familiar with them, however.

You don't have to be the founder of a computer company in your garage. You don't have to play third base for the Yankees. You don't have to make a rap album that goes platinum. Those folks are outliers.

To build a seven- or eight-figure net worth, all that's necessary is to maximize your income, live beneath your means, invest your money wisely, and let compounding work its magic.

It should build confidence to learn that many tens of millions of Americans have already reached this goal. And to know that the path is open to all of us.

Unfortunately, many Americans have been told that capitalism is all about selfishness, greed, and exploitation. Yet that mischaracterization doesn't stand up to a moment's scrutiny.

Yes, everyone is self-interested. But you don't build wealth in a capitalist economy by focusing on yourself. You build it by figuring out what other people want or need – and delivering it better, faster, cheaper, or more reliably than the next person.

As for greed, even if you're the greediest person in the world, no one is going to give you a dime until you provide them with a product or service of value. The free-market system is based on voluntary exchanges for mutual benefit. That's why the first thing you hear when you walk into a store is, "How may I help you?" It's also why you always hear two thank-yous at the checkout counter. You say thanks because you value the merchandise more than the cash. The store owner says thanks because they value the cash more than the merchandise. Both sides win.

As for exploitation, if you don't want to work for a company, sell to a company, buy from a company, or own its shares, you don't have to. And if you do and you're not satisfied, you are always free to make a change. Where is the exploitation in that?

Capitalism promises that you can have anything you want if you just provide enough other people with what *they* want. Where is the harm in any law-abiding individual doing that?

Anti-capitalists insist that businesses charge as much as they can while doing as little as they can for their customers, suppliers, and employees. Let me assure you that the good ones do not. Businesses focused solely on short-term profits don't last long. If you cut corners on quality, your customers will leave you. If you bargain with your suppliers too hard, they won't trade with you. If you undervalue your employees, they will take their talents elsewhere. It is in the best interests of business owners to make sure that all stakeholders – employees, suppliers, customers, and communities – are satisfied.

Now, here's a news flash: businesses are run by fallible human beings. Sometimes they make mistakes, breach contracts, use poor judgment, harm individuals, or damage the environment. When they do, the transgressors should be punished. But that doesn't make capitalism *wrong* any more than democracy is wrong when some politician cheats or breaks the law.

The simple truth is that most wealthy Americans achieved their affluence not by inheritance or speculation or luck but by owning a piece of profitable businesses. Most of us don't have the time, money, or experience necessary to start and run a business ourselves. Yet we can still own a piece of one – or a portfolio full of businesses – through the quintessence of capitalism: the stock market.

With just a modest amount of money, any individual can accumulate a stake in many of the world's great businesses. And it's easy. A click of the mouse and you're in. Another click, and you're out. (Compare *that* to your typical real estate closing.)

And owning a piece of a company is a whole lot simpler than running one. You don't have to sign personal guarantees, hire or fire employees, grapple with an avalanche of federal mandates and regulations, pay lawyers and accountants, or even show up for work. How great is that?

Some Americans today obsess over the issue of fairness. Yet the stock market shines here, too. If you own shares of Tesla or Microsoft, for example, your gain over the next year will be just the same as two the world's richest men: Elon Musk and Bill Gates. Sure, they may own a few more shares than you do, but your percentage returns will be the same.

We are living in a golden age for investors. Forty years ago, I wrote research reports for an international brokerage firm. This generally required multiple phone calls to investment banks and trading houses where I coaxed, cajoled, wheedled (okay, begged) other analysts to send me what I needed.

When the information arrived – usually days later – it required follow-up calls to update the data. The internet changed all that. Research that once required hours in the periodical room at the library or days sifting through reports is done in minutes. Information and ideas scattered or hidden around the globe can be accessed instantly. Plus, it's generally free and easily available to anyone who takes the time to learn where to look.

You used to have to hunt for stock prices in the business section of the newspaper. (When was the last time you did *that*?) Or you could call your broker, get placed on hold, and eventually get a quote that – by the time you received it – was no longer current. After getting a quote, you could place a trade with your broker, who would put you on hold again while they jotted it down and hustled it over to the firm's trading desk.

In those days, a market order was a real roll of the dice. Today you don't think twice about getting a real-time quote, placing a trade with a mouse click, and getting a near-instantaneous confirmation.

Costs used to be exponentially higher, too. Brokers routinely sold mutual funds with front-end loads as high as 8.5%. (That's not a misprint.) And prior to May 1, 1975, brokerage commissions were fixed at high levels, too. Deregulation – and the debut of Charles Schwab – changed that.

The bid/ask spreads on share price are far thinner today, too. When I started in the money management business almost 40 years ago, a large stock might have a spread of an eighth of a point and a small one a quarter of a point. Tack on a 2% or 3% commission and you were already down 5% by the time you received your trade confirmation.

Today liquidity is much greater, bid/ask spreads are often a penny, and trade commissions are zero. In short, your investment choices have never been greater. Information has never been more widely available. Monitoring your portfolio has never been simpler. Spreads have never been thinner. Executions have never been faster. And commissions have never been lower.

Yet I often hear people with little or no experience in the stock market moaning that "the little guy doesn't have a chance." Not true. You have all the tools you need. But you may still lack the essential knowledge to take advantage of them. (I address this with specific investment advice in Chapter 16.)

Chris Hogan, the bestselling author of *Everyday Millionaires*, is a long-time speaker, television personality, and financial expert. His message is addressed primarily to Americans who have little or no assets and are generally buried in debt as well.

No one is in more dire need of straight talk than stressed-out men and women. And Hogan gives it to them. He points out that while we have a record number of millionaires in this country, the number of people living paycheck to paycheck is also at a record.

Yet Hogan has made a successful career of showing everyday folks how to reach financial independence. The Ramsey group surveyed and/or interviewed more than 10,000 American millionaires. (Just so we have our terms straight, a millionaire is not someone who has an income of a million dollars or more. It is someone with a net worth – total assets minus total liabilities – of $1 million or more.)

He points out that many Americans are not even working toward this financial goal because they are consumed by myths about the affluent.

According to Hogan, the top three are:

1. The wealthy didn't earn and don't deserve their money.
2. The wealthy take big risks with their money.
3. The wealthy have a leg up in education and careers.

Hogan counters these myths with facts discerned from the more than 100,000 millionaires surveyed. (You'll find a big overlap with the Credit Suisse Global Wealth Survey.) For example, 79% American millionaires received zero inheritance, meaning only 21% received any inheritance at all. (The vast majority of millionaires are first-generation rich. That means they worked hard, made sacrifices, and lived on a plan.)

Eight out of 10 millionaires come from families at or below the middle-class income level. In most cases, their relatives had nothing to leave them. In fact, 48% described their parents' household as middle class, 27% described it as lower middle class, and 4.25% described it as lower class. He also found that 76% of millionaires say that anyone in America can become a millionaire with discipline and hard work.

Degrees from prestigious private schools – where students are often taught to hate our economic system if not the country itself – weren't necessary. Seventy-nine percent of millionaires did not attend private schools. Sixty-two percent graduated from public state schools, 8% attended community college, and 9% never graduated from college at all.

One-third of millionaires *never* had a six-figure household income in a single working year. Only 31% of them averaged $100,000 household income a year, and only 7% averaged over $200,000 household income over the course of their career.

Becoming wealthy *doesn't require* a high-paying job. Hogan notes that someone with a US household income of just $59,000 a year could start investing 15% of their income at age 30 and – if they earn the long-term return of the S&P 500 – have over $1 million by age 55. So much for millionaires taking "big risks" with their money.

Most millionaires *do not* use leverage (i.e., borrow money to invest). In fact, 90% have never taken out a business loan. Nor did they get rich trading penny stocks, options, or crypto. In fact,

79% of millionaires reach the seven-figure mark through their employer-sponsored retirement plan.

While we can see the advantages that most millionaires *didn't have* – a big inheritance, a degree from a prestigious institution, or a high-paying career – there are several habits and attitudes that the wealthy *do have* in common.

Hogan calls them *the five key attributes of millionaires*:

- They take personal responsibility.
- They practice intentionality.
- They are goal-oriented.
- They are hard workers.
- They are consistent.

Let's start with personal responsibility. Many folks prefer to blame their financial circumstances on their parents, their spouse, their "ex," their children, their boss, "the breaks," our economic system, even the country itself. Yet here's the reality. You control your choices and behavior. You don't control anyone else's.

Whether the problem is joblessness, overspending, a lack of saving, or poor investment decisions, you move closer to a solution the moment you take responsibility for your actions. As Hogan puts it, "You can make progress or you can make excuses. You can't make both."

The Ramsey group found that 97% of millionaires agree with the statement "I control my own destiny." And 95% of them are willing to quickly admit when they are wrong. That's taking responsibility.

Millionaires also practice intentionality. Nobody accidentally ends up retiring with millions in their bank or brokerage account. When they're starting out – and even after they've achieved financial independence – these folks live well within their means. They save regularly. They take prudent risks to earn high returns. And they leave their investments alone, so they keep compounding.

Millionaires are goal-oriented. Ninety-two percent of them develop a long-term plan for their money, compared to just 60% of the general population. They make financial goals and stick with them. Seventy percent of millionaires save more than 10% of their income throughout their working years. They also tend to pay off their homes. Sixty-seven percent of millionaires live in homes with paid-off mortgages. (Note: this isn't possible if they trade up to a bigger house every few years.)

Millionaires are also hard workers. This doesn't mean that you need to work 60-hour weeks. It means working smarter, better, and more efficiently in the hours you're already on the job. It may also mean upgrading your skill set. The world changes constantly and the most valuable employees adapt to it.

Eighty-six percent of millionaires believe that challenging themselves makes them smarter. Ninety-six percent of them are always learning new things, many of them job-related. The more valuable you are to your employer, the greater your earnings potential. That's hardly rocket science.

Millionaires are also consistent. They don't make smart financial moves occasionally. They make them a habit. They save regularly. Their contributions to their employer-sponsored retirement plan are deducted automatically. They minimize their financial costs and investment taxes. And when they need financial help, they seek it out.

Their sites are firmly set on the long-term goal – financial freedom that will enable them to live the life of their dreams – not the latest bauble. This mindset and these habits enable ordinary people to become extraordinarily wealthy.

There is another important reason to reach your most important financial goals, aside from the security and peace of mind it brings. Research shows that people with a higher net worth live longer. According to a study in *JAMA Internal Medicine*, once Americans make it to their late 50s, the wealthiest 10% live to a median age of about 86 years. That's approximately 14 years longer than the least wealthy 10%. People with more money can afford healthier food, more health care, and a home in a safer, less-polluted neighborhood. They also favor purchases that help track their health, stay active, and reduce stress.

Bottom line? If you want to become a millionaire, you need to start acting like one. Given the amazing power of money compounding, sooner is better than later. Compounding your wealth is like improving your health. It's never too late to get started.

CHAPTER 10

How Wealth Is Created

> Too many people are thinking of security instead of opportunity.
> They seem more afraid of life than death.
>
> —Supreme Court Justice James Byrnes

It never ceases to surprise me how little most people understand about how wealth is actually created in a capitalist system.

Successful businesses help people solve problems, save time, live better, or fulfill a dream. U2 singer Bono once said, "It's just foolishness not to recognize the creativity you can unlock in the corporate world." He added, "Some of the most selfish people I've met are artists – I'm one of them – and some of the most selfless people I've met are in business, people like Warren Buffett. So, I've never had that clichéd view of commerce and culture being different."

Microsoft founder Bill Gates notes that businesses underwrite many thousands of ideas that don't work out – but the handful that do revolutionize our world. The Industrial Revolution transformed people's lives, but our current information revolution is creating a sort of worldwide superintelligence that is making enormous contributions to humanity, some in ways that we can't imagine yet.

One of the biggest challenges that businesses face is retaining their most talented employees. The best managers treat and pay their staff exactly the way they would want to be treated themselves.

Jacqueline Novogratz, founder of Acumen, said that successful entrepreneurs don't worry about reputation. They focus on character. (Reputation is what people think you are. Character is what you really are.)

Warren Buffett advised, "Don't just satisfy your customers – delight them. They're gonna talk to other people. They're going to come back. Anybody who has happy customers is likely to have a pretty good future."

The internet and social media have created a new era of product transparency. Consumers now share their likes (and dislikes) so broadly and rapidly that there is far greater opportunity for great products or services to achieve widespread adoption and far less opportunity for shoddy ones to succeed.

Businesses drive innovation, create jobs, improve our quality of life, and elevate our standard of living. And the stock market – capitalism's great equalizer – lets everyday Americans own a piece of this engine. Not everyone can start a business. But anyone can own one.

This is something we should remember. Because there are voices – loud ones – that constantly try to undermine the system that creates the very prosperity they benefit from. But let's get real: no one saves or invests money in a country they believe is fundamentally broken. If America were, our markets wouldn't lead the world.

Once you realize how journalists distort and sensationalize the news – because negativity attracts eyes, ears, clicks, likes, shares, and retweets – you're in on the game. And that means you can profit from it.

We live in a world where people compete for scarce resources: money, power, prestige, you name it. But obtaining these things requires something essential: accurate information. If you listen to news that is sensationalized, biased, overly negative, or out of context, it leads to bad decision-making. Good information, however, leads to better decisions. And improved outcomes.

That's why it's crucial to limit your consumption of cable news, social media blather, and partisan propaganda. It may seem that everyone else is wallowing in the stuff. But avoiding it – or sharply limiting it – will help you see the world as it really is and succeed.

If you want to upgrade your information sources, you might start by visiting websites like Our World in Data or Human Progress. They tell the other side of the story: the optimistic, data-backed side.

Problems and setbacks are real and continuous. They have always been with us – and they always will be. But challenges also contain the seeds of opportunity. Your best life is generally realized not by pursuing a farfetched and unrealistic dream but by following your opportunities.

Here's an example. Each May, ceremonies are held across the country for graduating college seniors. Before these new graduates can toss their caps in the air and ride into the sunset with their freshly minted diplomas, however, they are generally subjected to a commencement speech that encourages them to "pursue their dreams" or "follow their bliss."

This is terrible advice for most 21-year-olds. (Not all, but most.) If you are a graduating senior and your lifelong dream is to become a physician . . . or an engineer . . . or an Air Force pilot . . . or to enter some other skilled profession – and you're on track to do that – more power to you. But a lot of graduating seniors are more like me.

After completing 16 years of formal education, I hadn't the foggiest idea what I was going to do next. I earned a Bachelor of Arts from Furman University in Greenville, South Carolina, with majors in business and psychology. (A perfect foundation for analyzing the stock market, although I didn't know it at the time.)

I had interviewed with a few firms at my college, and we quickly came to an agreement. They didn't see any value in me, nor I in them.

The idea of moving back home with my parents – though I love them dearly – was unthinkable. I was too independent for that. Relying on the government? That never even entered my mind. That was for the unfortunate folks that then-president Ronald Reagan called "the truly needy."

I mulled over my limited options. Then it dawned on me. When I grew up in Virginia, we'd load up the family station wagon every few years and drive 12 hours to visit relatives in Florida. (It was all we could afford.) At college, I spent spring break every year in a dive motel at some beach in Florida. With no job skills, connections, or money (aside from what I'd earned working part time in school), I packed up my beater car – the stereo was worth more than the vehicle – and drove to Florida to seek my fortune.

I'm sure my parents were less than proud to tell their friends that their son – the new college graduate – was now waiting tables at a tavern in Daytona Beach.

I worked a few hours each night – and threw the frisbee with bikini-clad women on the beach all day. I was a 21-year-old who had followed the age-old commencement address wisdom. I had followed my bliss. I was living the dream. And, of course, going nowhere. That's the problem with pursuing your dream when you're young, whether you want to be a singer-songwriter, a playwright, or a beach bum. There's usually no money in it.

After paying the expenses on the crummy apartment I shared with coworkers I didn't enjoy living with, there was nothing left. An empty stomach is a great motivator, however. It concentrates the mind. And it made clear something that adult children who receive financial outpatient support from their parents are often slow to understand.

I realized that it really didn't matter what kind of work I might find personally fulfilling. I had to find someone who needed something done. . . and was willing to pay me to do it. That was my first real epiphany. Success is not about fulfilling my own wants or needs. *It's about serving someone else.*

Commencement speeches often note the value of service, but almost always in the context of charitable work. Yet serving others is the key to success in the private sector, too. The key question most graduating seniors should answer is, "Who needs something done that I might be able to do?"

I'm not suggesting that readers should selflessly devote their lives to helping other people fulfill their dreams. But when you're starting out? Absolutely. Certain jobs – and sometimes entire industries – will turn out to be dead ends. When you recognize that, it's time for a change. But once you find something you're good at – and stick with it for a while – you'll obtain knowledge. You'll gain experience. You'll develop a reputation as someone who can be relied on to get things done. And – if you have a bit of ambition – someone who leads and motivates others, as well.

For most of us, it's not about doing what we love. It's about loving what we do. It's not about following your dreams. It's about following your opportunities.

Of course, you can't possibly see all the opportunities that will arise in advance. The world – and life itself – is far too unpredictable for that. But by showing up every day – and reliably doing whatever needs to be done – you'll eventually find yourself in the right place at the right time. And be able to capitalize on it.

My advice to young people is not to follow your dreams. Or, at least, *not initially*. Get busy . . . work hard . . . show up every day . . . and follow your opportunities instead.

Something else young people should realize – something that probably runs counter to everything their professors taught them – is that we live in the best economic system in the world.

Socialism doesn't work. It's been tried many times in many places, but it always fails. Proponents can't point to a single example of a socialist system that has increased the overall prosperity of the people who live under it.

I would love to live in a world where everyone gets a free college education, complementary health care, and a full-time job with high wages, short hours, generous benefits, and early retirement. Unfortunately, I live in a different world. It's called *the real one*, where people respond to incentives, income is earned rather than merely "distributed," and the word *free* just means someone else is paying for it.

Critics of capitalism argue that there is less economic inequality in socialist countries. What they rarely point out is that in every one of them, the average citizen is much poorer than in free market nations. As Winston Churchill famously put it, "The inherent vice of capitalism is the unequal sharing of blessings. The inherent virtue of socialism is the equal sharing of miseries."

Yet polls show that more than half of Americans believe "the rich get richer and the poor get poorer under capitalism." That reveals an astonishing ignorance about how the US economy works. Ours is a knowledge-based society where individuals with the most education and skills are the highest compensated. But, make no mistake, the poor are getting richer, too.

And not just here at home. Around the globe, poverty has declined more in the last 50 years than in the previous 500. According to the latest World Bank data, more than 100,000 people are being lifted out of poverty every day.

It's a sad fact that most Americans don't recognize the free enterprise system as an incredible source of prosperity. Economies expand over time. Incomes grow. And so does household wealth. The Federal Reserve recently reported that US household income and net worth are at all-time records and a multiple of what they were 50 years ago in inflation-adjusted terms. That is a testament to the strength of our economic system.

Every day, US companies are knocking themselves out to deliver products and services that are better, cheaper, and longer lasting. It's a highly competitive world and most new products (as well as new businesses) fail. But the ones that succeed improve our lives immeasurably.

Corporate failures are tough on employees and business owners. Creative destruction generates innovation and prosperity. But it also means job insecurity. Capitalism is a profit *and loss* system. Market failures are inevitable.

Some folks don't like this. They want a different economic system, one with guaranteed employment, a high level of financial security, and little or no economic inequality. Yet the countries that have gone down this path have only immiserated their citizens. To maintain order, they must strip them of their political freedoms as well as their economic freedoms.

The best part of our free market system? Anyone who is willing to work, save, and invest can become not just financially independent but a card-carrying millionaire or multimillionaire. In the process, you will become not a "greedy SOB" but *a public benefactor.*

For example, when you buy or sell shares of stock, your actions are almost certainly based on self-interest. You want to buy a company at a good price. And you want to sell it at an even better price. Yet many shareholders – perhaps most – don't realize that they are actively promoting the public good when they act for personal financial gain.

As I've pointed out, in a free enterprise system like ours, every transaction is based on mutually beneficial exchange. The only way a business attracts customers – and makes money – is by enticing them to buy its products and services. If they sell those products and services for more than they cost, they earn a profit. And if they can't, they don't.

Not making a profit is more common than non-entrepreneurs realize. Most businesses fail within five years of opening. A profitable firm is the exception, not the rule (especially in the world of startups). Business owners – the shareholders – eat the losses. They are entitled to the profits if there are any.

At a successful business, the incentives are aligned for everyone to benefit, not just the shareholders. However, the business and its assets do *not* belong to the other stakeholders. They belong solely to the shareholders. Many people lost sight of this a few years ago, when some of the world's largest asset managers pressured firms to pursue not sales and earnings but various social responsibility objectives – better known as ESG (environmental, social, and governance) or DEI (diversity, equity, and inclusion). Fortunately, the pendulum has finally begun to swing back the other way.

The best companies seek to maximize long-term gains not short-term ones. If this were not the case, they would not invest billions each year on equipment, factories, technology, research and development, marketing, and employee benefits. Instead, they would distribute all that money to the shareholders, either in the form of dividends or share buybacks. But they don't. Because they expect their investments to pay off in even bigger profits down the road.

Thousands of firms opt to raise money in the stock market. The funds are raised in an initial public offering or secondary offerings. If you're buying shares in the market on a typical trading day, your money does not go to the company itself but to someone who is selling their shares. You are not providing capital to the firm. You are providing liquidity to other shareholders, as you are again when you sell your shares.

Think about this for a moment. Public companies provide us with most of the things we want or need. They provide jobs and training for employees. They are sources of sales and profits for suppliers. They support and enhance their communities. And they pay billions each year in taxes.

Who makes all this possible? The shareholder, who is willing to accept the risks and potential rewards of a business owner – and who provides liquidity for other investors. So please don't buy into the false narrative that stock market investors are greedy and selfish. They are public benefactors.

It's yet another reason – if you needed one – to get out there and make some serious money.

The Key to the American Dream: Personal Responsibility

The difference between a successful person and others is not a lack of strength, not a lack of knowledge, but rather a lack of will.

—Coach Vince Lombardi

As I've discussed, hard work and wages are not enough for most to realize the material aspects of the Dream. It also requires saving, which means living within your means, something tens of millions of Americans have trouble doing.

However, for those disciplined enough to live on less than they earn, the return on risk-free savings is low. Your money will barely keep up with inflation and sometimes – depending on the level of interest rates – it might not even do that. Your savings need to be invested, which requires two things: intelligent risk-taking and patience.

The first stumbling block? Surveys show that many Americans are financially illiterate. They don't understand risk and reward, stocks versus bonds, or the incredible power of money compounding. Moreover, they want to get rich *yesterday*. That doesn't work.

Jeff Bezos once asked Warren Buffett, "You are the second richest man in the world and yet you have the simplest investment thesis. How come others didn't follow this?" To which Buffett responded, "Because no one wants to get rich slowly."

Too many Americans are out on a frantic snipe hunt for Powerball tickets, the hottest crypto play, or the meme stock du jour. Yet those bets don't generally pay off. Investing in high-quality companies with superb management, rising sales and earnings, and defensible profit margins generally does.

And while patience is required, time is your ally. The American Dream is something you work toward. Unless you were born with the proverbial silver spoon in your mouth, no one is going to hand it to you. (This realization is sometimes lost on the "Everyone Gets a Trophy" generation.)

Many young Americans are not even aware of what social scientists call *the success sequence*. It consists of three milestones:

1. **Finish high school.** Getting a high school diploma increases your job opportunities and earnings potential, which is essential for financial stability.
2. **Work a full-time job.** Securing full-time employment, even at an entry-level position, provides both a steady income and the work experience necessary to move up.
3. **Wait until marriage to have kids.** It's hard – if not impossible – to work a full-time job and raise an infant, unless you have a committed partner. A stable family structure is a great benefit. (However, if you're not marriage-minded and can receive or afford all the help you need, that's different.)

Again, it's pretty simple: stay in school, get a job, and wait to have children. According to a Brookings Institute report, 97% of adults who follow these three steps avoid poverty and eventually enter the middle class.

Conversely, skipping or reversing these steps *increases* the likelihood of economic hardship. Of course, these are just the first steps. There are other actions you can take *today* to live your version of the Dream.

While campaigning for president, Donald Trump struck a positive note when he promised that he would "bring back the American dream, bigger, better, and stronger than ever before."

Vice President Kamala Harris took the opposite tack. At the Congressional Hispanic Caucus Institute's Leadership Conference just before the election, she said, "the American Dream is elusive for far too many people increasingly." In an interview with MSNBC, she expanded on that, saying, "Gone is the day of everyone thinking they could live the American Dream." She then tripled down in an NBC interview, saying, "You know, the idea of the American Dream was something that previous generations could count on, not as much anymore."

This was an odd sentiment for someone whose administration had been in charge for four years. No wonder she lost. Of course, as Ronald Reagan warned us, the government is usually the problem rather than the solution. The public school monopoly, high taxes, mounting federal regulations, needless licensing requirements, the absence of right-to-work laws, and the ever-metastasizing national debt are more a hindrance than a help to everyday Americans who want to get ahead.

Too many feel that financial security is completely out of reach, especially since spiraling inflation, higher mortgage rates, and a tight housing market have made getting on the property ladder increasingly tough. Polls show that just 21% of young people today think the American Dream is attainable. Yet millions are on their way to achieving it.

The ones making progress are those willing to embrace *radical responsibility*. If you're unfamiliar with it, the story of Fleet Maull is instructive. In 1985, he began serving a 14-year sentence for drug trafficking. During his incarceration, he completed a PhD in psychology, authored a well-received book, became an ordained priest, founded a prison hospice program, and launched the Prison Dharma Network, a nonprofit organization that supports prisoner rehabilitation through contemplative spirituality.

Today Maull is a personal effectiveness coach, lecturing at leading universities, in corporate boardrooms, high-risk areas like Rwanda and the Middle East, and what he calls "the forgotten world" inside our jails and prisons. Maull has plenty of wisdom and experience to share. But he sums up his core message with those two simple words: *radical responsibility*.

He believes we create everything that is happening in our lives, good and bad. It is only when we accept complete responsibility that we take the giant step from childhood to adulthood. Self-responsibility is the key to personal effectiveness in every sphere of life.

However, many choose to embrace the psychology of helplessness and victimhood, preferring to explain all their struggles in terms of the actions of others.

Like you, I meet many middle-aged people who are still grumbling and complaining about earlier unhappy experiences, who are still blaming their problems on other people or "the breaks." They are angry with their parents, fuming at an old boss, still simmering over their ex-spouse. They are trapped in the past and can't get free.

Yet the great enemy of success and happiness is *negative emotions*. Fear, self-pity, envy, jealousy, and anger hold us back, tie us down, and suck the joy out of life. Studies show that there are four root causes of these emotions. Once you identify them, you can begin to banish them:

- **Justification.** You can be negative only as long as you convince yourself that you are *entitled* to be angry. Unhappy individuals will always be found explaining and elaborating on the profound unfairness of their situation.
- **Rationalization.** Rationalization is self-deception, an attempt to create a plausible explanation for a socially unacceptable act. (As in "If I don't show up for the Zoom meeting, no one will notice anyway.")

- **Blaming.** There is no quality more closely associated with unhappiness than the habit of blaming others for our difficulties.
- **Poor self-esteem.** Low self-esteem is generally characterized by a hypersensitivity to the opinions of others. No one wants to lose the respect of others, but conscientious people don't need to fret about what other people think.

Author and management consultant Brian Tracy points out that there is a simple antidote to these factors that create negative emotions. You need only say three words: "I am responsible."

Whether your problem is joblessness, addiction, overspending, obesity, or a damaged personal relationship, you move closer to a solution the moment you say three magic words: "I am responsible." It is not possible to say these words and still feel angry. The very act of taking responsibility short-circuits and cancels out negative emotions.

As Tracy says,

> Every time you blame someone else or make excuses, you give your power away. You feel weakened and diminished . . . . Without the acceptance of complete personal responsibility, no progress is possible. On the other hand, once you accept total responsibility for your life, there are no limits to what you can be, do and have.

Yet many would rather train for the Boston Marathon in three feet of snow than say those three words. Why? Psychologists say human beings have a natural propensity to accumulate pride and shun regret. Whether we recognize it or not, we tend to take responsibility for the positive developments in our lives and attribute unfavorable developments to others or circumstances.

This is not to say there aren't times when our lives are significantly influenced by outside forces. Maybe you're a great worker who lost your job due to a corporate downsizing or the poor economy. Maybe your parents really were poor role models. But victims don't create change. It's only when you choose to focus on what you can do and how you should act that you gain power.

Businesses and other organizations today are looking for people who are willing and able to think, who are self-directing and self-managing, who respond to problems proactively rather than merely waiting for someone else's solutions.

A study done in New York a few years ago found that people who ranked in the top 3% in every field had a special attitude that set them apart from average performers in their industries: they chose to view themselves as self-employed throughout their careers, no matter who signed their paychecks. These are people who set goals, make plans, establish measures, and get results.

Radical responsibility changes everything. It means you own your thoughts, impulses, feelings, and actions. *You* are accountable for the consequences they bring and the impact they have on others.

This is not a burden, incidentally. It's a privilege and an honor to take ownership of your actions. It creates freedom and control. It gives meaning to life. Self-reliance is the great source of personal power. We create ourselves, shape our identity, and determine the course of our lives by what we are willing to take responsibility for.

Want to change your life and solve your problems, starting today? Then say those three simple words: "I am responsible." It means taking ownership of every sphere of your life – from your health and well-being to your business and personal relationships to your saving and investment goals.

Why is this so important? Because if you blame your current circumstances on other people, bad luck, or lousy circumstances, you relinquish your power. Your ability to change others' behavior – not to mention "society" or "the culture" – is minimal. But your power to change yourself is limitless.

This is where you can make a real difference, particularly when it comes to saving and investing. Don't listen to the pessimists and complainers who insist that this is no longer the land of opportunity, that the American Dream is dead, and that we face a diminished future.

It's not true. Successful people take responsibility for their lives and develop habits conducive to asset accumulation. In his classic bestselling book *The Millionaire Next Door*, mentioned in Chapter 7, Stanley lists seven attributes of the affluent:

- **They live well below their means.** Most of us quickly learn that expenses rise to meet the income available. But millionaires tend to maximize their income, minimize their expenses, and religiously save and invest the difference.
- **They allocate their time, energy, and money efficiently in ways conducive to building wealth.** As the old saying goes, "Rich people plan for three generations. Poor people plan for Saturday night."
- **They believe that financial independence is more important than displaying high social status.** So who is buying all those luxury cars, powerboats, top-shelf wines, and expensive bling from Tiffany? "Wannabe's" or "aspirationals." These are folks who have high incomes – and the desire to appear rich – but can't get there thanks to their spending habits. (The Texas term is "all hat, no cattle.") Stanley discovered that the average millionaire in this country doesn't own a second home, has never owned a boat, is more likely to wear a Timex than a Rolex, drives a Mazda rather than a Mercedes, and spends very little on prestige brands and luxury items.
- **Their parents did not provide economic outpatient care.** They learned responsibility, frugality, and self-reliance at an early age.
- **Their adult children are economically self-sufficient.** Take note if you currently have a millennial living in your basement.
- **They are proficient in targeting market opportunities.** In our competitive economy, success accrues to those who figure out what people want or need and then move heaven and Earth to deliver it.

- **They chose the right occupation.** If your fervent desire is to be an archaeologist, a hairdresser, or a high school basketball coach, more power to you. You will fill an important need and might live a thoroughly enjoyable life that others can only envy. Yet if financial security is an important goal, recognize that some professions are more conducive to wealth building than others.

What careers are in greatest demand today? Carpenters, electricians, plumbers, engineers, computer support specialists, software developers, health-care workers, sales representatives, doctors and registered nurses, to name just a few. Or consider a career in heating, ventilation, and air conditioning. The demand for those who can sell, install, maintain, and repair these systems will always remain strong, regardless of the health of the economy. If financial freedom is important to your kids or grandkids, have them look at this list before declaring a major in Egyptian Art or Women's Studies.

In short, the path to financial freedom is bound to be bumpy. But it is straightforward. (As I've said from the beginning: simple but not easy.) Most people just don't understand what's required – or have trouble getting started.

In the next few chapters, however, I'll describe the concrete steps you (or your offspring) can take – starting immediately – to reach a place where money is no longer a concern.

CHAPTER 12

How to Make Success a Habit

> You don't get in life what you want. You get in life what you are.
> —Author Les Brown

As a young man fresh out of college, I had no money and no serious job prospects. Most of my fraternity brothers – who made up my social group at school – had gone on to law school or med school or taken a professional or business management position somewhere.

Things were a little different for me. I was waiting tables six nights a week in Daytona Beach. Despite my inauspicious start, I did have three things going for me: an insatiable curiosity about how the world works, a strong desire to improve my circumstances, and a passion for reading. That last factor is probably the biggest determinant of the success I've experienced professionally, financially, and even personally.

Every time I would take a new job in some new industry, I would look around at my colleagues and think, "You may be smarter than me. You may have more experience than me. You may work harder and longer than me. But you know what? I'll bet I can out-read you."

I was a sponge, learning everything I could about every job I took, every company I worked for, and every industry I entered. I even told my kids as they finished up their own time in college, "If you don't read passionately, I can't really give you any career advice. Because that – and showing up every day – is how I managed to get ahead everywhere I went."

Today when I need information quickly I turn to artificial intelligence (AI) platforms like ChatGPT, Claude, Copilot, and Perplexity. The idea that you can ask a chatbot whatever you want and have it spit out an answer in seconds is pretty close to my idea of heaven on Earth. (Although those answers need to be verified.)

As a young man, of course, there were no AI platforms. So I bought every book I could find on personal development, business success, and wealth-building. I read dozens of them, everything from old classics like *Think and Grow Rich* by Napoleon Hill and *How to Win Friends and Influence People* by Dale Carnegie to *Psycho-Cybernetics* by Maxwell Maltz and *The Seven Habits of Highly Effective People* by Steven Covey. I wore out a highlighter on each of them. And, after I finished, I would read the highlighted parts again and again.

(That is a habit I started in college and have continued to this day. It's surprising how much more information you will retain if you highlight nonfiction and then reread it.)

Driving in my car, I also listened to motivational cassettes by Earl Nightingale and Zig Ziglar. They were not a hit with passengers, but I didn't care. I was earning little and going nowhere yet determined to live some version of the American Dream.

Since I didn't know a soul who was financially successful themselves – at least not well enough to ask them for advice – I relied on books and tapes to provide me with knowledge and inspiration. They were all short on specifics, of course. But that was fine because the authors didn't know what was happening in my life anyway. I figured that I could just take their general principles and apply them to my specific circumstances. And that intuition proved correct.

Some people scoff at the self-help section of the bookstore, but I don't know where I'd be today without it. There's also the library, of course, but I wanted to *own* this knowledge. Plus, libraries don't look kindly on dedicated highlighters like me.

I relied on these books because I didn't have a mentor, a role model, or business and family connections – and I was too much of an introvert to be a successful networker. Besides, anyone in my "network" would have been an inexperienced and financially challenged young person like me.

If you need good advice today, however, it's a whole lot easier. You don't have to read an entire book. Or take a course on career advancement or financial planning. There is plenty of basic saving and investing advice on websites and podcasts.

But you don't have to take generic advice from some dubious influencer. And you don't have to take personalized investment advice from a high-paid professional who is trying to maximize their "production" by turning a substantial portion of clients' assets into the firm's income.

You can just hop on a free AI platform – like ChatGPT, Perplexity, or Copilot – and ask for advice tailored to your specific situation. For example, I asked ChatGPT this: "I'm a single mom with two young children who makes $35,000 a year and has no savings. What should I do to become more financially secure and start working toward financial independence?"

Here is the excellent response I received:

> Thanks for sharing that – it's incredibly courageous, and I want you to know that it *is* possible to build financial security, even from a place like this. You're already doing the hardest part: **showing up every day and providing for your kids**. That's your foundation.
>
> You're in a tough – but very solvable – situation. Here's a step-by-step plan tailored to your situation:
>
> **Step 1: Stabilize and Protect**
> **Goal:** Get a clear picture of where things stand and protect against emergencies.

- ☑ **Make a simple monthly budget**
  - **Start with needs:** rent, food, childcare, transportation, etc.
  - Use the **50/30/20 rule** as a guide if possible:
    - 50% needs
    - 30% wants
    - 20% saving/debt repayment
    (For now, even saving 2% counts – we'll build!)
- ☑ **Use free tools**
  - **Apps:** Mint, YNAB (free trial), or Goodbudget
  - **Paper method:** Just jot it down – no shame in low-tech
- ☑ **Start an Emergency Fund (tiny is fine!)**
  - Open a **separate savings account** – even $5 a week helps
  - Look into **high-yield savings accounts** (Ally, Capital One 360, etc.)
  - **Goal:** $500 to start. Then $1,000. Small steps.
- ☑ **Protect what you have**
  - **Check for government assistance** (SNAP, WIC, Medicaid, childcare subsidies)
  - **Low-cost life insurance:** Term life (20- or 30-year) for peace of mind
  - Build a **community safety net:** friends, local charities, mom support groups

Step 2: Reduce Financial Pressure
Goal: Free up cash flow and reduce stress.
- ☑ **Lower your biggest expenses (without drastic change)**
  - **Housing:** Are you eligible for housing assistance or tax credits?
  - **Childcare:** Explore:
    - **Local nonprofit daycare**
    - **State vouchers or subsidies**
    - **Family share/co-op childcare**

- **Debt?** If applicable, look into:
  - Debt consolidation
  - Credit counseling (nonprofit orgs like NFCC)

Step 3: Increase Your Income (Even a Little)
Goal: Build more breathing room and opportunity.

- ☑ **Upskill or reskill**
  - **Free/affordable training:**
    - Google Career Certificates (IT, data analytics, etc.)
    - Coursera (many free courses)
    - Local community college scholarships
    - Job training programs (check your local workforce development office)
- ☑ **Side income ideas (time-permitting)**
  - **Remote freelance work:** customer service, virtual assistant
  - **Weekend gigs:** selling on Facebook Marketplace, babysitting, tutoring

Step 4: Plan for the Future – Slowly
Goal: Lay the groundwork for long-term security.

- ☑ **Open a Roth IRA (eventually – even with $50!)**
  - Grows tax-free for retirement
  - Many brokers like Fidelity or Vanguard have no minimums
- ☑ **Set small financial goals**
  - First: $500 savings
  - Then: 1 month of expenses saved
  - Eventually: 3–6 months saved, investments, etc.
- ☑ **Dream big, plan small**
  - Your long-term financial independence may take 10 years – that's okay
  - Focus on **consistency over perfection**

Bonus: You're Not Alone
- Connect with **other single moms or support networks**

> - Resources:
>   - **Single Moms Planet**
>   - **Modest Needs Foundation**
>   - **Local community resource centers**
> - Consider **therapy or mental health support** if stress feels overwhelming
>
> Would you like help putting together a **custom monthly budget**, or want help researching **side gigs or job training in your area**? I'm here for that – and anything else you need.
> You've got this – one step at a time. 🖤

How great is this? The advice is practical. And the empathy – even though it's not human – is amazing.

Any technical jargon you don't understand can be explained by simply asking more questions. Each step of the process can be broken down further. And if you run into any stumbling blocks along the way, the AI platform will help you deal with those, too.

Here are some other questions that a chatbot could answer and elucidate quickly and at zero cost:

- How should I set up my first basic budget?
- What's the best way to build an emergency fund on a low income?
- How can I earn more money without going back to school full-time?
- What side hustles are realistic for a busy single parent (or someone with limited free time)?
- What are inexpensive ways to upgrade my skills and qualify for better jobs?
- How can I negotiate a raise or promotion at my current job?
- How should I prioritize paying off different types of debt?
- Should I focus on paying off debt or saving money first?
- How do I build (or repair) my credit score wisely?

- What is a Roth IRA, and should I open one?
- How do I plan for big expenses (like buying a car, paying for childcare, or buying a house)?
- How should I think about retirement when I feel like I'm just surviving day-to-day?
- How do I stay motivated when progress feels slow?
- What habits separate people who stay broke from people who build wealth?
- How do I avoid lifestyle inflation as I start earning more?
- What mistakes should I watch out for on the road to financial independence?

Let's recall that even most of the people living under the poverty line in the United States have a smartphone. The AI apps are free to download and free to use. There is no reason for anyone to feel stymied because they "don't know where to start."

You can put in all your personal details and financial issues. Unlike a gossipy friend, you can tell ChatGPT about your low income, your high bills, your student loans, your credit card debt, even your spouse with a shopping or gambling addiction. In each case, you'll receive a smart response and a fresh direction – with follow-up information available on request.

All that's necessary is a desire to understand what is necessary and the willingness to start the journey. As I've said from the beginning: simple but not easy.

I mention these chatbots, in part, because I often have parents come up to me and say, "My kids have low-paying jobs, a high overhead, and a lot of debt to service. They are stuck. They don't know what to do – and I don't know how to help them, short of bailing them out."

Don't bail them out. If you do, the chances are that it won't be the last time. Help them figure out a way forward. But unless you've got tons of experience or some special connections, you aren't likely to give them better career, budgeting, and saving advice than a chatbot.

With the advent of AI, the excuse "I don't know what to do" sounds more than a little hollow. Anyone can easily find out what they should do. The tough part — for any of us — is actually doing it.

Returning to my own story, I studied for and received a Florida real estate license and made a mediocre living with it for five years. Then I got my Series 7 securities license and made a good living with it for 16 years. Throughout my business career, I continued to read books about personal success and wealth-building strategies, mainly because the people who wrote them knew a lot more about how to get ahead than my colleagues did.

However, it wasn't until relatively late in my life that I read what I consider to be the best book on personal development ever written: *Atomic Habits* by James Clear. If it had been available to me as a young man, I feel confident that I'd have gone further faster — in every aspect of my life. In fact, I can't imagine anyone who wouldn't benefit from reading it. This isn't exactly a secret. The book was a *New York Times* bestseller and has sold over 10 million copies worldwide.

Clear's premise is that your outcomes in life are a lagging indicator of your habits. (A habit is any routine or behavior that is performed regularly and, usually, automatically.) Your knowledge is the sum of your reading and learning habits. Your health is the sum of your eating and exercise habits. Your net worth is the sum of your saving and investing habits.

But here's where things get interesting. Clear points out that getting the results you want — financial or otherwise — is not about setting the right goals. It's about *following the right systems*.

For example, your office may be a complete mess. Your goal might be to have it neat and organized. You could take an hour or two and straighten up, throw things out, and organize what's left. When you're done, your office will look great. Except, if you don't change your habits — if you don't adhere to a system — it will soon be a disaster again.

Why is this so common? Because most of our daily behaviors are automatic. We follow unthinking routines because it frees up our minds to tackle the truly important issues we need to deal with. That's why it's crucial to put proper systems in place for the things that really matter. Like financial freedom. Tiny changes here can lead to dramatic results in your life. That's why Clear calls them *atomic* habits. Atomic means both extremely small and very powerful.

For example, if you go to the gym three times, you are unlikely to notice any real changes to your body except for an uncomfortable soreness. However, if you go to the gym three times a week for six months and follow a proven routine, you will see incredible changes. Not maybe. Definitely. And that uncomfortable soreness? You'll actually start to look forward to that pleasant "burn," which is your muscles breaking down before they build back up firmer and stronger.

What does this have to do with living the American Dream? A lot. In my previous life as a portfolio manager, prospective clients who came to me were often enormously frustrated. These were successful businesspeople or professionals – doctors, engineers, pilots – and plenty smart, but struggling to earn satisfactory returns with their investment portfolios.

Yet when I looked at what they were doing, it rarely made a lot of sense. They owned a bunch of securities. But they couldn't recall exactly why. They didn't have an asset allocation. They didn't have a buy or sell discipline for the individual stocks they owned. They often traded on emotion. And they paid way too much in fees and commissions, many of them hidden.

In short, they didn't have a system. Or they had one, but it wasn't comprehensible, it didn't work, and, not coincidentally, it was helping pay for their financial advisor's lavish home in a gated community. Is it any real surprise that things weren't working out?

My goal is to help everyday men and women reach financial independence, whether they define that as being happily debt-free or building a seven- or eight-figure net worth. The minimum goal is to no longer worry about money. The more usual goal is to have enough to make their dreams a reality.

The way to do this is to unleash a new set of habits. For example, you can automate money so that once your bills are paid and your investments are allocated, you can spend anything left over guilt free. No shame, no chiding, no arguments. Just create a formula that works and stick with it.

Over the course of the next few chapters, I'm going to explain the simplest way I know it to make your investment dollars work for you. Wealth is created by following a system, using proven habits that lead to uncommon results. Yes, there are other ways. But the simplest system is the one I'll describe in the pages ahead.

What are these other pathways to wealth? According to billionaire money manager Ken Fisher, there are – after discounting things you can't control like a lottery win or a big inheritance – essentially 10 ways to get rich:

1. **Start a successful business.** Prime examples are Bill Gates, Charles Schwab, Sam Walton, Jeff Bezos, and Elon Musk. Of course, you're unlikely to do nearly as well as any of these guys. But that isn't necessary. With enough time and effort, you can get plenty rich filling a need for a local product or service in your hometown. (That includes starting a plumbing business or putting braces on kids.)
2. **Become CEO of an existing firm and juice it.** This was the method for Steve Balmer, Tim Cook, and others. This requires many years of experience – and generally a lot of loyalty to one company. But if you have the drive and ambition, the salary and option compensation can make it well worth your while.
3. **Hitch your wagon to a star.** This method involves tying your fortunes to a successful business visionary. Charlie Munger did with Warren Buffett, Jeffrey Skoll with Jerry Yang, and Peter Chernin with Rupert Murdoch. This is a tough one, though. You have to recognize a visionary early – offer them something of value and stick with them. Not easily done.
4. **Turn celebrity into wealth.** We all know that celebrities are loaded. But unless you're a world-class athlete, a terrific singer/songwriter, or George Clooney, you might give this one a miss. Yes, it's possible to become an "internet influencer." But with more than eight billion people on the planet, the competition is ferocious.
5. **Marry well – really, really well.** This may seem shallow, but a *Wall Street Journal* poll found that two-thirds of

women said they'd be "very" or "extremely willing" to marry for money. Half of men surveyed said they'd marry for money, too. (The downside? Expect a prenup.)

6. **Steal it, legally.** Some people think plaintiff's lawyers are crusading saviors. Fisher sees them as bloodsucking leeches and extortion artists. (He quotes the age-old Mexican curse: may your life be full of lawyers.) But if you can handle law school and pass the bar, this method is another possibility.

7. **Use other people's money.** This is the most common road for the ultra-wealthy. Managing other people's money is how bankers, brokers, insurance companies, mutual fund managers, hedge fund managers, and personal money managers like Ken Fisher make their millions.

8. **Invent an endless future revenue stream.** In this scenario, you create something – a book, a movie, a Broadway play – and find a way for it to create long-term royalties. This, admittedly, is a long shot. If you're going to try this path, says Fisher, "think lunch boxes." Products that end up on lunch boxes – Spider-Man, Star Wars, and so on – are the really big moneymakers.

9. **Monetize unrealized real estate wealth.** Millions of Americans have gotten rich in real estate. And many will in the future. But Fisher says skip the idea of flipping houses and condos – the transaction costs alone will kill you – and concentrate on good properties in desirable areas with predictable cash flows.

10. **Take the "road more traveled."** This is the method we'll focus on here because anyone can do it. It's about maximizing your income, controlling your outgo, saving religiously, and then managing your investment portfolio in a smart and disciplined way.

The road more traveled is the classic way for everyday people to get rich. Most of us don't have the time, the capital, or the expertise to own our own business. But we can always use the stock market – the quintessence of capitalism – to become business owners. This takes patience and equanimity. But it is the surest way to long-term wealth.

This is not the route for high-paid professionals only, incidentally. Fisher's firm doesn't accept accounts starting at less than $500,000. But he has plenty of former middle-class workers as clients. In his book *The Ten Roads to Riches*, Fisher writes, "If your passion is truly social work, teaching kindergarten, or quilting – fine. Then focus on frugality. It can be done! I have clients who were postal carriers, teachers, cops, etc. They did it. Frugal!"

How is this possible? There's no magic. These people live beneath their means and save. "Skip mocha-caramel-triple-lattes," says Fisher. "Pay off credit card debt. Avoid designer labels. Buy used cars. Eat in more, out less. Total no-brainers. Yet some can't do this – just can't." If you can, you have a good chance of becoming "the millionaire next door." If you can't, Fisher warns, you better find a higher-paying alternative. (In other words, see nos. 1–9.)

I made my fortune by concentrating on no. 10 – and it's not difficult if you adhere to proven wealth-building habits. Let me give you an example from my own experience. As a young man, I hired an accountant each year to prepare my federal tax form. It's not that my finances were complicated – far from it – but I am form-a-phobic. I hate filling out the annual 1040 and still believe the IRS makes paying taxes needlessly complicated.

When my accountant did the calculations and told me how much extra I owed each year, it irked me. She'd ask why I didn't save some taxes – and plan for retirement – by making an IRA contribution of $2,000. That was the maximum back in those days. (I had no employer-sponsored plan.)

"Why don't I? That's easy," I said. "I don't have $2,000."

She shrugged and said she had no other suggestions to offer. However, I did some research and discovered that there was a fund family called 20thCentury – now American Century – that would allow investors to open an IRA account with no minimum investment. (No minimums are common now but were virtually nonexistent 40 years ago.)

I did a quick calculation and found that $2,000 divided by 12 months is $166.66 a month. So I sent 20th Century a check for that amount and signed up to have them automatically draft my bank account for another $166.66 each month.

This is a widely known investment technique called *dollar cost averaging* or DCA and – while I'd never heard the term back then – it has several advantages. By investing a fixed amount at regular intervals, it smooths out the effect of market fluctuations. When prices are high, you buy fewer shares; when prices are low, you buy more. Over time, this will lower your average cost per share.

DCA eliminates market timing, which can't be done successfully, and reduces emotional decision-making, such as overconfidence during stock market rallies and panic selling during downturns. The habit of making regular contributions instills discipline and helps investors stick to their investment plans. And automating your investments ensures that funds are consistently allocated toward building wealth rather than being spent elsewhere.

History shows that stocks rise over the long haul, reflecting the growth in the economy and corporate profits. Spreading out investments over time ensures consistent participation in the market. Dollar cost averaging is an ideal investment technique for small investors, most of whom don't have a lump sum to invest anyway.

Over time, I began dollar cost averaging with other funds – and with greater sums – and watched as my account values grew from tens of thousands to hundreds of thousands of dollars.

I let the bank drafts continue in both good times and bad – including after the stock market crash of 1987 – always reminding myself when the market was down that I was buying more shares with the same amount of money.

Here's the surprising part. I made a single initial decision – to open an account and invest what amounted to little more than the monthly beer money – and then watched my net worth rise as the years went by.

Note that I didn't do anything brilliant. Nor did I do anything terribly brave. I just made it a decision to have my bank account debited monthly and then just let it happen automatically. James Clear would recognize why I succeeded. I let a habit become a system, one that required zero effort on my part.

Usually I say, "simple but not easy." But dollar cost averaging is simple *and* easy. The only other requirement is patience. It's not rocket science. And it's a great way for small investors to get started on the path to the American Dream.

Part of the American Dream: Home Sweet Home

There is no passion to be found playing small – in settling for a life that is less than the one you are capable of living.

—State leader Nelson Mandela

Homeownership has long been viewed as one of the most important aspects of the American Dream. In Chapter 4, I explained how housing became *more affordable* to blue-collar workers between 1980 and 2020, when measured in time prices. In recent years, however, the housing market has become tight. Interest rates have risen, and there is less affordability.

Over the past 15 years, home prices have approximately doubled. (As of January 2025, the median home-sale price was $396,900, according to the National Association of Realtors.) And fixed-rate 30-year mortgage rates have risen from a historic low of just 2.65% in January 2021 to a recent average of 6.72%, a 154% increase.

That has made it tough for young people and lower-income households – two overlapping groups – to buy a home and start building equity.

However, there are pros and cons to homeownership. And ways to buy a house even if you don't have good credit or the income to afford current mortgage rates, which most people *don't know*.

Let's start with the state of homeownership in the United States. According to the National Association of Home Builders, as of the fourth quarter of 2024, the US homeownership rate stood at 65.7%. That's only slightly below the 25-year average of 66.4%. However, the homeownership rate for those under 35 dropped to 36.3%. That's the lowest level since the third quarter of 2019.

High mortgage rates and rising home prices have created a multi-decade low in housing affordability. There are other factors as well. Limited inventory, especially for entry-level homes, has made it difficult for first-time home buyers to enter the market. And concerns about the economy – and the changing nature of work – may also cause potential buyers to hesitate. For example, some jobs require employees to move periodically or even frequently. It's not easy to get in and out of a house quickly, while covering all closing costs and turning a profit, or at least breaking even.

There are other downsides to homeownership. Purchasing a home generally requires significant up-front expenses, including a down payment and closing costs. Homeowners are responsible for all repairs and maintenance, which can be time-consuming and costly.

Homeowners must pay annual property taxes – which are substantial in some areas – and banks generally require property insurance, which can also be expensive. Owning a home can make it more challenging to relocate for a job or capitalize on other opportunities, reducing the homeowners' flexibility. And, while home values generally appreciate over time, there's always a risk of market downturns affecting property values.

Given these challenges, some families – and especially young people who are not yet settled – may opt to forgo homeownership, at least in the near term. Yet most Americans want to own a home and enjoy the many advantages. The biggest? Homeownership enables individuals to build wealth over time as they pay down their mortgage and the property appreciates in value.

Aside from building equity, there are tax benefits. Homeowners can deduct mortgage interest and property taxes, providing financial advantages. Fixed-mortgage rates offer predictable housing costs over time, unlike rising rents. Homeowners have the freedom to customize their living space, adding to their quality of life. And owning a home often leads to stronger community ties, which are important to many people.

Despite these many advantages, it's important to realize that houses are not always great investments. This may come as a surprise to homeowners who have benefited from the hot housing market recently, but – historically – the typical home has only slightly outpaced inflation. Of course, most homeowners use leverage. They put down only a fraction of the cost of the house as a down payment. That means even a modest uptick in the price can result in an attractive return on the total dollars invested.

But leverage is a double-edged sword. A downturn in the price of a home can quickly exceed the value of the money invested, resulting in a serious loss, although history shows this is the exception not the rule.

The stock market has provided a far superior return to most real estate. For example, the S&P 500 – while more volatile than home prices – has delivered a long-term average annual return of slightly over 10%. (Plus, index funds are far more liquid than real estate, have dramatically lower transaction costs, and require no active management or out-of-pocket expenses.)

Many renters have earned higher returns over the past few decades by buying a diversified portfolio of stocks rather than making mortgage payments . . . and preserved their freedom and flexibility along the way. As a friend of mine likes to say, "Live like a king . . . rent *everything*." That's fine for some people. Others want the stability, equity, and other financial and aesthetic advantages of homeownership.

That can be difficult when home prices are near record levels and mortgage rates have more than doubled since 2021. Moreover, many folks – and especially young people – feel they lack the money or credit score necessary to buy a starter home and move onto the property ladder. Yet, in some cases, this is more a mental stumbling block than an actual one.

A story from my own past will help explain. I grew up in a middle-class household. My parents knew almost nothing about wealth building. That meant they had no advice to give in this department.

However, my dad did offer that one pearl: buy a home rather than throwing your money away on rent year after year.

This wasn't brilliant advice, but it was practical. There were a few problems, however. A young man in my early 20s, I had no experience with homeownership, no savings, and virtually no credit score since I had never bought anything on credit. I was also fortunate that my parents never offered any economic support after I finished school. (I say "fortunate" because I feel that helped make a man out of me.)

I did have two things going for me: a full-time job and a credit card. However, with no savings I had nothing for a down payment. I also didn't have enough job experience or credit to qualify for a mortgage.

I should add that this was the early 1980s, when mortgage rates peaked near 18%. That meant that – aside from lacking a down payment, an income history, and the credit score to qualify for a mortgage – I couldn't have afforded a monthly mortgage payment at prevailing rates anyway.

Most people would assume they were locked out of the housing market. And their friends and associates would agree. Yet I remained undeterred. I visited a local bookstore and my eyes fell on a business book with the generic title *How to Buy Real Estate with No Money Down*. I bought it immediately. But when I showed it to my friends, they laughed.

"Everybody dreams of buying a house with no money down," one said. "But it's not possible. You're going to need to put up a substantial down payment to satisfy the bank, cover the real estate commission, and pay closing costs. So how the heck are you going to buy a house with no money down?"

His skepticism sounded reasonable. But I read the book anyway – and my eyes were opened. The author freely admitted that most houses could never be bought with no money down for the very reasons my friend enumerated. Instead, the author advised that I look for a home with three special circumstances.

The first? The sellers had to be what he called *don't-wanters*. They had to be strongly motivated to sell the house quickly. Maybe it had already been on the market a long time and the upkeep had become a pain in the neck. Maybe they had already bought another house elsewhere and couldn't afford to make two mortgage payments. There are endless potential circumstances that can create a don't-wanter.

I happened on mine in the real estate listings of the local paper. It was a brand spanking new, never occupied, three-bedroom townhouse that a merchant marine had bought pre-construction and planned to occupy. Then he got the order to move overseas.

Because mortgage rates were in the high teens – destroying the residential real estate market – he had been unable to unload it. That – and his travel plans – made him a serious don't-wanter.

The second set of circumstances I needed was for the property to be for sale by owner. The reason is simple. Without a realtor involved, there is no real estate commission to cover.

Third, the sellers had to be willing to carry the financing. In other words, rather than me going to the bank and taking out a mortgage to cash them out, they had to be willing to let me make the payments directly to them. (Which they would then pass along to the lender.)

Why would a seller agree to such an arrangement? As I mentioned, my seller really wanted *out*. If carrying the financing were necessary, he was willing to do it. I, however, wanted *in*. I especially wanted to take over his older, lower-interest mortgage, since I could neither afford nor qualify for a new mortgage.

However, the seller wasn't *so desperate* that he was willing to simply let me take over the payments. (Although I've since met folks who have bought a home that way in a really bad market.) He wanted $3,000 down as security.

Unfortunately, that was $3,000 more than I had on hand. But I got a $3,000 cash advance on my MasterCard – and gave it to him after I paid a lawyer a few hundred dollars to draw up what is known as a contract for deed, or land contract. The contract stipulated that if I continued to make the mortgage payments in a timely fashion – or wanted to sell it – the property was mine. But if I fell even 60 days behind, he could take the property back and keep the accumulated equity.

Our rights and responsibilities were clearly defined. And both sides were happy, as is the case with every free-market transaction. I was delighted: a young, single guy with a brand-new three-bedroom place.

I took the master bedroom and then invited a couple of buddies to move in. Their rent covered most of the mortgage payment. They also paid two-thirds of the utilities. And I got all the tax breaks, writing off the mortgage interest and property taxes each year.

It was my first taste of capitalism. And I liked it. I was building equity while paying less each month than when I was a renter.

I sold the place for a tidy profit five years later and avoided a capital gains tax by buying a larger lakefront home . . . also with no money down. Why am I sharing this story? Because most people in my situation would have said they didn't have the money or credit to buy a house. End of story. Yet all it took was a strong desire, a bit of creative thinking, and some pluck.

Can you buy your dream house this way? Perhaps. (That was my modest dream house at the time.) Then again, maybe not. But you can almost certainly find *some home* in your area this way – and start building equity.

A contract for deed is a great vehicle for getting a seller out of a house they no longer want. And it allows the buyer to take over the old lower-interest mortgage in the process. (Moreover, the seller could potentially use a contract for deed to buy their next place, whether they are upsizing, downsizing, or just relocating.)

A contract for deed is just one of several ways to buy a house when interest rates have spiked. However, there are other steps a potential homeowner could take:

1. **Check your credit score.** A higher credit score improves your chances of qualifying for a mortgage and securing a better rate. Most conventional loans require a minimum score of 620.
2. **Save for a down payment.** The minimum down payment for a conventional loan is 3%, while FHA loans require 3.5%. VA and USDA loans may allow for zero down payment, but eligibility requirements apply.
3. **Manage debt.** Lenders assess your debt-to-income ratio. Keeping below 45% for conventional loans improves your chances for approval.
4. **Research assistance programs.** Investigate first-time homebuyer programs, down payment assistance, and grants that are available at the state and local levels.
5. **Get your mortgage preapproved.** This clarifies your budget and strengthens your offer.
6. **Consider creative financing.** I've already discussed a contract for deed. But consider lease-to-own programs, alternative mortgage products (like interest-only loans), and hybrid options, as well.
7. **Build an emergency fund.** As I've mentioned, homes come with plenty of expenses both expected and unexpected. Having a cash reserve is essential.
8. **Adjust expectations.** Many buyers opt for smaller homes, condos, manufactured homes, or properties that need renovation to stay within budget. Co-buying with family or friends is another option.

It's important to realize that most Americans had to make sacrifices to get into their first home. It takes time to establish good credit, save for a down payment, and research the best opportunities in your local market.

Homeownership, like virtually every other aspect of the American Dream, starts with believing in the possibility, and following through with wise choices.

CHAPTER 14

Savings: The Seed Corn of the American Dream

> Discipline is doing what you really don't want to do so that you can do what you really want to do.
>
> —Author John Maxwell

What does it mean to be "rich"? I took an informal poll of friends and associates, and most responses fell into one of three general categories. The first group said being rich means not having to stress about their bills. The second group said it means being able to spend avidly – or give generously – without feeling guilty. The third group said being rich means having the wherewithal to live the life of their dreams.

These are three good answers that pretty much define the essential levels of financial freedom. But how much money does each level require? That will depend on the individual. We all have basic needs, but beyond that some folks have simple wants that are not difficult to accommodate. Others have a taste for finer things and exceptional experiences. Still others want to see, do, enjoy, and have it all.

Young people – who are highly influenced by social media – often make a priority of living a lifestyle comparable to their friends. For example, 61% of millennials and Gen Zers said, "Being able to afford a similar lifestyle to my friends makes me feel wealthy." Just half as many baby boomers felt that way.

Approximately half of millennials and Gen Zers also said, "I make purchases based on what I see my friends and other influencers share on social media." Only 10% of baby boomers agreed.

Part of the problem for many young people these days is that they are constantly connected. Retailers use affiliate links and algorithms to target customers. Buy Now buttons make purchases as frictionless as possible. Emails and texts provide constant nudges. And social media – like Instagram and TikTok – sell the dream of a perfect product leading to a perfect life.

The problem is particularly acute among Gen Z and millennial shoppers. A third admitted to being addicted to shopping, according to a 2024 survey conducted by Qualtrics for Intuit Credit Karma.

They can fight back, however. It starts by removing saved credit cards from phones, uninstalling shopping apps, disabling location-finding technology, and unsubscribing from commercial email lists.

Young folks with out-of-control spending are heading down a treacherous path. The fear of missing out – or the desire to keep up – makes them feel pressured to spend money on things that don't have long-term value. The more they spend, the less they can save and invest. As their debts mount, they are squandering the one big advantage over the rest of us: more time for their money to compound.

For example, a 25-year-old who saves $400 a month until age 65 – and earns nothing more or less than the 10% average annual return of the S&P 500 – will have $2.24 million. However, if someone waits until age 35 to save $400 a month – and earns the same return – it turns into just $832,340 by age 65. Wait until 45 to get started and that $400 a month turns into only $289,811.

These numbers reveal how young people are undoing themselves when they spend all their take-home pay to keep up with the Joneses on Instagram.

Social media has its advantages. But I have zero regrets about growing up without it. As a young man, I knew that some of my contemporaries had way more money (and stuff) than me, but I spent no time dwelling on it.

My buddies and I had little discretionary income. But it didn't make any difference. A fun night was buying a couple of six packs and having friends over to watch the ball game (on a small tube with grainy reception). And I learned that some women don't care how much money you make if you can work small miracles on the grill.

In many ways, those were some of the best years of my life. I learned that it really doesn't take a lot of money to have a lot of fun.

Schwab's Wealth Survey confirmed that most of us realize what's truly important. When asked what wealth means, 70% chose enjoying experiences over owning nice things. Seventy percent also said not having to stress over money is more important than having more money than most people they know. Sixty-nine percent said having a healthy work-life balance was more important than maximizing their earnings. Sixty-seven percent prioritized being generous with loved ones now versus leaving an inheritance. And 62% said enjoying healthy relationships was more important than having a lot of money. In short, nonfinancial assets – like health and family – resonate more than large sums of money when defining true wealth.

However, life takes money. And financial independence is a worthy goal. It's just that most Americans have little understanding of how to get there. The Securities and Exchange Commission (SEC) recently released a wide-ranging report on financial literacy in the United States. And the conclusion is clear: we're not there yet. Not even close.

Yet the consequences have never been greater. Corporate pension plans have gone the way of the passenger pigeon. And without serious reform, Social Security – according to that agency's own website – will eventually be done in by time and arithmetic. At the very least, the age of initial eligibility is likely to be raised substantially in the years ahead to adjust for greater longevity.

This means Americans are largely on their own. We need to understand basic financial concepts – and apply them. Yet the SEC report and others like it show that the vast majority aren't ready. A Health and Retirement Survey concluded that most Americans "lack even a rudimentary understanding of stock and bond prices, risk diversification, portfolio choice, and investment fees." The most common response to most questions in the survey was "do not know."

It's a shame that students routinely graduate from high school today without understanding compound interest, variable-rate mortgages, Roth IRAs, what a bond is, or why we have a stock market.

Teachers will argue that students suffer from historical or scientific illiteracy. But being unable to identify Jonas Salk or Winston Churchill will not cost you hundreds of thousands of dollars over your lifetime. When it comes to money basics, ignorance gets expensive, fast.

Here are just a few highlights from that SEC report. When asked the primary benefit of portfolio diversification, respondents were given three choices: (A) risk reduction, (B) increased returns, or (C) reduced tax liabilities. Only 56% knew the answer is A. Even if they had no idea whatsoever, respondents had a 33% chance of getting it right. The reality is that most participants didn't even know this most basic piece of financial wisdom.

When asked whether a young investor willing to take moderate risk for above-average growth should invest in (A) Treasury bills, (B) money market funds, or (C) balanced stock funds, 63% of respondents chose the wrong answer. Even 49% of mutual fund owners didn't know the correct answer is C. When asked whether a traditional IRA, a 401(k), or a Roth IRA offered withdrawals that are tax-exempt, only 44% knew the correct answer is a Roth.

This is a shame, especially in a country like ours where citizens are given the freedom and opportunity to pursue financial independence. As a result, too many learn the hard way, falling for the siren song of an expensive insurance agent or transaction-based broker . . . or committing hari-kari in a discount brokerage account.

What is the solution? Teaching basic financial literacy in every public high school in the country would be a good first step. But education reform is slow and difficult, not least of all because fewer than 20% of teachers polled said they felt competent to teach saving and investing.

You can work hard for a long time, earn a decent living, and live a good life. But to feel secure, enjoy peace of mind, and live the Dream? It's vital that you save and invest. For more than two-thirds of elderly Americans, Social Security is their major source of income. (For a third of them, Social Security is their only income.) If you are retired or close to it, you can count on Social Security to help meet your financial needs. But it's tough to imagine living on nothing more.

Inflation – the thief that robs us all – is slowly but steadily driving up your cost of living. Your eroding purchasing power means you'll have to devote more of your budget in retirement to housing, utilities, insurance, health-care costs, and other monthly expenses.

Unfortunately, polls show that over half of Americans believe it is the responsibility of the government or their employer to take care of them in retirement. These folks are in for a rude awakening. You may indeed get benefits from your employer and the federal government. But neither is likely to provide you with a cushy retirement.

When you take control and accept full accountability for your own financial welfare, you let go of the idea that it is someone else's obligation to provide for you in retirement. You let go of the idea that your broker or financial planner will ensure your financial independence. Ultimately, your financial welfare is up to you. You need to plan. You need to save. And you need to manage your money intelligently.

Let's acknowledge a fundamental truth. There can be no long-term security without saving. So why don't people save more? That's easy. Consumption is easy and fun. Saving – the conscious deferral of present comforts for future gains – is hard. Yet financial freedom starts with setting aside enough money each month to begin reaching your financial goals. Yes, it's partly about planning. But it's mostly about having the discipline to follow through.

A few years ago, a survey by Bankrate.com found that 68% of adults avoid news about the cost of retirement. Why do so many Americans have their heads in the sand? There are various reasons. Some see their parents getting by on Social Security and pensions. Others simply lack the discipline to save.

These folks might want to go back and read Aesop's fable about the ant and the grasshopper. Americans are living longer than ever thanks to healthier lifestyles and modern medicine. If you're likely to live longer, you need a hardworking investment portfolio (one that can duck into a phone booth and come out with a red cape unfurled). But to truly maximize the size of that portfolio, you'll need to save as much as you reasonably can, as soon as you can, for as long as you can.

Most people know this, of course. They just have trouble doing it. Especially young people.

Like many readers, as a young man I was essentially broke. Forty years later, I'm decidedly not. But even when I had a net worth of zero, I believed fully in the American Dream. I didn't have the first clue how I would get there. But I had no doubt that I eventually would.

I think having confidence – a sense of optimism – is essential to achieving the Dream. And there are indications that young Americans are taking their financial future into their own hands.

According to that 2024 Charles Schwab survey, for Gen Zers (those born in the United States between 1997 and 2012), the average age for their first investment is just 19. That's excellent. For millennials (1985–1996) it is 25. For Gen Xers (1965–1980), it's 32. And for baby boomers (1946–1964), it's 35.

Getting a head start on investing is undoubtedly a good thing. Easy access and no minimums make wealth building possible for everyone. (Even if you don't have a few hundred dollars to buy a share of one of the big tech leaders, you can own a fractional share and still participate in their growth.) The downside? Multiple surveys show that too many young people – and especially young men – with access to all sorts of risky products and strategies are taking big chances.

Thanks to smartphones, zero-commission trading, and the growing "gamification" trend, young folks are amping up the risk in their portfolios . . . and with entirely predictable results.

They're gambling, not investing. Millions of young men opened brokerage accounts during the pandemic and gravitated toward highly risky investments. They chased meme stocks. They traded on margin. They bought and sold crypto. And they became active option traders.

Let's start with margin. Borrowing money from a broker to trade or invest – making purchases "on margin" – can magnify losses as well as gains. While the ability to trade on margin has been around since before the stock market crash of 1929, it is risky. Yet it has gained popularity with next-gen investors. In 2021, 23% of investors ages 18–34 said they had made purchases on margin, compared with 12% of respondents ages 34–54 and 3% of respondents age 55 and older. (With age comes wisdom.)

Options can be even riskier. An option contract gives an investor the opportunity to buy or sell a security by a specific date. They can be used to generate income, hedge risk, or engage in speculation. Take a wild guess which young traders went for?

Option trade volumes have soared since the pandemic, when young men – unable to visit a casino or sports book – became enamored with them. A 2021 investor survey by the Finra Education Foundation discovered that 36% of respondents ages 18–34 said they had traded options. That compares with 21% of respondents 35–54 and just 8% of respondents ages 55 or older.

While an options trader can close out their positions on any market day – at a profit or a loss – approximately 80% of all stock options expire worthless.

As if these odds weren't daunting enough for anyone but hardcore speculators, the young and the restless have begun experimenting with zero-dated options. These options expire at the end of the day, enabling traders to bet on intraday market moves of major indexes and related exchange-traded funds (ETFs). A trader can potentially earn a quick windfall or rapidly lose an entire position. Excitement? Guaranteed. Profits? Not so much.

If you have plenty of options trading experience, and a high tolerance for risk, knock yourself out. If you're a low-net-worth young person who likes to gamble, strap on your protective gear. The sad thing, especially since these individuals have so much time ahead of them, is what they're giving up in future returns.

For example, most young people can bounce back from losing $5,000 in zero-dated options (or on a typical gambling junket to Atlantic City or Las Vegas). But I wonder how many of them stop to think that it's not just the $5,000 that's gone. It's the $234,000 it would have turned into over the next 40 years if the money earned nothing more than the historic return of the S&P 500.

As the Renaissance genius Leonardo da Vinci said, "He who wishes to be rich in a day will be hanged in a year." (Although, in this case, it's your portfolio that will be swinging at the end of a rope.)

This goes for crypto traders, too. Most young people saw that bitcoin – while highly volatile – mostly trended up for several years. Yet economists at the Bank of International Settlements – an institution widely considered the central bank of central banks – analyzed data on investors in cryptocurrencies in 95 countries between 2015 and 2022. Their conclusion? "Around three-quarters of users have lost money on their bitcoin investments."

Moreover, they found that "as prices were rising and smaller users were buying bitcoin, the largest holders (the so-called whales or humpbacks) were selling – making a return at the smaller users' expense." The study also found that the biggest segment of cryptocurrency users – roughly 40% – were extreme risk-seekers, men under 35.

The Bank of International Settlements study is a few years old. But it dovetails with Bank of America's 2024 Study of Wealthy Americans. The new study found starkly different views on asset allocation between Americans over the age of 44 and those between the ages of 21 and 43.

Both groups thought that real estate investments should make up 31–32% of their portfolio. I have no real quarrel with that. But the older and more experienced investors thought they should have 41% of their portfolios in US stocks. The younger investors thought only 14% was right.

The real divide? Older investors thought they should have just 4% in crypto and other digital assets. Young people thought they should have a whopping 28% of their portfolio in this sector.

Crypto is a solution in search of a problem. If you're not an extortionist, bribe taker, kickback payer, tax cheat, drug cartel, terrorist network, heavy weapons dealer, human trafficker, or country trying to evade economic sanctions, crypto does nothing to make your life simpler, easier, or better. It's just something to bet on, although three-quarters of the bets – apparently – are not paying off. If I were to hazard a guess, I'd say a much larger percentage will fail in the future. For law-abiding citizens, crypto is a speculative asset and nothing more.

A currency – any currency – is supposed to facilitate transactions. In 2021, 2% of US adults used cryptocurrency for payments. The same percentage did so in 2022. But by 2023, only 1% did. While crypto ownership has grown over the years due to the availability of ETFs and other vehicles, the percentage of Americans using cryptocurrencies for purchases or sales has remained low and even decreased.

Young people have plenty of time for appreciating assets to deliver the high net worth they ardently desire, but many are squandering that opportunity by investing a substantial portion of their portfolios in long shots that are more likely to deliver capital losses.

However, these folks are at least *trying* to get ahead. A big percentage of them are not even making an attempt. In 2022, for example, Fidelity Investments conducted a Money Mindset study that examined the challenges and perceptions of 18- to 44-year-olds when it comes to their relationship with money.

One in four said they would rather run a 5K on Thanksgiving morning than cut back on spending. One in three would rather deep-clean their bathroom than check their savings account.

Here are some other clarifiers:

- Fifty-nine percent cringe at the thought of checking their bank account balance.
- Fifty-one percent don't pay attention to spending, as long as they have money in the bank.
- Sixty-five percent say they know they should save more but are so stressed out about their finances that they avoid thinking about them altogether.
- Fifty-seven percent dread the thought of budgeting.
- Fifty-four percent believe it's easier to follow a strict food diet than a monthly budget.
- Sixty-one percent admit the fear of missing out has them spending more money than they intended.

Let's pause here to note that this list doesn't just represent the views of *some* 18- to 44-year-olds. It is a representative sample of *all of them*.

Yet I still haven't covered what I call *the startling statistic*: 71% said they know they need to save for the future but are unwilling to make changes to their current lifestyle. This is more than 7 in 10 young Americans. (And how many of the 29% who answered yes are merely dreaming about their willingness to forgo spending now to meet long-term financial goals?)

Houston, we have a problem.

As entrepreneur Roger Babson says,

> *Experience has taught me that there is one chief reason why some people succeed and others fail. The difference is not one of knowing, but of doing. The superior man is not so superior in ability as in action. So far as success can be reduced to a formula, it consists of this: doing what you know you should do.*

Most Americans will not reach financial independence – or even some level of financial security – without investing. But there can be no investing without first saving . . . which means deferring gratification and living beneath your means. Anyone unwilling to do that is unlikely to meet their most important financial goals.

Who is to blame? Parents? Teachers? The government? Employers? Rich people? The free-enterprise system? Of course not. We are all individually responsible for our choices and behavior.

As I said previously, the American Dream is an achievement, not an entitlement. Moreover, the people who have given up on achieving it are missing out on the best part: not the destination but *the journey*. Working harder, saving more, and investing wisely are struggles, yes. But it can be an enjoyable struggle that pays off enormously in the end.

Arthur Brooks, a social scientist and former president of the American Enterprise Institute, emphasizes the concept of "earned success" as a key driver of human happiness and fulfillment. He defines earned success as the belief that you create value in your life — and in the lives of others — through effort, skill, and perseverance.

Money alone doesn't make anyone happy. It is a means to an end, not an end in itself. Financial success does not guarantee happiness. Instead, people find lasting satisfaction when they achieve something through their own efforts, in their careers, their relationships, and in their personal growth.

People who survive on parental or government handouts — or other unearned rewards — often lack meaning and purpose in their lives. They lack dignity. Why? Because their success is unearned. When you master a marketable skill, build a career (or a business), or raise a family, you have a sense of progress and achievement, not just material wealth.

Anyone, regardless of their background, can achieve success in this country. But it does require hard work, perseverance, and self-reliance. (As the old saying goes, the only place success comes before work is in the dictionary.) Let me reassure the young people who are struggling that I know it's tough out there. Paying your bills and getting ahead can be difficult. But you can start by reframing your thoughts.

Instead of being afraid to look at your bank balance or overwhelmed by the complexities of investing, you can begin to think of achieving your dreams as an enjoyable challenge. Embrace *the journey*. And when you get to the destination – the place where money is no longer a major concern in your life – remember that the biggest payoff won't be where you are, what you own, or what you can afford.

It will be that feeling of earned success.

Investing: How to Sow What You'll Reap

We know that investing entails risk. But we also know that not investing dooms us to financial failure.

—Vanguard founder John Bogle

Let me summarize: to enjoy financial security, you need to maximize your income, live within your means, and save regularly. Now we get to the part where so many Americans stumble: actually putting their money to work.

This doesn't need to be a complicated subject. Successful investing is about the intelligent management of risk. You can't avoid risk or eliminate it. You have to take it by the horns and deal with it.

Every investment choice entails risk. Even if you're so conservative that you keep all your money in cash investments like T-bills and certificates of deposit – not a terribly good idea, incidentally –

you are taking the sizable risk that your purchasing power fails to keep pace with inflation and you outlive your money.

Yet, terrified of seeing the value of their investments decline even temporarily, plenty of investors err on the side of conservatism. This is understandable at first blush. After all, it's not easy watching your nest egg get scrambled as the stock market spasms in reaction to every piece of bad business news or new government statistic.

But history shows that over the long run, you are well compensated for withstanding the vicissitudes of the market. If, by contrast, you seek stability in your investments first and foremost, your returns are guaranteed to be low. Investments in money market funds and certificates of deposit return very little after taxes and inflation. Over the past 90 years, T-bills have returned approximately 3.8% per year. Most short-term bond funds and money market accounts offer very little real (after-inflation) return on your money.

Don't get me wrong. If you're saving for a short-term goal like a new car or a down payment on a house, you can't get safer than 30-day T-bills. Unless the American flag is no longer flying over the White House a month from now, your investment is secure. Over the long haul, however, that kind of safety comes at a steep price. A portfolio that takes an ultraconservative approach to market risk exposes the investor to a high degree of shortfall risk.

When you own a share of stock, you will capture the return that these businesses generate in the form of earnings growth and dividends. And thanks to the miracle of compounding, the accumulations of wealth that are generated by those returns over the years have been little short of fantastic. Thanks to the growth, productivity, resourcefulness, and innovation of our corporations, equity ownership has been a winner's game.

Stocks have given far superior long-term returns over other asset classes, like bonds, real estate, or commodities. Yet many investors are frightened of them. They view the market as a giant casino (and it often acts that way from hour to hour and day to day). But, over the long term, nothing could be further from the truth.

Historically, the odds of making money in the US stock market are 50–50 in one-day periods, 68% in one-year periods, 88% in 10-year periods, and 100% in 20-year periods.

This should not surprise you. Stocks are not simply slips of paper with corporate names on them. A share of stock is a fractional interest in a business. When a corporation issues stock, it is offering each purchaser the right to share in the fortunes of the business.

Once the initial stock offering is complete, shares are then bought or sold on an exchange. That's when things get interesting. Stocks move each market day based on news or investor perceptions about inflation, interest rates, economic growth, commodity prices, the dollar, consumer confidence, technological developments, business conditions, government policies, and many other factors.

This causes a company's share price to fluctuate more dramatically than the prospects for the underlying business. That's because stock prices are determined "at the margin." Only a small fraction of a company's shareholders sell their shares in the market each day. Yet that tiny fraction determines the value of the entire company – at least temporarily. Sudden imbalances in buy or sell orders can quickly push a stock dramatically higher or lower.

Sometimes these price swings are triggered by a change in the company's fundamentals. But a company's daily share price can rise or fall for reasons that have nothing to do with the outlook for the company, or even the economy. Individual stock prices can be pushed around, for example, by rumors, official buy or sell recommendations by major wire houses, short sellers, high-frequency traders, tax selling, good or bad publicity, insider transactions, fads, takeover speculation, or bad news elsewhere in the sector. Short-term momentum traders often pile on, too, creating even more volatility.

For short-term traders, these are issues that must be understood and dealt with. But for long-term investors the daily trading activity can be conveniently ignored.

Why? Because over the long term there is one thing about equities that you can safely take to the bank: share prices follow earnings. (Earnings, of course, are the net profits of a business.) Look back through history and try to find even a single company that increased its earnings quarter after quarter, year after year, and the stock didn't tag along. Conversely, try to uncover one whose earnings declined year after year and the stock continued to move up. It just doesn't happen.

That's why Benjamin Graham famously said of the stock market, "In the short run it's a voting machine, but in the long run it's a weighing machine." And what it weighs is corporate earnings both actual and prospective. Regardless of what the market does next week or next month, you can count on it to reflect earnings over the long haul.

When results are measured not in months or years but decades, nothing has rewarded investors better than common stocks. Not cash, not bonds, not real estate, not gold, not collectibles, nothing. That's why I call common stocks the greatest wealth creators of all time.

THE BEST INVESTMENT . . . EVER

Jeremy Siegel, a professor of finance at the Wharton School of the University of Pennsylvania and author of *Stocks for the Long Run: The Definitive Guide to Financial Market Returns & Long Term Investment Strategies*, has done a thorough historical study of the returns of different types of assets over the past couple hundred years.

What he discovered is dramatic: $1 invested in gold in 1802 would have been worth $103 at the end of 2024. The same dollar invested in T-bills would have grown to $9,649. A $1 investment in long-term bonds would have been worth $53,114. And $1 invested in a diversified portfolio of common stocks with dividends reinvested – drum roll, please – would have been worth more than $64 million.

The odds are good, of course, that you weren't around more than 200 years ago. And, unless something truly exciting happens soon in the field of cryogenics, you won't be around two centuries from now, either.

However, it's not necessary to think *that* long term. Start whenever you choose, and you'll find that when measured in decades the investment returns for different asset classes are remarkably consistent. Stocks are the big winner. Since 1926, the stock market has generated a positive return in 72 out of 98 years.

But those inevitable down years quickly take the fun out of the stock market for many investors. Since 1945, the S&P 500 has tumbled 26%, on average, in the periods leading up to and during recessions.

These bear markets often drive investors to the sidelines, where they miss the ensuing rally. Running to bonds or cash when a recession looms might be a fine idea, if only recessions were predictable. They're not. Statistics show that recessions tend to be identified weeks or months after they begin. By the time headlines confirm that a recession has arrived, the damage in the stock market is usually done.

Even if you somehow knew what was going to happen in the economy, you still wouldn't necessarily know what was going to happen in the stock market. Perversely, stocks often fall during the good times and rally during the bad times. Billionaire money manager Ken Fisher doesn't call the stock market *the great humiliator* for nothing.

And even if you make a good call and get out of the market before a downturn, how do you know when to get back in? Wait too long and you can miss a substantial part — or all — of the next bull market. That can be costly.

It is clear to anyone who takes the time to investigate that stocks have outperformed all other liquid investments — and illiquid ones, too, including real estate and other tangibles. And while no one can tell you with certainty what investment returns will be in the future, most investors need a good percentage of their portfolio invested in stocks to meet their long-term goals. And they need to stick with this stock market exposure to avoid missing the good times. Never forget that the greatest risk you face as an investor is the possibility that your investments won't last long enough to meet your long-term spending requirements.

In short, you are well compensated for enduring the constant ups and downs of the stock market. Yes, you're likely to get the sweats from time to time. But whether you're able to meet your spending commitments in retirement is more important than what the stock market does this year or next. This is especially true because, while asset returns have been relatively stable over the past couple hundred years, human life spans have lengthened dramatically.

What does this have to do with your investment strategy? Quite a bit. The whole point of financial planning is to make sure your investment portfolio doesn't kick the bucket before you do. If you're in good health, you may live a lot longer than you think – or than you're counting on, financially. This means that unless you're independently wealthy – and can live happily ever after with your money tucked away in Triple-A, insured, tax-free bonds – stocks should play an important part in your retirement planning.

This thought scares the bejesus out of novice investors – and a few old hands as well – especially when the market, with no notice whatsoever, begins rumbling like Krakatoa.

This is the norm, however. Investors who expect to earn the generous returns only a diversified stock portfolio can deliver while watching their net worth rise as smoothly as a bank balance are either uninformed or unrealistic. "Steady as she goes," has never described long-term equity investing.

Despite the inevitable volatility, there are good reasons to be grateful for the stock market. Capitalism does a better job than any other economic system of alleviating poverty, raising our standard of living, and creating prosperity. The essence of capitalism is the private ownership of the means of production and distribution. Most of us, however, don't have the capital or the experience to run our own business. The stock market is what makes capitalism truly democratic.

Virtually anyone can own a piece of a thriving business. With even a modest amount of money, an individual can accumulate a stake in many of the world's greatest companies and most profitable businesses.

Yet how quickly this notion of owning great companies gets lost in the daily headlines, where the focus is constantly shifting from Fed policy to Wall Street downgrades to the latest hedge fund blowup. Yes, the stock market can be frightening at times. But it is essential that you understand that nothing offers you the prospect of earning higher long-term returns. That's why stocks are a key component of your long-term investment plan.

"Shouldn't we wait until the coast is clear before investing?" some will ask. The answer is no. Waiting for everything to look better before you invest is a bit like waiting for all the traffic lights to turn green before pulling out of your driveway. It doesn't happen. And no one ever sounds an "all clear" for the stock market, either.

To successfully time the market requires you to buy low, sell high, and then buy low again (while covering all spreads, trading costs, and taxes on capital gains). Fail, and you'll get left behind while the equity train rumbles on.

For example, assume you invested $10,000 in the S&P 500 in 1991 and just left it alone through the end of 2024. If you stayed fully invested, it grew to about $109,000. If you missed the 10 best days – out of 7,500 trading days – it only grew to $49,000. If you missed the best 20 days, it only grew to $28,000. If you missed the best 30 days, it only grew to $17,000. And if you missed the 40 best days, it only grew to $11,000.

Clearly, attempting to move in and out of the market to catch the best possible returns can easily derail your investment plans.

Yes, the stock market is unnerving and unpredictable in the near term. But inflation makes your future financial requirements unpredictable, too. That's why you need to generate the higher returns that only equities can give.

When Siegel's book first came out, detailing the returns of various asset classes, it caused a bit of a sensation. Not because he pointed out that stocks have given the best historical returns. That was already common knowledge, at least among students of the market. The real bombshell was the following statement from the first edition, based on a thorough examination of two centuries of financial data:

> *Although bonds are certainly safer than stocks in the short run, over the long run the returns on stocks are so stable that stocks are actually safer than either government bonds or Treasury bills. The constancy of the long-term, after-inflation returns on stocks was truly astounding, while the returns on fixed-income assets posed higher risks for the long-term investor.*

Stocks are safer than T-bills? To many investors, that sounded like lunacy. But for long-term investors who measure their returns in decades, it has been the case for more than two centuries now. Is it likely to remain that way in the future? It is safe to assume so. Let me explain why, not in financial terms but in human ones.

We all have economic needs: food, clothing, shelter, utilities, health care, and so on. It is business – not government – that fills those needs. As long as there are human beings – and the population continues to grow – businesses will prosper by filling those needs. Many investors would benefit from thinking not about the stock market, but about the advantages of owning a portfolio of thriving businesses. This is likely to remain the most assured route to financial independence.

Any academic can tell you how much stocks have returned in the past. No one can tell you exactly what stocks will return in the future. But when estimating future long-term returns, it is reasonable to expect that they will not be significantly higher or lower than past long-term returns.

History clearly demonstrates that no other asset class returns more than stocks over the long haul. Once you understand this – and accept the steep odds against timing the market – you've made the first step toward adopting an investment strategy that can generate high returns with an acceptable level of risk.

Given equities' superior long-term results, a few bold investors may ask, "Why not invest 100% of my portfolio in stocks?"

You can do this – as some investors do. However, people are not unfeeling automatons. You have to consider the likelihood that you will stay the course after you've set up a workable strategy. My many years as an investment advisor clearly demonstrated to me that most investors have a low pain threshold when it comes to tolerating market declines.

Many felt an overwhelming urge to "do something." And that something was invariably to "sell!" when most of the damage was already done. However, there are ways to reduce the volatility of your portfolio – and thus your propensity to panic – and still meet your most important investment goals.

History clearly demonstrates that common stocks should provide the foundation of any portfolio designed to maximize total returns. The first question, of course, is how many stocks should you own, and which ones? For the purposes of this book, the answer is simple: *all of them*. We're going to capture the performance of every major public company on the world's leading stock exchanges.

This may come as a surprise to regular readers of my newsletters and trading services. After all, I spend several hundred hours a year researching, recommending, and monitoring a few dozen individual stocks that I believe are the best of the best. And we've had our fair share of success.

However, it's not possible to give shorter-term trading recommendations in a book. Besides, achieving the American Dream doesn't require you to be a trader, but it does require you to be an investor to meet your long-term investment goals.

It's not necessary to buy and sell individual stocks. You can own mutual funds or exchange-traded funds instead.

THE MUTUAL FUND ADVANTAGE

According to Statista, nearly half of American households own mutual funds. Most investors are already familiar with them. As you may know, they offer several important advantages:

- **Diversification.** The risk of owning a whole portfolio of stocks is considerably less than the risk of holding any one individual stock. But it can take quite a bit of money to build a diversified portfolio of stocks or bonds. You get instant diversification with each mutual fund share.
- **Professional management.** Whether you own an index fund or an actively managed fund, there is a professional manager overseeing the portfolio.
- **Low minimums.** Each fund establishes its own investment minimum. But minimums have come down dramatically over the past few years.
- **No financial advisor required.** You can buy mutual funds that charge no loads (commissions) directly from the fund companies.
- **Liquidity.** Mutual fund companies will allow you to redeem (sell) all or part of your shares on any day the market is open for trading.
- **Automatic reinvestment.** You can arrange for all your fund's dividends and capital gains to be automatically reinvested in the fund – or directed to other funds – without charge.
- **Convenience.** You can buy and redeem fund shares online, by phone, or by mail. You can arrange automatic purchases

from your bank account or you can arrange regular periodic withdrawals. You can also arrange that the proceeds from your funds' redemptions or distributions be deposited in your bank account.
- **Simplified recordkeeping.** You will receive regular statements showing the value of your account and any activity. At the end of each year, you'll receive the tax-reporting information you need, too.
- **Customer service.** If you have a question or a problem, or need to make changes to your account, you can call your fund's toll-free customer service line and get the help you need at no additional cost.
- **Time.** Owning shares of a mutual fund saves you the trouble of researching, constructing, and monitoring a portfolio of individual stocks.

THE WISER BET

There are essentially two types of mutual funds: index funds and actively managed funds:

- **Index funds.** With indexing, the fund manager attempts to replicate the return of a particular benchmark, such as the S&P 500 or the Bloomberg Barclays Aggregate Bond Index. Index fund managers generally do not buy stocks or bonds that are not included in the benchmark.
- **Actively managed funds.** Active managers try to outperform a benchmark by selecting the best-performing securities or trying to time the market. Or both.

Some readers may question why any investor would settle for the performance of an index when you can opt for a fund manager who is willing to swing for the fences.

However, you may not realize just how exceptional – or rare – great managers are. Investing in actively managed funds is generally an exercise in futility. The overwhelming majority of actively managed funds fail to beat their benchmark.

I wish I could tell you the story was different with fixed income funds, but it's not. The vast majority underperform their benchmark.

Is this just a recent phenomenon? An aberration, perhaps? Hardly.

In 1967, academic Michael Jensen decided to evaluate mutual fund managers, testing for evidence of the ability to consistently beat the stock market averages. What he discovered – and scores of studies have subsequently confirmed – is that the average fund produces roughly the same gross return as the market. Unfortunately, the average investor receives a *net* return that is lower, thanks to expenses. Those costs add up quickly, dramatically reducing the final value of your portfolio. Expenses alone prevent most actively managed funds from keeping pace with index funds.

When the fund industry prints its famous disclaimer, "Past performance is no guarantee of future results," that's not just boilerplate. Past is not prologue when it comes to the performance of the best actively managed funds. That's why it's estimated that more than half of all institutional monies are now invested using indexing strategies.

Even investment greats like Warren Buffett and Peter Lynch agree with the power of indexing. In the April 2, 1990, issue of *Barron's,* Peter Lynch said, "[Most investors would] be better off in an index fund." In his 1996 letter to Berkshire Hathaway shareholders, Warren Buffett said, "The best way to own common stocks is through an index fund . . . ."

The question you should ask yourself is, "If the nation's most sophisticated institutions and the most successful investors of our era are advocating an indexing strategy, should I be using one?"

The answer is an unequivocal yes. Actively managed funds are laden with higher management and administrative fees. These funds may also charge front-end or back-end loads and 12b-1 fees (annual marketing or distribution fees) – expenses that will make your head spin. There are other costs, too. And oftentimes they are not itemized neatly for you. Instead, the specifics are buried in fine print in the prospectus.

Way back in 1320, William of Occam set forth a precept, commonly known as Occam's razor: when there are multiple solutions to a problem, choose the simplest one. By far the simplest way to own the world's best businesses is to own a total stock market portfolio. As John Bogle put it, "Don't look for the needle. Buy the haystack."

Of course, selecting the so-called best performing funds may be the way your broker or financial advisor makes a living. But the sooner you realize these funds are unlikely to outperform their benchmarks, the quicker you'll be on your way to securing your financial freedom. It's a straightforward equation, really. The fees you pay directly reduce your investment portfolio's returns. More money in expenses means less money in your pocket. It's that simple.

Yet, despite load funds' high costs and poor performance, investors still plunk hundreds of billions of dollars into them every year. In fact, broker-sold stock and bond funds regularly attract more money from retail investors than lower-cost no-load funds.

With Vanguard, you know exactly what you're getting. Vanguard stock and bond funds stay fully invested in their target markets. Their managers do not try to time the market. Vanguard does not advertise its funds' past returns or peer rankings, which are based on past performance and can mislead investors.

In short, the interests of Vanguard shareholders and fund managers are completely aligned. That means lower fees, less hassle, no sales pressure, and higher net returns.

Why don't you see more about this in the mass media? You do, occasionally. But the overriding goal at *Forbes, Fortune, Businessweek,* and similar publications is not to make readers wealthy. Their goal is to attract paying subscribers, rent lists, and sell advertising. Actively managed funds and brokerage firms are among their largest advertisers. Why alienate them? And how can these publications devote space to a complete investment strategy like this one every month, when the goal is to keep tantalizing readers with ever-new ways of getting rich?

Sadly, few stand to profit from telling the truth. Not brokerage firms. Not the mutual fund industry. Not the mass media. Everyone has an agenda, it seems. You, however, have an agenda of your own: financial freedom. And that requires shutting out the noise and confusion created by the mainstream media, Madison Avenue, and Wall Street's attempt to grab your assets.

SIX CRUCIAL FACTORS

Let's get down to brass tacks. There are only six primary factors that determine the long-term value of your investment portfolio:

- How much you save
- How long your investments compound
- Your asset allocation
- Your portfolio's annual return
- How much you surrender in annual expenses
- How much you pay in annual taxes

That's it. Whether you're investing $10,000 or $10 million, these six factors will determine what your net worth eventually becomes. So let's take a closer look at each.

How Much You Save

I've already devoted an entire chapter to saving. It's important to save as much as you can, starting as soon as you can, and continuing for as long as you can. Understand, too, that it's tremendously beneficial to keep saving even as your portfolio takes wing.

Realize that you can have the world's most sophisticated investment strategy, but if you've saved only a pittance, it won't make much difference. Before you can invest seriously, it is essential to forgo nonessential spending.

It's also important to save in a qualified retirement plan first, where your money compounds tax-deferred and your contribution may be tax-deductible. This is especially true if you contribute to an employer-sponsored plan that provides matching benefits.

How Long Your Investments Compound

There are two ways to let your investments compound longer. You can start investing sooner or work and save longer. Or both. If you're 20 years old, for example, you need only have $31,327.88 compound at 8% to accumulate $1 million at age 65. At 40, you need to have $146,017.90 compounding at 8% to reach $1 million by age 65. At 55, the number turns into $463,193.49. Clearly, it's in your interest to let money start compounding as soon as you can – and leave it alone as long as you can.

This requires more than a little discipline. But it's imperative that you adopt a hands-off mentality toward your investments. You can't enjoy the benefits of compounding if you interrupt the process by tapping your portfolio from time to time to buy the latest and greatest object of fascination. Albert Einstein famously said that the most powerful force in the universe is money compounding. Let the force be with you.

Your Asset Allocation

Investors are often surprised to learn that their most important investment decision is not which securities they own but the asset allocation they represent. Your asset allocation is how you divide your portfolio among different imperfectly correlated assets like stocks and bonds. (Imperfectly correlated means they don't necessarily move in the same direction at the same time.) As we've seen, stocks give the greatest return over the long haul. The trade-off is high volatility. Blending different types of stocks with safer assets – like bonds – can generate excellent returns with less risk than being fully invested in stocks.

Your Portfolio's Annual Return

This is the great unknown, of course. Outside of low-returning, risk-free assets, you cannot know with any certainty what your returns will be in any year or even decade. But over the long haul, the returns on various asset classes are remarkably stable. Your goal should be to generate higher than average returns while keeping risk carefully controlled.

How Much You Surrender in Annual Expenses

All things being equal, the higher your investment costs, the lower your annual returns and the longer it will take you to reach your financial goals. Keeping investment expenses to a minimum is crucial, although I can guarantee it's not your investment advisor's biggest priority. As Vanguard founder John Bogle writes in *The Little Book of Common Sense Investing*, "In the casino, the house always wins. In horse racing, the track always wins. In the Powerball Lottery, the state always wins. Investing is no different. In the game of investing, the financial croupiers always win, and investors as a group lose." Successful investing, then, is about minimizing the share of your returns consumed by Wall Street.

How Much You Pay in Annual Taxes

The government requires revenue to fund its various spending programs. But regardless of how patriotic you are, when financial independence is your goal, the IRS is not your friend. The tax collector can take good returns and make them mediocre very quickly. Yet many investors fail to consider the tax consequences of their actions. They needlessly fork over many thousands of dollars each year by failing to tax manage their investments. Fortunately, index funds are highly tax efficient. Because the index rarely changes, there are seldom any realized gains – that is, gains taken by the portfolio manager – to distribute each year.

★ ★ ★

These seven crucial factors will determine both the long-term value of your portfolio and your quality of life in retirement. Note that of these seven factors only one is beyond your control: your portfolio's annual return. No matter how proficient you are as an investor, you cannot control your portfolio's annual investment returns. Yet this is the factor so many investors spend their time fretting about. What will the stock market do? When will my bonds bounce back? You might as well ask what the weather will be six weeks from Saturday. Nobody knows.

Fortunately, I'm going to recommend a simple strategy that eliminates the perpetual guessing game about what lies ahead for the economy and the markets. Instead, you accept what you don't know (and can't control) and focus on those things you do know and can control — specifically, saving, compounding, asset allocation, minimizing costs, and avoiding needless taxes.

Armed with the investment basics and a little discipline, you can manage your serious money yourself — and save many thousands of dollars in the process. The folks on the other side of the desk may argue that the world of investing is so complicated — and your financial circumstances so distinctive — that it's foolhardy to consider managing your money yourself.

Investing can, of course, be a complicated subject. But you also have the choice of keeping it simple. And that's what we're going to do with the portfolio I recommend here.

If you like short-term stock trading as a hobby, continue to enjoy it. I do it myself. This is something you don't generally hear from die-hard asset allocators. But you can invest your long-term growth money safely and have some fun in the market, too. The two activities are not mutually exclusive.

It is important, however, to separate your long-term core portfolio from your short-term trading portfolio. This keeps things uncomplicated. Plus, it ensures that you don't start trading your long-term positions or find yourself clinging to positions that were designed to be short-term trades.

In my view, even the most dedicated short-term traders need an effective long-term strategy for their serious money. But my hunch is that most folks have better things to do than watch the stock market bounce up and down all day. It's for these folks that I've written this book. And for those, too, who want some insurance to back up their trading activities.

In the next chapter, I'll discuss a concrete investment plan that will allow you to live your dreams. I call it *the world's simplest investment portfolio*.

CHAPTER 16

The World's Simplest Investment System

A low-cost index fund is the most sensible equity investment for the great majority of investors. My mentor, Ben Graham, took this position many years ago, and everything I have seen since convinces me of its truth.

—Investor Warren Buffett

Successful investing is about reaping the rewards of owning the world's leading corporations. By putting your money into well-diversified, tax-efficient index funds, you can reach your goals with just as much sophistication as the country's leading money managers — and get better results than the vast majority of them.

Managing your money this way is likely to lead to satisfactory long-term investment returns. And the strategy I'm about to reveal is designed to make sure you don't lose. We will have removed three layers of risk – active manager risk, individual security risk, and high expenses – that could potentially derail your retirement plans or defeat your investment objectives.

Our goal here is not the testosterone-fueled desire to slay the market by the largest margin in the shortest period. Rather, it's to enable you to achieve financial independence and its main by-product: peace of mind.

Before we move forward, let's take a moment to review what we've established so far:

- The living standards of Americans today are among the highest in the world.
- Rapid progress is occurring. Most things are getting better for most people in most places in most ways.
- The future is always uncertain. No one can accurately and consistently forecast interest rates, inflation, the economy, or the financial markets.
- Investment success begins with meaningful saving. You need to save as much as you can, for as long as you can, beginning as soon as you can.
- No one cares more about your money than you do. That's why you should take responsibility for your portfolio yourself.
- Americans are living longer, healthier lives. Many baby boomers retiring at age 65 will spend up to three decades in retirement. You need to maximize your total return so that your money lasts as long as you do.
- There are six factors that will determine the long-term value of your portfolio: the amount you save, the length of time it compounds, your asset allocation, your portfolio's annual returns, your investment expenses, and your annual taxes on interest, dividends, and capital gains.
- Your asset allocation is your most important investment decision.
- No-load index funds with low annual expenses and high tax efficiency are the best vehicles for implementing your investment strategy.
- The best investors are not necessarily smarter, just more disciplined.

By sticking to this strategy, you can look forward both to reaching your long-term investment goals and outperforming most professional money managers.

Your success will depend on how diligently you save, how long your investments compound, whether you stick with the system during sudden or protracted downturns, and – not least of all – whether you have the discipline to keep from spending your fortune as it grows.

How much is *enough* is for you to determine, not me. But I have a few thoughts on how to make your dreams a reality. And it starts with having realistic expectations.

To manage your serious money successfully, you should aim at a specific target. You need a goal, a number.

Goals are dreams with deadlines. This is especially true in the case of financial dreams. Ideally, your financial goal should be clear and specific. It is not enough to say, "I'd like to have a lot of money someday." It is far better to say, "I intend to have $2.5 million on my 65th birthday." Now that's specific.

How you're going to get there should be quantifiable, too. For example, visit Investor.gov and navigate to the Savings Goal Calculator. It will show you exactly how much you'd need to set aside each month in order to achieve your goal.

The beauty of these calculators is that you can change the inputs to fit your personal circumstances. If you have more time before you retire – or less – you can adjust for that. If you are able to invest more each month – or each year – you can adjust for that as well.

The important point is that you're more likely to achieve your goal if it's specific and you know exactly how to achieve it.

First, however, you need to decide how much you need to retire comfortably. When I was growing up, a million-dollar net worth seemed unspeakably rich. People with that much money, I imagined, had no concerns about money whatsoever. (Presumably, they spent their days smiling, whistling, and counting their blessings.)

Today the situation is different. Yes, a million dollars is still a substantial sum. And by the standards of most of the world's population, millionaires are not just affluent. They are exceedingly wealthy. But most folks with a million-dollar net worth do not consider themselves rich.

My favorite activities, for example, are playing golf and pickleball, hiking, reading, listening to music, and spending time with my family and friends. The required annual cost of pursuing these interests – except for the occasional greens fee – is essentially zero. That has made it easy for me to live beneath my means and save regularly.

Someone whose interests lean more toward yachting, raising thoroughbreds, or collecting vintage cars has a different perspective on the cost of their hobbies. If you have the income to pursue these interests and still meet your financial goals, more power to you. But, for most of us, a simpler, less materialistic lifestyle could be the biggest liberating factor in our lives.

As Albert Einstein once wrote, "I believe that a simple and unassuming manner of life is best for everyone, best both for the body and the mind."

HOW TO CALCULATE YOUR NUMBER

Ultimately, you'll decide what kind of lifestyle you want to live and how much income is necessary to support it. But here's a quick-and-dirty calculation that financial planners use to determine how much money a person needs to reach financial independence. Take your required annual income – apart from Social Security and any pension income you may receive – and multiply it by 25.

Want $50,000 a year? You'll need to accumulate $1.25 million. Need $100,000 a year? Make it $2.5 million. Need $200,000 a year? It's $5 million.

Why multiply times 25? Because a good rule of thumb, if you want to be conservative, is to draw down no more than 4% of your portfolio each year in retirement.

You should expect the annual return on your portfolio to well exceed that, of course. But the returns above 4% will keep your portfolio rising in value so that you get a cost-of-living increase over the years as you continue to make withdrawals.

Some financial advisors will argue that 4% is too conservative. They believe that considers too many worst-case scenarios where the market behaves badly or tanks just when you reach retirement. And they may be right. If they're wrong, however, you'll have taken a very bad gamble. You run the risk of *lifestyle relapse*. You may be unable to live in the style to which you've become accustomed.

For example, imagine drawing down your retirement portfolio while the stock market is in a multiyear tailspin. That's why some percentage of a retiree's portfolio should be invested in bonds.

You can always draw down more than 4% of your investment in retirement. But the higher the percentage you take out, the greater the chance your portfolio will kick the bucket before you do. Especially if you withdraw funds from a shrinking portfolio early in your retirement.

The goal is to make sure your invested assets are doing the hard work, so you can eventually leave your job – or do only work you enjoy – and live your version of the American Dream.

Knowing exactly what you want – and how you plan to get there – will go a long way toward helping you reach your target. Make your number realistic. Make it specific. And, most important, give it a deadline. That's how to turn your dream of financial freedom into a reality.

Investment success is often more attributable to your emotional quotient than your IQ. When the investment sailing gets choppy, here are four ways you can keep your emotions under control:

- **Do a reality check.** Recognize that investing in stocks means your portfolio value is bound to sustain wide fluctuations from time to time. It's unrealistic to think that you're going to earn the superior returns only stocks can give while watching your funds rise as steadily as a savings account.
- **Automate your investments.** If you're in the early stages of wealth accumulation, use a discipline like dollar cost averaging – investing a consistent amount at regular intervals – to take advantage of the market's occasional swoons.
- **Act unemotionally.** Buying what everyone else is running from takes courage. But history shows you will be well rewarded for doing so.

- **Sit on your hands.** Warren Buffett once said, "Inactivity strikes us as intelligent behavior." During volatile periods, you must resist the urge to "do something." It's one thing to feel fearful about the market. It's quite another to let that fear upend your well-laid investment plans.

Studies in behavioral finance clearly demonstrate that it's not your store of market knowledge that is most likely to determine your success as an investor. It's whether you let your emotions dictate your actions.

I'm not saying you shouldn't feel emotional from time to time. That's too much to ask. But if you let those emotions control your investment decisions, eventually you're going to feel something entirely different: regret.

This is not just my perspective. In *The Four Pillars of Investing*, William Bernstein writes,

> *It is not uncommon to meet extremely intelligent and financially sophisticated people, oftentimes finance professionals, who are still emotionally incapable of executing a plan properly – they can talk the talk, but they cannot walk the walk, no matter how hard they try. The most common reason for the "failure to execute" shortcoming is the emotional inability to go against the market and buy assets that are not doing well. Almost as common is an inability to get off the dime and commit hard cash to a perfectly good investment blueprint, also called "commitment paralysis."*

Most investors don't realize that their biggest obstacle to success is not inflation, bad markets, the tax collector, or Wall Street. As Benjamin Graham wrote back in 1934, "The investor's chief problem – and even his worst enemy – is likely to be himself." (Or, as the comic strip *Pogo* once put it, "We have met the enemy and he is us.")

The other pitfall, one that keeps investors from even getting out of the blocks, is procrastination. Many of us have big plans that – due to a lack of action – never get beyond the planning stage. Resolve that you will take responsibility for your success by understanding the timeless principles at work here – and move forward.

Don't make the mistake of waiting until the "right time" to get started. There will always be troubles in the economy and challenges facing the stock market. Trying to time your entry point in the market is a mug's game. There is no bad time to start a disciplined long-term investment program.

Ultimately, following this strategy is about waking up and taking the reins of financial freedom. The essential truth of modern economic life is that money gives you choices. Chief among these is the opportunity to do what you want, where you want, with whom you want. That's what financial freedom is all about.

It's a shame, really, that more of us don't recognize this when we're young. But then, it's never too late to begin an investment education.

What will your portfolio return in the future? The historical returns for each asset class are well known. It is reasonable to expect that they will be similar in the future, but certainly not in the short term. And perhaps not even over the longer term. Investing is always a challenge, and "the answer" is always qualified.

As Peter Bernstein warned in the Foreword to *Stocks for the Long Run*,

> *The returns derived from the past are not hard constants, like the speed of light or gravitational force, waiting to be discovered in the natural world. Historical values must be tempered with an appreciation of how investors, attempting to take advantage of the returns from the past, may alter those very returns in the future.*

No matter how thoroughly you understand historical asset returns and essential investment principles, it's important to realize that uncertainty will forever be your inseparable companion.

And that's okay. All asset classes go through up and down cycles. By investing in a globally diversified equity portfolio – like the one I'll reveal in a moment – you will always have a stake in whatever markets are performing best.

To gird you through the inevitable market declines – including serious bear markets – let me remind you of two important points:

- When you own a diversified stock portfolio, you own an interest in a broad selection of the world's biggest and most profitable companies. If you take a moment to recognize, for example, that your holdings include a slug of Amazon, Apple, Procter & Gamble, McDonald's, Johnson & Johnson, and other high-quality companies, you're likely to sleep better and hang in there long enough for time to work its magic.
- Don't waste time looking at your portfolio too often. Sure, it's fun to watch your account rise when times are good. But it does no good whatsoever to dwell on your portfolio's daily fluctuations in a market downturn, watching in anguish as your net worth declines – at least temporarily.

When I worked as a money manager, many of my clients would take a mental snapshot – if not an *actual* one – of the best statement they ever received. During market corrections, they would often remind me how much they had "lost in the market," failing to understand that nothing was truly lost unless they sold and abandoned their strategy. They also forgot that their account would never have reached that high-water mark if they hadn't invested in stocks to begin with.

With an investment strategy that is designed to last decades, you will see your share of bear markets. If it makes you feel better, remember that each one for the past 200 years was a buying opportunity. Recognize this and it becomes tougher to believe that the next one is any different.

As an investment advisor, I tried valiantly to get clients to increase their exposure to stocks during market downturns. The ones who did prospered. But, for many, hanging on was all I could get them to do. Adding to assets that were down was generally out of the question.

Of course, when times in the market were good, many assured me they would welcome the chance to buy in a downturn. But that's when we were talking in the abstract. When the bear market showed up, they sang a different tune. "I never imagined that 'this' would happen!" they'd say in frustration. And, of course, "this" is something different each time.

Yet history demonstrates that common stocks are nothing if not resilient. The economy will suffer the occasional recession. And the market will stumble. Expect it. And remember that you're using a system that enables you to capitalize on these inevitable downturns. In fact, the odds are good that the long-term value of your portfolio will be greater because of them. After all, it's during down markets that you get an opportunity to buy what's cheap and prosper during the recovery that follows.

In my last investment book *The Gone Fishin' Portfolio: Get Wise, Get Wealthy . . . and Get On with Your Life*, I recommended that readers invest in 10 different index funds that represented 10 different asset classes in different percentages that added up to 100%. Then all they had to do was rebalance the portfolio each year – return to the original percentages – by selling back the asset classes that had appreciated the most and adding the proceeds to the ones that had lagged the most. The strategy has worked well, delivering satisfactory returns with a low level of risk. An investor who put $100,000 into the strategy as its inception in 2002 had well over a half million dollars by the end of 2024.

Over the years, I've received two primary pieces of feedback on this strategy from readers. The first was "I can't believe sophisticated investing can be made this easy." The other was "This is still way too complicated for me."

Apparently, a substantial fraction of the public has a tough time calculating fractions. And that's required when you rebalance each year.

In this book, I want to give that second group of readers – the mathematically challenged – concrete advice about how to manage their portfolios as simply as possible. I thought about using fewer funds, for example. That wouldn't make the strategy better, but it would make it simpler. However, even using two funds would require investors to rebalance periodically; otherwise, the asset allocation would get riskier as the investor got older. And that's the opposite of what most people want.

After giving this issue considerable thought, I finally came up with what I call *the world's simplest portfolio*. To give credit where credit is due, Vanguard came up with the strategy.

It turns a single decision – buy and hold – into an effective, real-world investment strategy. The portfolio is completely liquid, asset allocated, broadly diversified, regularly rebalanced, professionally managed, carries no commissions or sales charges, and has annual operating expenses of 0.08%. That's a piddly 80 cents on every $1,000.

The investment minimum is low: $1,000. And you can add to it in any amount, even as little as a dollar. You can have the distributions automatically reinvested if you prefer. And you can add to your holdings periodically. (Or not.)

So, what is this single-decision portfolio? I'm referring to Vanguard's Target Date Retirement Funds. There are several to choose from based on your projected retirement date. Each fund offers a diversified portfolio within a single fund that adjusts its underlying asset mix over time. Each gradually decreases its exposure to stocks and increases its exposure to bonds as the target retirement date approaches.

While the allocation to fixed-income investments reduces overall risk, investors in the funds still need to be able to tolerate the volatility of financial markets. (This is true of any investments beyond low-returning, super-safe choices like Treasury bills, certificates of deposit, or money market funds.)

The target funds are globally diversified and invest primarily in four stock and bond index funds: the Vanguard Total Stock Market Index Fund (VTSAX), the Vanguard Total International Stock Index Fund (VTIAX), the Vanguard Total Bond Market II Index Fund (VTBIX), and the Vanguard Total International Bond II Index Fund (VTIIX).

Let's take the Vanguard Target Retirement 2045 Fund as an example. As I write, it has approximately 50% invested in the US stock market, 33% in foreign stock markets, 12% in the US bond market, and 5% in international bond markets. It also keeps a fraction of 1% of the assets in a cash reserve to meet redemptions.

Some readers will insist they don't want or need global diversification. They say that because international stock and bond funds have underperformed US financial markets in recent years. From 1971 to 1990, however, the MSCI EAFE index of developed international markets outperformed the S&P 500 by an average of

4.2 percentage points annually. The case for global diversification over the long term is solid.

Investing internationally helps reduce overall portfolio risk by spreading investments across different economies and markets. When one region faces economic challenges, others may thrive, balancing out potential downturns.

For example, during a US economic slowdown, a portfolio with exposure to European and Asian markets could offset losses from American equities. There are unique sectors and innovative companies that are not available in our domestic market, such as wind energy in Scandinavia or rare earth minerals in Brazil. Emerging markets in Latin America, Eastern Europe, and the Pacific Rim have high economic growth rates, potentially leading to better stock market returns.

Holding assets in multiple currencies can protect against fluctuations in an investor's home currency. This adds an extra layer of stability to the portfolio, especially during periods of domestic currency weakness or high inflation.

While international diversification doesn't always increase short-term returns, it has been shown to reduce "deep risk" – the risk of severe, long-lasting losses – over the long haul. This can lead to a more stable portfolio performance and better risk-adjusted returns over time.

In short, a globally diversified portfolio offers the benefits of reduced risk, increased growth opportunities, and improved long-term stability.

That's why Vanguard constructs all its Target Date Retirement funds this way. Investors can make an initial investment and then have Vanguard debit their bank account for a certain amount each month. This is the technique called dollar cost averaging that I described in Chapter 12. (By investing a fixed amount at regular intervals, investors end up buying more shares when they are low and less when they are high, improving their cost basis.)

In that same chapter, I talked about adopting positive habits. James Clear, the author of *Atomic Habits*, notes that the best way to make positive habits stick is to make them as easy to follow as possible. That's what dollar cost averaging does. It makes your investment program dead simple because once you've made the initial decision to have your bank account automatically drafted each month, you're on your way. All that remains is to not interfere with the system you've set up.

You just estimate an approximate retirement date, choose the Vanguard target date retirement fund that comes closest to it, and make the decision to dollar cost average that fund monthly by having your bank account drafted. And you're done.

You've used the world's simplest portfolio and the world's simplest investment technique – dollar cost averaging – to create the world's simplest investment system.

If you have an emergency and need to stop the monthly investments or liquidate your holdings, you can do that. But you'd be blocking your path to financial independence – and undoing your good work – so don't do it unless there is a genuine emergency.

I recommend Vanguard's Target Date Retirement Funds because – after 40 years as an investment advisor – I know no other way that smart investing could be made *simpler*. The funds are diversified, convenient, cost-effective, and offer an automatic glide path from higher risk to lower risk as the investor grows closer to retirement.

Is it the best portfolio that any investor could have? No, it's not. The funds offer limited control, are not personally tailored to the individual, and are less tax efficient in taxable accounts. But they are a heck of a lot better than what most investors do on their own – or what high-paid investment "professionals" would do for them at a much greater cost.

The funds offer a carefully calibrated balance between risk and reward that is backed by decades of research. And the proof is in the pudding: Vanguard's target-date funds, on average, have performed in the top quartile among their peer group for 10-year returns.

Complexity and confusion are big stumbling blocks for young, new, or unsophisticated investors. These funds eliminate this. Moreover, Vanguard's target-date funds have historically provided higher returns with less volatility than their peer averages.

If I had a friend or relative who wanted to invest but didn't have the time or inclination to become an expert on the subject, I would strongly encourage an investment in one of these funds, which currently go out as far as 2070.

(Even sophisticated investors might recommend it to their kids or grandkids who are likely to take a "hand's-off" approach.)

There is no muss and no fuss. All you need to do is make an initial investment and then add to it or over time, whether its monthly, quarterly, annually, or sporadically. And if you have a lump sum to invest, just plunk it in the fund and leave it alone. That's simpler still.

If an investor is already retired, there is also a "simplest" portfolio for retirement income: the Vanguard Target Retirement Income Fund (VTINX). And while it has a conservative asset allocation, I think most readers will be surprised at its construction.

The fund's goal is to provide current income and some capital appreciation by investing in Vanguard index funds. Its current asset allocation is approximately 38% in US bonds, 16% in international bonds, 17% in short-term inflation-protected securities, 17% in US stocks, and 12% in international stocks. In other words, the fund has approximately 70% in global bonds and 30% in global stocks.

Some readers will be surprised to find that the fund has nearly a third of its assets in equities. But there are good reasons for this. The fund is classified as "conservative to moderate" risk. It is designed for investors with a medium-term (4- to 10-year) investment horizon. Portfolios that have some allocation to stocks are less risky over the medium term than funds that invest solely in bonds.

Why? Because one of the biggest threats to financial security – over the medium to long term – is inflation. During inflationary times, companies can raise prices to protect earnings. But bonds pay a fixed interest rate. As consumer prices rise, those fixed rates are worth less in real terms, so bond prices decline (at least temporarily).

The Vanguard Retirement Income Fund is designed for investors who want income but have a low tolerance for short-term price fluctuations. Extreme market volatility is the last thing anyone wants to deal with when they're trying to preserve retirement savings. And the Vanguard Target Retirement Fund performed strongly against its peer group average during not one but four severe market downturns since it was introduced in 2003.

The goal is to sleep at night even when the market outlook is anything but sunny.

As you'd expect, the fund's total return has been modest. It has returned just over 5% annually since its inception in October 2003. This still puts it among the top-performing funds in its category. And a primary reason is the expense ratio.

Vanguard is a nonprofit organization. The shareholders own the company – and all its funds are run at cost. Vanguard has cut fees more than 2,000 times since 1975. The most recent fee reduction, announced in February 2025, was the largest in the company's history, affecting 87 funds.

The annual expense ratio of Vanguard's Target Retirement Income fund is 0.08%. (Again, just 80 cents a year on every $1,000.) The average expense ratio of similar funds is 0.7%, almost nine times higher! The difference between 0.7% and 0.08% makes a huge difference over time. For example, $100,000 invested in the fund in 2004 – with dividends reinvested – was worth $265,329 at the end of 2024. Another fund that earned the same return but charged the typical 0.7% in expenses would be worth $30,000 less. Costs matter. Especially when investing for income, where returns are lower.

Incidentally, if you wonder what happens to the Vanguard Target Retirement Date Funds after the target date is reached, the answer is they gradually morph into the same portfolio as the Vanguard Retirement Income Fund. So even if you're completely asleep at the switch – and don't adjust your portfolio as you move into retirement – Vanguard is still looking out for your interests.

I'll repeat here what I said about Vanguard's target date growth funds. This is not the best or most sophisticated thing you could do with the income portion of your retirement portfolio. You can, for example, take greater risks in credit quality or duration and earn higher yields. Or you could lighten your equity exposure and have less risk. But every investor must choose some combination of risk and reward at a reasonable cost.

Vanguard offers solutions that aren't perfect but that offer investors a simple path to their most important investment goals. The biggest challenge for participants is that they will need to stick with the program even when the skies look stormy. There will be no one to hold your hand and implore you to stick with the program when the next crisis hits. (And that's assuming your paid advisor *would*. Many earn heftier fees – or justify them – by moving money around on virtually any pretext.)

On the plus side, you will not pay the high fees that handholders charge. As with most things in life, success boils down to commitment and personal responsibility. Unforeseen national and international crises are bound to arise in the future. And – as has always been the case in the past – those crises will eventually fade.

Those tempted to abandon this investment strategy during difficult times should heed the words of Benjamin Franklin: "Those who would give up essential liberty, to purchase a little temporary safety, deserve neither liberty nor safety." He was talking about political freedom. But the same principle holds true for financial freedom. Long-term financial success is about *time in the market*, not *timing the market*.

If fear and anxiety cause you to bail on your well-conceived investment plans, you risk giving up reaching financial freedom. As I said previously, simple doesn't always mean easy. Or quick.

Here's an analogy: each day we either consume more calories than we burn or burn more calories than we consume. Doing the first will cause you to put on weight. Doing the latter will cause you to lose weight. If you are disciplined enough to lose even a single ounce a day, over a year you will lose almost 23 pounds. Simple? Yes. Easy? No.

Financial freedom is also simple but not easy. It means working steadily, maximizing your income, living within your means, saving regularly, investing wisely, and avoiding the temptation to spend your wealth as it grows. Simple, but not easy. However, for those who have the desire and fortitude to stick with the program, the result is freedom, security, and peace of mind.

That's the American Dream . . . and worth a bit of sacrifice.

CHAPTER 17

Staying the Course to Achieve the Dream

> We do not have to be smarter than the rest, we have to be more disciplined than the rest.
>
> —Investor Warren Buffett

There's a specific reason why I recommended the world's simplest investment strategy in the last chapter. Many Americans struggle with what they need to do to translate their savings into financial security. There are a lot of complexities and investment jargon that can be off-putting to the average investor.

But you no more need to master all this arcane knowledge to manage your money effectively than you need to understand how a combustion engine works to drive from here to the post office. Successful investing does not need to be complicated. It isn't necessary to do extraordinary things to get extraordinary results.

Yet studies show that most investors struggle, earning low returns or even losing money over the years. That's because investing is essentially the transfer of wealth to those who have a process and can execute it from those who do not or cannot. Investors fail because they either aren't using a proven strategy or can't adhere to it. There is more than just anecdotal evidence to support this.

Since 1984, analysts at the independent investment research firm Dalbar Inc. have published an annual Quantitative Analysis of Investment Behavior report. The study examines investor performance in mutual funds. The findings are not salutary.

Over the 30-year span ending in 2021, the average equity fund investor earned 7.13% annually compared to the S&P 500's 10.65%, a gap of over three percentage points a year. That means that over the three-decade period, an investor's initial investment grew to $789,465 versus the $2,082,296 they would have earned in the S&P 500. They would have earned almost $1.3 million more if they had invested in the S&P 500 and just sat on their hands.

The Dalbar study confirms that most people are their own worst enemies when it comes to investing. They succumb to market timing, performance chasing, and panic selling, thereby lowering – if not decimating – their returns. To avoid this, you need a process, a coherent plan.

No one can tell you with any certainty what the economy or the stock market will do from week to week, month to month, or year to year. People who say they do know are either fooling you or kidding themselves – or both. I am a militant agnostic when it comes to the future performance of the economy and markets. (I don't know and no one else does, either.) This means we can avoid economic forecasters, market timers, and the psychic network.

Our philosophy is further underpinned by an optimistic, real-world sensibility – one that polls show is *not* shared by 94% of the American public. What is it? An acknowledgment that the world is getting better in most ways for most people in most places, thanks to the triumph of reason, science, democracy, innovation, and capital markets.

Why do only 6% of Americans agree with the sensibility that life is getting better for most of us? Because it runs totally against the mainstream media's meta-narrative.

Some aspects of life are certainly getting worse. Human carbon emissions, the national debt, and popular music spring immediately to mind. And even as the world progresses, some people are dealing with unfortunate breaks or tragic circumstances. And that's in addition to the work issues, health problems, relationship frictions, and financial setbacks that we all deal with from time to time. But we can't let these issues color our perception of the state of the country – or the world.

It's easy to be optimistic when the economy is strong, inflation is low, the country is at peace, corporate profits are up, and stocks are trending skyward. The real challenge arises when the opposite occurs, which is often the case.

Here is a quick review of just a few of the hurdles investors faced since I started in the money management business in 1985:

- On October 19, 1987, the stock market crashed. It was global, sudden, severe, and entirely unexpected. Yes, program trading played a role, but analysts still argue about what caused it. After all, no politician was assassinated that day. No government failed. No currency collapsed. Yet the Dow finished the day down 22.6%. Many clients at the time told me it was the start of the "Greater Depression."
- In August 1990, Iraqi President Saddam Hussein decided he would like to own Kuwait and its tremendous oil wealth. As his tanks rolled into the country, energy prices spiked and US stocks entered a bear market. It was the beginning of the first Gulf War.
- In March 2000, the bubble in internet and technology shares popped, sending the S&P 500 down 49% over the next 2½ years and the technology-heavy Nasdaq down 77% over the same period.
- On September 11, 2001, a group of religious zealots hijacked four commercial aircrafts and crashed them into the World Trade Center, the Pentagon, and a field near Shanksville, Pennsylvania. It was the beginning of the Afghan War, the Iraq War, and the broad-based War on Terror, also known as the Forever War.

- In 2008, the housing bubble popped, leading to the collapse of Bear Stearns and Shearson Lehman. This kicked off the Great Recession. By March 2009, the stock market had lost more than half its value, unemployment peaked at 10%, and household net worth took a 45% haircut. Many homeowners — especially those who hadn't made down payments on their purchases — mailed their keys to their banks. There were more than 200 bank failures.
- That same year, in response to the loss of business and consumer confidence, the Federal Reserve took interest rates to zero and embarked on ambitious large-scale asset purchases known as quantitative easing, eventually inflating its balance sheet by more than $5 trillion.
- In 2010, the Flash Crash took the value of the S&P 500 down 9.6% in less than an hour, as trading algorithms rocked the market, even disconnecting some exchange-traded funds from the value of their holdings.
- In 2011, a sovereign bank crisis roiled Europe. And, for the first time in history, US Treasury debt was *downgraded*. (For the record, it has not been upgraded since.)
- In 2014, the Islamic State group gained global prominence after driving Iraqi government forces out of key cities and capturing a large swath of eastern Syria. At its peak, the world's largest and most powerful terrorist group ruled millions of people, controlled billions of dollars, and maintained a force of more than 30,000 fighters.
- Also in 2014, oil and gas prices collapsed as formerly inaccessible deposits became commercially viable due to technological advances like hydraulic fracturing and horizontal drilling.
- In 2016, the United Kingdom — defying the pollsters — voted to leave the European Union. Stocks sold off on the Brexit news.
- In early 2020, the novel coronavirus began to circulate widely. The global pandemic forced a shutdown of most of the world economy, threw millions of people out of work, caused tens of thousands of small businesses to close their doors (many of them for good), was responsible for the biggest economic contraction in history, and led to the fastest bear market ever.

- In 2022, inflation spiked to its highest level in 40 years. As the Federal Reserve began raising interest rates aggressively to respond, the stock market and bond markets tanked simultaneously. Long-term Treasuries experienced a record-breaking drop of 29.3%.
- In April 2025, President Trump announced "reciprocal tariffs" on all our trading partners. Economic forecasts and corporate profits plunged. So did stocks. The Nasdaq and the small-cap Russell 2000 fell into a bear market.

In each case, the stock market bounced back – as it has every other time in history – demonstrating the incredible resilience of equities.

Since the end of World War II, the S&P 500 has lost between 5% and 10% 63 times, and it has dropped between 10% and 20% 25 times. It's plunged at least 20% 14 times. And three of those were epic losses of 40% or more.

With the declines of at least 40%, the downdrafts lasted an average of 23 months and stocks took an average of 58 months – almost five years – to gain back their losses in full. (If you include dividends the recoveries were a little shorter.)

Through all of this, it took more than just intestinal fortitude to stay invested in stocks. It took an abiding faith in the ability of entrepreneurs, investors, businesspeople, and, yes, policymakers to tackle the problems of the present to create a more prosperous tomorrow.

During these crises, optimists didn't sell in a panic, run to cash, or hoard gold and silver. Rather they patiently and selectively took advantage of some of the greatest buying opportunities of our lifetimes. And reaped the benefits.

The world's leading investors and business leaders understand the importance of a prosperity mindset. Microsoft founder Bill Gates says,

> *By almost any measure, the world is better than it has ever been. People are living longer, healthier lives . . . . You might think that such striking progress would be widely celebrated, but in fact . . . many people think the world is getting worse. [This] isn't just mistaken. It's harmful.*

Benjamin Graham, the father of value investing and Warren Buffett's mentor, famously said, "Without a saving faith in the future, no one would ever invest at all. To be an investor, you must be a believer in a better tomorrow."

In a *Barron's* cover story, mutual fund great Peter Lynch said, "The thesis underlying everything . . . is that the U.S. will be OK. If you don't believe that, you shouldn't be in the stock market."

And in a Berkshire Hathaway annual report, Buffett said,

> *Many Americans now believe that their children will not live as well as they themselves do. That view is dead wrong: The babies being born in America today are the luckiest crop in history . . . .. America's economic magic remains alive and well.*

The best investors understand that we will always have serious problems but that the world is improving. Yet an overwhelming majority of investors don't realize it.

This lack of understanding causes negative consequences, from fear and anxiety to feelings of helplessness and depression. It also causes investors to misconstrue the economic outlook and believe that investment opportunities are far riskier than they really are.

What is the cure for this? A solid grounding in the facts is a good start. An understanding that "the daily news" is sensationalized and negatively biased is also helpful. But the best piece of advice I can give you is this: follow the trend lines, not the headlines.

To do this, you need to accept a few basic realities:

- Media stories, anecdotes, and headlines are not necessarily accurate, objective, or contextual.
- A "fact" – true or false – does not make a trend.
- Just because something isn't perfect today doesn't mean that it was better in the past or won't be improved in the future.
- What some people call problems or crises are often opportunities in disguise.
- Human beings, technology, and capital markets operate as a comprehensive problem-solving machine, improving our lives in almost every way imaginable: faster communications, more powerful computers, safer transportation, lifesaving drugs and medical devices, and so on.

- There is no limit to the improvements we can attain if we apply knowledge, innovation, and free markets to enhance human flourishing.

I challenge you to approach everything you read and hear with a deep sense of skepticism — and a few basic questions like these:

- Is this story based on verifiable facts . . . or opinions?
- Does it include counterbalancing facts or just hand-picked, one-sided ones?
- Has the journalist made a reasonable effort to tell multiple sides of the story?
- And could this narrative be overly pessimistic?

If you're going to invest money that you've earned, paid taxes on, and saved instead of spending, you need to feel a sense of optimism about the future.

That's a tall order for people who consume the daily litany of all the sad, tragic, or unfortunate events happening — or that could happen — in politics, economics, and business. Studies show that even highly educated individuals who watch cable news or read national newspapers hold worldviews that are unduly pessimistic.

If you kick yourself because you've been underinvested in a stock market that — with dividends reinvested — has risen more than 10-fold since the bear market bottom in 2009, recognize that your failure to take advantage of these opportunities is due, at least in part, to saturation news coverage that is not just negative but perversely so.

There will be more bad economies, down markets, and awful uncertainties in the future. The question is will you maintain a prosperity mindset and take advantage of the opportunities that unfold? Or will you fall prey to the prophets of doom?

Heavy media consumption is a detriment to investors. Part of this is just due to the nature of the news, of course. Nobody wants to hear each day about all the buildings that didn't burn, the planes that didn't crash, and the crops that didn't fail.

But cable channels highlight a fresh litany of woes each day. My advice? Combat this by acquainting yourself with the essential facts. You can do that by browsing websites like

Human-Progress.org, Gapminder.org, and OurWorldInData.org, or by reading books like *The Prosperity Paradox* and *It's Better Than It Looks* by Gregg Easterbrook, *The Rational Optimist* by Matt Ridley, *Factfulness* by Hans Rosling, *Ten Global Trends Every Smart Person Should Know* by Ronald Bailey and Marian Tupy, *Superabundance* by Gayle Pooley and Marian Tupy, and, of course, *Enlightenment Now*, which ought to be required reading in every high school in America.

Studies consistently show that we have enjoyed fantastic improvements in longevity, poverty, health, education, living standards, and wellness. Denying the progress we've experienced is not pessimism – it's ignorance.

Equanimity, discipline, and patience are all that's necessary to prosper from the world's simplest portfolio. And you don't need a high-priced investment advisor to put it together – or to run it.

You can generate satisfactory returns without divining the future – and without guessing about it, either. You need only understand what part of the investment process is knowable and unchanging, and what factors, such as economic growth or market fluctuations, can never be known in advance.

You can live with that uncertainty when you know that most major trends are most definitely your friends.

How to Enjoy and Preserve the American Dream

CHAPTER 18

The Power of Optimism to Attain the American Dream

It's not what you look at that matters; it's what you see.

—Henry David Thoreau

Views about the state of the country – and the world – are bound to vary. Some see the glass as half-full. Some see it as half-empty. Still others are completely jaded. They think the cup is cracked, the water is filthy, and, of course, the glass is half-empty, too. That's not a great way to live – or to achieve your dreams. Psychologists have discovered that most healthy, successful individuals are optimistic, *even when it doesn't seem warranted.*

A positive outlook motivates us to be proactive. This is particularly true in the investment arena. As we've discussed, history's greatest equity investors – from Warren Buffett to Peter Lynch and Sir John Templeton – all had a deep optimism about the future. That doesn't mean you shouldn't hedge your bets or take concrete steps to reduce risk and volatility. You should. That's why asset allocation, diversification, and rebalancing are all part of our simple portfolio.

However, you also need an abiding faith in the ability of democratic institutions, technology, innovation, and capital markets to meet society's needs and solve our most pressing problems.

Rational optimism doesn't mean turning a blind eye to negative circumstances – or never entertaining darker possibilities. But there is a huge payoff in seeing gray skies as just passing clouds. Optimism is a source of courage and confidence. It motivates us to set goals, to take risks. It encourages persistence in the face of obstacles.

Investors with a positive outlook don't sell in a panic. Nor do they turn up their noses at opportunities in a down market. Aside from death and taxes, few things in life are guaranteed. That is why I recommend that investors embrace "epistemic humility."

We are all swimming in an ocean of ignorance about future inflation, interest rates, economic growth, geopolitical developments, commodity prices, currency fluctuations, business developments, scientific innovation, corporate earnings, new and proposed legislation, tax rates, and much, much more.

No one knows how all these market-moving factors will work out. And no one ever will know, even with the help of artificial intelligence and quantum computing. The world is too messy, too complicated – and thanks to human emotions and behavior – too unpredictable.

However, there are a few important things we *do know*. People everywhere have economic wants and needs and businesses compete to meet them. Men and women who want to build a fortune will be incentivized to take the risk of starting or running a profitable business that creates as many satisfied customers as possible. And owning a fractional interest in several businesses in different industries – a diversified portfolio of stocks – is the least risky way to earn high returns.

Still, long-term success takes time and patience. And that epistemic humility will come in handy from time to time. In the financial markets, arrogance and big egos get taken down like the Berlin Wall. That means your investment approach should combine an understanding of the present, optimism about the future, and a deep skepticism about our ability to predict or control events. As much as any strategy or recommendation, this realization will be responsible for your success.

Some may say that I'm giving the many problems we face short shrift. I'm not. I've already noted many of the serious challenges we face – and the media delivers a fresh update every day. I'm only recommending that – if you want to achieve your dreams – you should look at these problems in a different light.

I view the world's problems as opportunities. And you should, too. Nationwide troubles, personal setbacks, corporate challenges, even global crises are an inevitable part of life. They always have been. And they always will be.

However, history shows that problems are a catalyst for progress. Companies that successfully identify and solve them not only unlock new avenues for profitability. They help our country – and the world – move forward.

Problems create opportunities for innovation, learning, and growth. You may have heard the old saying that you can cry because rose bushes have thorns or laugh because thorn bushes have roses. By the same token, you can frown because the world has countless problems to solve – or smile because humanity will never run out of opportunities to improve and advance.

Problems lead to breakthrough innovations by spurring the development of new products, processes, and services that shape entire industries.

Consider how companies in the technology, health-care, and energy sectors have thrived by addressing ever-evolving challenges.

- The tech industry, for example, has flourished by solving communication, information, and automation challenges. Companies like Apple, Google, and Microsoft identified inefficiencies in how we access and process information, leading to revolutionary products such as the iPhone, 5G, and cloud computing services.
- In health care, problems such as disease, inefficient care delivery, and high costs have prompted significant innovation. The COVID-19 pandemic accelerated vaccine research,

telemedicine, and diagnostics technologies, creating massive profits for some health-care companies while solving pressing global health challenges.
- As the world grapples with the negative effects of carbon emissions, energy companies are pivoting to renewable sources. Yes, we still rely on fossil fuels to grow the economy and improve our standard of living. But the need to decarbonize presents a major business opportunity. Companies investing in clean energy solutions are positioned to capture new markets. Solving a global problem often leads to substantial profits.

Overcoming obstacles is central to human flourishing. And with the right knowledge, no problem is unsolvable. However, each solution leads to new challenges, creating a continuous cycle of discovery and improvement.

Companies that recognize that there is always another problem to solve position themselves for long-term success. Instead of fearing disruption or change, they realize that every obstacle offers a fresh opportunity for innovation and growth.

The key takeaway here? Progress is a continual process. In a world where challenges evolve rapidly, companies that can anticipate, identify, and solve emerging problems will outperform their competitors.

For instance, Tesla disrupted the automotive industry by solving problems related to fossil fuel dependence and automotive efficiency. Through continuous innovation in electric vehicles and battery technology, Tesla has become one of the most valuable companies in the world.

Amazon recognized early on the inefficiencies of traditional retail and logistics. By continually addressing issues related to customer convenience, shipping times, and supply chain management, Amazon transformed the global retail landscape and achieved massive financial success.

Companies that adopt a problem-solving mindset do not simply react to a crisis. They proactively look for the next one. Since troubles and complications are never-ending, progress is open-ended. And so too are the opportunities for businesses that thrive on problem-solving.

Innovative companies adopt an agile approach, enabling them to pivot quickly when new challenges arise. The continuous emergence of fresh obstacles is not something for investors to fear. It is something to embrace.

Problems push us to innovate, experiment, and find new solutions. For businesses, this means that the future is chock-full of opportunities. And the best part? In a world where challenges are constant, businesses that thrive on solving them will lead, grow, prosper, and deliver great investment returns.

I've made it clear that I'm a rational optimist. If you want to be a better investor, you should be, too. Yet year after year and decade after decade, Americans consistently tell pollsters that the country is on the wrong track.

Why the disconnect? As I see it, there are 10 major reasons:

- **Ignorance of the facts.** Most of us simply aren't aware of the true state of the world. In his book *Factfulness*, renowned public educator Hans Rosling explains how he posed hundreds of questions to thousands of people in dozens of countries.

    Respondents everywhere thought the state of the world was much worse than it is. He concluded, "Everyone seems to get the world devastatingly wrong. Not only devastatingly wrong, but *systematically* wrong . . . worse than the results I would get if the people answering my questions had no knowledge at all."

- **Lack of perspective.** Few of us truly appreciate just how tough life was for our ancestors. Most men and women worked long hours doing hard physical labor. (That includes homemakers.) Your great-grandparents would view your life today – with all its modern conveniences (microwaves, dishwashers, coffee makers, lounge chairs that give massages) – as the realization of some utopia.

- **Habituation.** Whenever new products or developments appear, we rapidly adopt them and just as quickly take them for granted. Heart transplants, space probes, high-speed internet connections, smartphones, 70-inch ultra-HDTVs, immunotherapies, artificial intelligence, quantum computers. Ho-hum. What else is new?

- **The hedonic treadmill.** In some ways, human beings are hardwired to feel dissatisfaction. We strive to achieve what we desire. Those things satisfy us for a while. But nothing ever quite does it. And so we yearn for something more: a better-paying job, a new car, a bigger house, a firmer abdomen, a sexier spouse. It's a recipe for continual unhappiness.
- **Status anxiety.** Researchers have discovered that, to an astonishing degree, our life satisfaction is tied to how we evaluate our position in society relative to others. Honoré de Balzac called envy "the most stupid of vices for there is no single advantage to be gained from it." If you insist on doing this, at least do it right. The median global income is reported to be about $10,000 a year. Half the world lives on less than that. But I'll bet you're doing a lot better.
- **Media negativity.** Our mediocre public education system combined with biased journalism creates and reinforces an unduly pessimistic worldview. Future peace and prosperity are not guaranteed. But it's worth remembering that we've always pulled through before.
- **Abundance denial.** Millions of men and women construct elaborate mental rationales for considering themselves materially deprived. To the extent that they succeed, they make themselves envious and unhappy.
- **The revolution of satisfied expectations.** There can be an uneasy feeling that accompanies achieving your dreams. Do I really deserve this? Is this what it's all about? People can feel guilty for creating the prosperity and leisure that allows them to live better than others.
- **A lack of spiritual significance.** A decline in religious faith has led to a fundamental shift – from "material want" to "meaning want." As living standards rise, people can still feel that they lack significance in their lives. Meaning can be more difficult to acquire than material possessions.
- **Collapse anxiety.** Despite peace and widespread prosperity, many cannot enjoy them thanks to the coming (take your

pick) economic meltdown, currency collapse, political crisis, terrorist attack, population explosion, bird flu epidemic, mineral shortage, war in the Middle East, debt default, government shutdown, global pandemic, or environmental catastrophe.

It's important to realize that some people try to signal *how much they care* by continually emphasizing all the world's woes. Yet alarmists of all stripes have been telling us to cup our groins and curl into the fetal position for many decades, and things really haven't gone their way.

Human intelligence, technology, and capital markets enable us to solve problems, improving our lives in almost every way imaginable: faster communications, more powerful computers, safer transportation, and lifesaving drugs and medical devices, to name just a few.

Risk is real, of course. And down markets – which are inevitable – inflict emotional and psychological pain. That's why most portfolios should be diversified with bonds. If they keep you from having to sell your stocks during a bear market, they will boost your returns despite their low risk. The ill-timed sale of stocks – turning a paper loss into a realized one – can do more damage to your long-term returns than any temporary bear market.

Remember, it isn't necessary to earn fantastic short-term returns to meet your long-term financial goals. Good returns compounded uninterrupted – especially during times of chaos – are all you need.

You can look back at every market sell-off of the last 200 years and see it was a buying opportunity. When markets get hit hard, however, people feel emotional. They feel a strong need to do something. And that something is usually the wrong thing.

It was never easy for investors to hang on during periods of disruption. But it was crucial. Staying invested when the outlook is good and running to cash when the outlook is poor may seem like a safe strategy to some. But it has never worked in the past. And it's unlikely to work in the future.

Most investment advice is geared toward what investors should do *right now*. But what you do most days isn't that important. It's what you do – or more to the point *don't do* – during that small number of days when you're terrified that is vital.

Heed the words of Daniel Goleman, the author who promotes the idea that success is more closely tied to your emotional state than education or knowledge. In his book *Emotional Intelligence: Why It Can Matter More Than IQ*, he writes, "As we all know from experience, when it comes to shaping our decisions and our actions, feelings count every bit as much – and often more – than thought . . . . Passions overwhelm reason time and again."

Goleman argues that two key aspects of emotional intelligence are impulse control and persistence. These are exactly the two qualities that will keep you from letting periods of poor market performance cause you to abandon your investment strategy in a panic.

There are plenty of other reasons to keep your cool and remain optimistic when the market – or life – gets you down. Researchers show just some of the benefits:

- Better heart health, enhanced immune function, improved longevity
- Reduced anxiety and depression, better coping mechanisms, increased happiness
- Better relationships, increased social connections and support
- Greater sense of control
- Increased motivation and persistence

Who wouldn't want to have all the benefits on this list? No one, of course. So why aren't people more optimistic? Because they don't think it's warranted. Yet – as I've demonstrated repeatedly throughout this book – it is.

And there are ways to let your optimism endure. Don't hang out with negative people. Don't spend hours a week doomscrolling on social media. Don't marinate in cable news.

Instead, clear your mind. Adjust your attitude. Focus on your goals. Maintain your strong habits. And you'll find yourself not just pursuing the Dream but living it.

To Live Fully ... Aim to "Die with Zero"

> The time to be happy is now. The place to be happy is here. The way to be happy is to make others so.
>
> —Orator Robert Ingersoll

As a young man, I held various positions at several companies. When I look back at my workplaces, I recognize two broad categories of coworkers: those who had to be goaded to work and those who had to be reminded to stop. There are a lot more people in the first group, especially in jobs that are not particularly interesting or challenging.

As I got to know my colleagues better over the years, I also found they had two general approaches to money. Some, including quite a few high-income earners, spent everything they made. Others, including many modest-income earners, lived beneath their means and saved religiously.

When money compounds over a long period of time, something amazing happens. It turns into a bigger pile than you would have imagined initially.

To illustrate, imagine that a wealthy employer offered you an important job for one month with two very different choices for compensation.

They offer to either pay you $1,000 a day for 30 days. Or . . . they would pay you a penny the first day and twice as much every day thereafter until the end of the month. In other words, you would receive two cents the second day, four cents the third day, and so on. You would earn $1.27 the first week and receive a total of $163.83 by the end of the second week.

Most people instinctively say they would take the first offer, knowing they would earn $1,000 a day . . . or $30,000 for the month. But compounding makes the second offer far better. You would earn more than $10.7 million.

(If that sounds impossible, I encourage you to get out your calculator.)

Of course, you will never compound your money at a 100% rate. Not annually and especially not from one day to the next. (On the positive side, your portfolio is probably worth a lot more than a penny.) Yet compounding money at even a single-digit rate can turn into a substantial sum over time. It turns into so much, in fact, that many people who work hard, save regularly, and invest smartly don't realize what will ultimately happen. They will die with an enormous amount of unspent wealth.

Shrouds don't have pockets. Hearses don't have luggage racks. You know that you can't take it with you. You understand that – despite bumper stickers to the contrary – those who die with the most toys *don't win*.

While it's crucial to plan for longevity, it's also important to enjoy retirement, when many people have the time, money, and wisdom to live the Dream in a way they never could before.

What is going on here? Why aren't retirees spending more rather than dying with all this unspent wealth? There are a few reasons.

Many don't realize that as their health inevitably begins to decline, their wants and needs will decrease as well. Meanwhile, their investments will keep compounding. That means they are not spending enough – or giving away enough – while they are young enough to enjoy it.

Bill Perkins, a successful hedge fund manager and tournament poker player, makes a provocative argument in his book *Die With Zero*. Rather than accumulating more and more wealth to enjoy during your so-called golden years, he suggests that people middle-aged and up maximize their spending while they're still healthy enough to create memories with the people they care about most.

This strategy is not for everyone, obviously. Folks who have saved too little – or didn't invest to earn higher returns – need to keep working, saving, and compounding to attain greater financial security. However, I know plenty of people who have done an excellent job of saving and investing yet developed a mentality along the way that prevents them from enjoying it.

For example, it makes perfect sense during the long wealth accumulation phase of life to keep a sharp eye on spending . . . to reinvest interest, dividends, and capital gains . . . and to never touch principal unless there is an emergency or financial necessity. But this is not the best mindset during the *decumulation* phase of life, when you have enough. Or more than enough.

Of course, no one knows exactly how long they'll live . . . or what their future expenses will be . . . or what their portfolio will return in the years ahead. So isn't it risky – or downright foolish – to start spending down what you've accumulated over a lifetime? Not necessarily. There are good ways to estimate how long you'll live and how much you'll need so that *you* can enjoy what you've accumulated – and not just your heirs. Yet living that life is difficult for some folks *even if they can afford it*.

These individuals are financially independent but highly reluctant to spend. Often they have strong self-control, which is how they ended up with more money than they ever imagined. They became wealthy over a period of decades – as most affluent Americans do – because of disciplined saving and investing. Their mantra was "avoid frivolous spending and never touch principal."

That makes perfect sense when someone is in the asset accumulation phase. But, after a certain age, it's no longer the case. After all, what is the point of accumulating wealth if you never enjoy it – or get to see others enjoy it?

But the main reason many affluent people never spend down their fortune is that they are afraid of running out of money. This concern is understandable for folks who think they may not have enough for a retirement that may last two or three decades.

But – like you, perhaps – I've known many men and women with more than enough who are still reluctant to spend and enjoy it. Yet no one need be financially paralyzed by uncertainty. It's quite possible to make reasonable estimates that will allow you to loosen your purse strings and enjoy. Let's start with how long you might live.

Sure, you could step in front of a bus tomorrow, but that isn't likely. Insurance companies have turned life expectancy into a science. And while you don't have all the tools available to an actuary, you can get a pretty good estimate of how many years you have left by using an online longevity calculator.

Blueprint Income offers a basic one online. And it's free. After calculating how long you might live, you can estimate what your portfolio will earn and how much you will receive in Social Security benefits. (The government allows you to estimate your Social Security benefits online as well.)

To best estimate what your portfolio will earn, look at historical asset class returns. From 1926 through 2024, for example, a portfolio that is 60% stocks and 40% bonds has earned 8.8% a year.

You can increase this return by owning a greater percentage of stocks, diversifying into higher-returning small caps, and/or beating the market with individual security selections. (That would mean moving beyond the world's simplest portfolio.)

Once you've made a reasonable calculation about how long you're likely to live and how much you're likely to earn (including pension benefits and any other sources of income), you need to calculate how much you're likely to spend. Here the estimation gets much more personal. Some folks are content to live simple lives based on low-cost activities like reading, watching TV and movies, browsing the internet, walking, swimming, and socializing.

Others want to travel to exotic locales, pursue expensive hobbies, and savor the finer things life has to offer. You are the best judge of which category you belong to or where you fall on the spectrum.

Yet Perkins points out that many folks make a crucial mistake that prevents them from enjoying the money they've accumulated. They fail to recognize that their material wants and needs will decline dramatically with age.

(He's right about this. My parents are currently 95 and 96 and in reasonably good health. But they are not shopping at the local mall. In fact, aside from the grocery store, they are hardly shopping at all. If they suddenly found an extra $10 million in their bank account, it wouldn't change their lives in the least.)

Most of us go through life as if we have all the time in the world. Yet your most valuable asset is not your house, your bank account, or your investment portfolio. It's the amount of time you have left on this little blue ball.

It makes no sense – especially if you've worked, saved, invested, and compounded your money for decades – to delay gratification for too long or indefinitely. You need to start converting your hard-earned money into the things that make you happy. Psychologists insist that people get more gratification from spending on experiences rather than on *more stuff*.

Look around your house – and in your closets – and you'll see countless items that seemed powerfully attractive before you bought them but now hardly elicit a shrug. (You might remember this before springing for the next object of fascination.) Maximizing your fulfillment from experiences – by planning how you will spend your time and money – is how you *maximize your life*.

Perkins points out that unlike material possessions, which quickly depreciate, experiences actually gain in value over time. That's because experiences pay what he calls a *memory dividend*. You don't just enjoy a great experience. You also enjoy the memory of the experience – often in the company of those with whom you shared it – year after year. (I'll add that I've found the *anticipation* of the experience is another part of the payoff.) You cannot overestimate the value of memory dividends. Nothing pays a higher rate of return. In the words of Carson, the butler of *Downton Abbey*, "The business of life is the acquisition of memories. In the end that's all there is."

One day when you're too frail to do much – if you're fortunate enough to live that long – the best part of your life will be your memories. You can already look back on your life and experience pride, joy, and the bittersweet feeling of nostalgia. But you can live more deliberately now by recognizing that as your health inevitably declines so will your capacity for new experiences.

Perkins suggests that you mentally divide your retirement years into three categories: the go-go years, the slow-go years, and the no-go years. The go-go years are when you're first retired and raring to have all those bucket list experiences you've been putting off. Later – depending on your health but typically in your 70s – you enter the slow-go years. You're still making memories but at a slower pace.

In your 80s and beyond, you may find that you don't have a lot of go left, no matter how much money remains. If you're planning to give money to loved ones and worthy causes, consider doing it now. Most would benefit from getting some of your wealth sooner rather than later. (I refuse to spoil my adult kids, but the last thing I'd want when I kick the bucket is for them to go, "Woo-hoo, we finally hit the jackpot!")

Don't deprive your current self to care for a much older future self who will have no need for all that money. Is this really a problem for retirees? You'd be surprised. Perkins cites studies that show most retirees are saving more aggressively, living more frugally, and decumulating their assets more slowly than necessary.

Retirees who had $500,000 or more at retirement had spent down a median of only 12% of that money 20 years later or by the time they died. Eighty-eight percent remained unspent!

Folks with less than $200,000 saved had spent down only a quarter of their assets after 18 years of retirement. And a study by an affiliate of Prudential Financial found that married 65-year-olds with at least $100,000 in financial assets withdrew an average of 2.1% of their savings annually. That is well below the 4% spending rate many advisors recommend, which would have protected retirees from running out of money in every 30-year period since 1926.

Of course, no one attempts to die with zero if they are consumed by fears that they will hit zero before they die. If you fall into this category, there are two things to consider. The first is that home equity can be earmarked for any long-term-care needs. If that isn't applicable – or reassuring enough – let me recommend a specific type of investment that guarantees you won't outlive your money.

It's called an immediate annuity. Many readers are thinking, "Oh, good. I own an annuity." Unfortunately, it is almost certainly a *variable annuity* rather than an immediate annuity. And the former is greatly inferior.

With an immediate annuity, you pay a lump sum up-front to an insurance company in return for a steady, guaranteed monthly paycheck that will provide income for life, no matter how long you live. It mimics the payout of a traditional pension plan. That is very different from a variable annuity, one of the worst investment choices you can make.

Variable annuity salespeople say, "It's like an IRA, offering tax-deferred compounding but with no investment limit. And you are guaranteed a lifetime of minimum withdrawals, no matter how long you live or how poorly the stock or bond market performs. No other investment product offers this combination of benefits."

Sounds enticing. Who would argue against these great benefits? Only those apprised of all the facts. For starters, you really shouldn't be plunking your hard-earned money into broker sold investment *products*. These are ideal for only one kind of person: the person who sells them.

Variable annuities offer the highest sales commissions in the industry and – believe it or not – the Securities and Exchange Commission doesn't even require them to be disclosed in the prospectus. Back when I was at Merrill Lynch, an annuity salesman dropped by our morning meeting one day and hit us with this pitch:

> *If your client puts $1 million into this annuity, we will pay you a $100,000 commission that day. Yet the annuity will still show up in his or her account as having a $1 million value. What's more, your client can take the prospectus to a forensic accountant and he will never discover that you earned 10% on this annuity. It's not disclosed anywhere in the paperwork. (What is disclosed is a massive surrender penalty if you try to cash out of the investment in the first few years.)*

Armed with this vital information, the brokers stampeded out of the meeting, got on the horn, and pitched the product to their clients. While brokers generally do a bang-up job of summing up the positives of variable annuities (and each one is different), they either ignore or don't fully understand all the negatives.

Let's consider them here:

- Annuities are not FDIC-insured.
- Withdrawals prior to age 59½ are generally subject to a 10% IRS penalty.
- These are the most fee-laden investment products in the financial industry. Average annual expenses are up to three times higher than a typical mutual fund and up to 30 times higher than a typical Vanguard index fund. This, of course, sharply reduces your future investment returns.
- If you cash in a variable annuity, the IRS will tax your gains (if you have any) at your income tax rate rather than at the lower capital gains tax rate.
- You can get most of the same tax-deferral benefits (at 1/30th of the cost) by simply buying and holding a Vanguard equity index fund or municipal bond fund. Or you can buy and hold individual stocks. (So much for the big "tax advantage.")
- And that principal guarantee? Your contract – contained in a two-inch-thick prospectus – will require you to hold the annuity for many years to realize that guarantee. If you cash it in sooner for some reason, you will be hit with an additional fee – called a surrender penalty – equal to up to 10% of your investment.
- Even if you hang in there for years or decades, a guarantee is only as good as the issuer. Understand that you are surrendering your principal to the insurance company immediately. So even with an immediate annuity, make sure it gets a top rating from AM Best.

So, yes, variable annuities offer certain advantages. But, in virtually every case, they are swamped by all the drawbacks. However, an immediate annuity is a different animal altogether. For certain investors – who have good reasons to believe they may outlive their money – they make sense as part of a diversified portfolio.

An objective, comprehensive website to compare immediate annuity rates is ImmediateAnnuities.com. The site offers extensive coverage, comparing annuities from more than 150 insurance companies, including major providers like New York Life, MetLife, MassMutual, Nationwide, and Pacific Life.

Users can quickly generate side-by-side quotes tailored to their age, investment amount, and income start date in less than three minutes. And the site offers something that annuity salesmen generally don't: detailed tables showing company ratings, surrender fee periods, minimum premiums, annual rates, and straightforward comparisons.

ImmediateAnnuities.com emphasizes the importance of choosing highly rated insurers to ensure long-term payment security. It's not just about chasing the highest payout.

There are essentially three stages of financial freedom: building a nest egg, keeping it, and enjoying it. An immediate annuity can allow even the most frugal, risk-averse retirees to relax and spend.

Sadly, many Americans never build a good-sized nest egg to begin with. Others are unable to keep it, thanks to poor investments or overspending. But, according to Perkins's research, even the majority of those who build it and keep it, die with most of their money unspent.

If your goal is to leave most of what you've earned to your heirs or a favorite charity, that's fine. The advice in this chapter is meant for those who have built it and kept it — or plan to — and want to enjoy it. An immediate annuity is a good solution for those who are afraid that enjoying their money means potentially outliving it.

As I've said from the beginning, wealth gives you choices. Instead of making more money, you can make more time. Instead of maximizing your profits, you can maximize your relationships. Instead of pursing goals of achievement, you can pursue goals of enjoyment.

Real success is not just about attaining the American Dream. It's about sharing it with others, too. And that makes "dying with zero" a worthwhile aspiration for the most economically successful.

CHAPTER 20

There Is No True Wealth Without Health

> The greatest of follies is to sacrifice health for any other kind of happiness.
>
> —Philosopher Arthur Shopenhauer

In Chapter 2, I detailed many of the ways that the United States is an exceptional nation. Most of them are positive. But there some negatives to American exceptionalism, too, particularly in health.

While Americans are living longer, they aren't necessarily living with more vitality. In a study, published in *Nature Medicine*, researchers defined healthy aging as reaching 70 in good cognitive, physical, and mental health and without developing a major chronic disease such as cancer, diabetes, or heart disease. Surprisingly, less than 10% of those tracked over a 30-year period hit that milestone.

The United States is arguably the best in the world at treating complex diseases. Yet Americans die earlier and are sicker than people in other high-income countries. This has been true for decades, but the trend is getting worse.

The US obesity rate is nearly double the average of peer nations. And about a third of US adults have multiple chronic conditions, the highest rate among peer nations.

In decades past, the deadliest scourges in this country were infectious, with influenza and tuberculosis topping the list. Better sanitation and advances in antibiotics and vaccines helped us win this war. Medical innovations and antismoking campaigns also spurred decades of progress against heart disease and cancer. But chronic diseases are undermining that momentum, contributing to our stalled life expectancy over the past decade. Much of this is due to a poor diet and sedentary lifestyle.

You've heard that if you've got your health, you've got everything. That's not exactly true. There are plenty of healthy people living with tragic or unfortunate circumstances.

But the reverse is certainly true: if you're in poor health, it's hard to live the Dream, regardless of the state of your career or the size of your bank account. There is no real wealth without decent health. The man in good health has a thousand dreams. The man without it has one.

A growing body of research on people's health spans – the number of years we live in good health – finds that there are four factors that can extend our vitality. I call them *the fundamental four*: a healthy diet, regular exercise, sufficient sleep, and close human connections. (And I'll add a fifth for investors in a moment.)

Let's start with perhaps the most basic building block: a healthy diet. Millions of Americans eat in a way that is literally killing them. Smoking used to be the leading cause of death in the United States, but it's moved to no. 2. The no. 1 killer, according to the Global Burden of Disease Study, is what we eat.

Smoking kills nearly half a million Americans every year. The standard American diet – rich in sugars, processed meats, and unhealthy fats – kills hundreds of thousands more. In fact, ultra-processed foods make up about 58% of the calories that US adults and children consume. (Foods are considered ultra-processed if they contain ingredients that you wouldn't find in a home kitchen, such as emulsifiers or high-fructose corn syrup.)

Recent studies have linked diets high in ultra-processed foods to increased risks of obesity, Type 2 diabetes, cancer, cardiovascular disease, and depression. We are literally digging our graves with our knives and forks. And the worst part is these deaths are entirely preventable.

I first got interested in this subject about 15 years ago, when my friend John Mackey, the founder and former CEO of Whole Foods, invited me to a social weekend at his ranch near Austin. There were quite a few foodies there. But they weren't the kind I was familiar with, most of whom were either connoisseurs rhapsodizing about their favorite new dish or weight-conscious men and women who obsessed over carbs, calories, sugars, and fat grams.

At John's, I heard people arguing about things like whether walnuts are healthier than almonds, blackberries are healthier than blueberries, and black beans are healthier than lentils.

I asked John what this was all about. He replied, "they're just interested in living the longest, healthiest, most disease-resistant life possible."

Well, who wouldn't be interested in that?

I spent years reading and researching, searching for the optimal human diet. I heard lots of opinions that seemed sensible but were contradicted by other credible sources. That's because there is no scientific consensus about the diet that leads to the greatest longevity. (Although if you had to pick one, you can't go too far wrong with the Mediterranean diet.)

However, there is a great deal of agreement on what kind of eating shortens your life. It's the standard American diet I described.

After listening to a lot of voices, I zeroed in on an especially credible expert in the field, Dr. Michael Greger. He is not only a practicing physician and internationally recognized nutrition expert but he is also the author of several books on the subject, including *How Not to Die: Discover the Foods Scientifically Proven to Prevent and Reverse Disease.*

Has he discovered the secret of immortality? Definitely not. But Greger has made it his mission to help Americans prevent, treat, and even reverse 15 leading causes of death: heart disease, lung diseases, brain diseases, digestive cancers, infections, diabetes, high blood pressure, liver diseases, blood cancers, kidney disease, breast cancer, suicidal depression, prostate cancer, Parkinson's disease, and iatrogenic causes. (Iatrogenic means "caused by diagnosis or treatment by a physician." Medical errors are the third-leading cause of death in this country.)

Greger argues that these deaths are preventable because they are related, at least in part, to how we eat. Some folks believe that premature death is just a matter of bad luck or bad genes. But the evidence shows that only about 10–20% of the risk of these diseases is related to genetics. Most of the rest is due to a poor diet.

Unfortunately, most people don't get the advice they need on this important topic from their doctor. Only a quarter of medical schools offer a *single* course in nutrition. And six out of seven graduating doctors recently surveyed felt they were not adequately trained to counsel patients about their diets.

When it comes to the profound connection between diet and disease, most of us are on our own. So let's start with the basics.

These simple, healthy lifestyle factors have a strong impact on the prevention of chronic diseases:

- Not smoking
- Not being obese
- Exercising at least a half-hour a day
- Eating a healthy diet

If you can check off all four, Greger says you've reduced your cancer risk by more than a third, your risk of stroke by 50%, your risk of a heart attack by 80%, and your risk of developing diabetes by 90%.

The first three lifestyle factors are straightforward. But healthy eating is a contentious subject. Even nutrition experts disagree on what constitutes the optimal diet. However, there is a broad consensus about one thing: you need to maximize your intake of whole plant foods – primarily fruits and vegetables – and minimize your intake of processed junk.

To increase your chances of spending more time with your grandkids and great-grandkids, consider heeding Greger's daily dozen. He recommends that every day you consume the following:

- Three servings of beans. The most comprehensive analysis of diet and cancer ever performed – a review of more than a half-million studies – was published in 2007 by the American Institute for Cancer Research. One summary recommendation was to eat whole grains and/or beans (legumes) with every meal. Not every week or every day. *Every meal.*
- Two servings of greens. That may include kale, arugula, sorrel, spinach, Swiss chard, mustard greens, or turnip greens. Dark green leafy vegetables are the healthiest foods on the planet, offering the highest nutrient density per calorie.
- Two servings of other vegetables, including asparagus, artichokes, beets, carrots, peppers, corn, onions, potatoes, snap peas, squash, tomatoes, or zucchini. A wide diversity of vegetables provides you with the greatest health benefits.
- At least one serving of berries. Strawberries, blueberries, and blackberries are the healthiest fruits – and loaded with anti-aging, anti-cancer antioxidants.
- Three servings a day of other fruits: oranges, apricots, bananas, grapefruit, peaches, pears, pomegranates, mangoes, and so on. (Greger says people who claim they don't have time to eat healthfully have never met an apple.)
- One tablespoon of ground flaxseed. You can sprinkle it on yogurt, salads, whatever. Flaxseed averages 100 times more lignans than any other food and may even reduce tumor-proliferation rates.
- Three servings of whole grains. These include brown or wild rice, barley, oats (or oatmeal), quinoa, millet, rye, whole-wheat pasta, and popcorn.
- At least one serving of cruciferous vegetables: broccoli, cabbage, collards, kale, or Brussels sprouts. Greger calls this the single most important change you can make to your diet. Cruciferous vegetables may cut the risk of cancer progression by 50%.

- One serving of nuts or seeds, including almonds, Brazil nuts, cashews, chia seeds, macadamia nuts, pecans, pistachios, pumpkin seeds, sunflower seeds, and walnuts. No food is more highly correlated with human longevity than nuts.
- One-quarter teaspoon of ground turmeric. Research shows that curcumin – the bright yellow chemical found in turmeric – may play a role in preventing lung disease, brain disease, and a variety of cancers, including multiple myeloma, colon cancer, and pancreatic cancer. Greger calls turmeric the closest thing he knows to "a magic pill."
- Five glasses of water. You can get some of that through coffee or – better still – green tea.
- One serving of exercise, ideally either 45 minutes of vigorous exercise (like running) or 90 minutes of moderate exercise (like brisk walking). In addition to helping you maintain a healthy body weight, exercise can ward off mild cognitive decline, boost your immune system, prevent high blood pressure, bolster your memory, enhance your mood, and improve your sleep quality.

This checklist may seem overly prescriptive for some. But too many Americans eat like the future doesn't matter.

Investment great Warren Buffett is one of them. He has battled prostate cancer and other health issues. Yet his beloved hamburgers and Dairy Queen sundaes are loaded with fat. His daily Cokes are chock-full of high fructose corn syrup, a substance linked to more health problems than sugar. And he insisted at a Berkshire Hathaway shareholder meeting that there is no evidence broccoli would help him live to 100.

He once quipped, "I checked the actuarial tables, and the lowest death rate is among six-year-olds. So I decided to eat like a six-year-old." His friend Bill Gates recounted how Buffett stayed at his house and had Oreos for breakfast. "He mostly eats hamburgers, ice cream, and Coke," Gates added.

Buffett might visit NutritionFacts.org, Greger's informative, entertaining, and commercial-free website offering the latest nutritional science. Greger scours the world's scientific literature to uncover the evidence-based diet that best prevents – and even reverses – the leading causes of death and disability.

No one needs to eat like a monk or obsess over their food choices. Your health is not determined by a particular treat or a special occasion. It's about how you eat day in and day out. There are hundreds of diets out there, of course, each claiming to be the best. So why use Greger's approach?

He answers that vital question in *How Not to Die*:

"Anytime anyone tries to sell you on some new diet, ask just one simple question: 'Has it been proven to reverse heart disease?'. . . If it hasn't, why would you even consider it?"

If that's all a whole-food, plant-based diet could do — reverse our no. 1 killer — then shouldn't that be the default position until proven otherwise?

The second leading disease-causing death is cancer. According to the World Health Organization, 30–50% of all cancers are preventable. And diet is one of the most impactful lifestyle factors in cancer prevention and survivorship. A diet rich in plant-based foods– like vegetables, fruits, whole grains, legumes, nuts, and seeds — provides essential nutrients that help reduce cancer risk. These foods are high in fiber, antioxidants, and phytochemicals, which reduce inflammation and protect cells from damage that could lead to cancer.

The fact that this diet is also effective in preventing, treating, and arresting other leading killers would seem to make the case for eating this way overwhelming.

I'm no saint when it comes to eating myself. (I call myself a "Mediterranean sinner.") But I try to remind myself that "fit feels better than anything tastes." It's never too early — or too late — to start eating healthier. It's a matter of life . . . or premature death.

Let's move on to the second pillar of the fundamental four. Imagine a pill that helps you lose weight; exchanges fat for muscle; strengthens your bones; fortifies your immune system; prevents heart disease, cancer, and stroke; relieves stress; improves your mood; helps you sleep; boosts your brainpower; keeps you looking younger; and significantly extends your life.

You can stop imagining now. There isn't any such pill. (If there were, I'm sure you'd have heard about it.) But the good news is you can get this whole smorgasbord of benefits – and more – from about a half-hour of daily exercise.

It's not breaking news that physical activity is good for you. However, scientists have recently discovered that exercise is far more beneficial than we previously realized. They're also learning just how unhealthy a sedentary lifestyle is.

However, the Centers for Disease Control and Prevention recently collected survey data from more than 450,000 adults across all 50 states and found that nearly 80% of Americans do not get the recommended amounts of exercise each week, setting themselves up for years of health problems – and fueling a national health-care crisis.

It's a shame, really. Exercise slows or reverses muscle loss, weight gain, artery hardening, joint stiffening . . . even glaucoma. Regular physical activity cuts your lifetime risk for general dementia by almost half. (It even lowers your odds of getting Alzheimer's by almost 60%.) It also makes you smarter. Studies show that exercisers outperform couch potatoes in reasoning, attention, long-term memory, and problem-solving tasks.

In *A Short Guide to a Long Life*, Dr. David B. Agus, one of the world's leading cancer researchers, wrote,

> *"There are 100 billion neurons in each of our brains, and they love a good physical workout. Studies now show that older people who still do vigorous exercise, play competitive sports, or just walk several times a week protect their brains' white matter from shrinking."*

Physical activity is an effective antidote for anxiety and depression as well. My friend Dr. Joel Wade, a practicing psychologist and life coach, once told me, "When I have a client who's feeling down, the first thing I tell him or her to do is get outside and get moving."

From an evolutionary perspective, we were made to exercise. Anthropologists say our ancestors on the plains of the Serengeti covered a lot of ground, walking as much as 12 miles a day. Why were we moving so far and so fast?

We needed to find new food sources, avoid predators, and escape enemies, problems that don't particularly trouble us today. Yet our brains – and our bodies – still crave exercise. Everything from diabetes to high blood pressure, heart attack to cataracts, and arthritis to macular degeneration can be reduced as much as 70% with exercise.

It's okay if you don't have a lot of time – or stamina. Research shows that while at least 30 minutes of exercise per day is ideal, the majority of the mortality reductions are due to the first 20 minutes of activity. However, if you exercise more, you may be on your way to a lifetime of enviable fitness.

Every bit of exercise helps. Here are the national exercise guidelines issued by the Department of Health and Human Services:

- 150 minutes (2½ hours) of moderate aerobic activity each week, such as brisk walking or lap swimming
- 75 minutes a week of more vigorous aerobic activity, such as running
- Weight training at least twice a week, to ensure that both bones and muscles are healthy

The inexorable loss of muscle mass that begins in our 40s is called *sarcopenia*. Over time, it robs us of independence . . . of the life we want to live. But weight training combats sarcopenia, changing the dynamics of aging.

However, it is aerobic fitness, not strength training, that is most closely tied to health benefits. You don't need fancy equipment or an expensive gym membership. Just a pair of comfortable shoes. Aside from walking or running, you can use your body's own mass for strength training – doing push-ups, pull-ups, squats, or planks – anywhere at any time, with all the same cellular benefits of free weights or Nautilus machines.

In short, physical activity is one of the best, easiest, and cheapest ways to decrease your mortality risk. It is one of the most powerful antiaging tactics we have. When combined with a plant-based, whole foods diet, exercise can dramatically improve the way you look, the way you feel and – not incidentally – how long you live.

Let's also consider the third pillar of health, one that researchers call "the most glaring omission in the contemporary health conversation."

There is nothing any of us wish for more ardently – for ourselves as well as our children and grandchildren – than robust health. So imagine your shock if – after a thorough examination of your newborn – the obstetrician said, "Throughout your child's life, he will repeatedly lapse into a state of apparent coma. It will sometimes resemble death. And while he lies there, his mind will often be filled with bizarre and unpredictable hallucinations. This state will consume a third of his life."

Doctors never say this, of course. They don't have to. Because we all understand the nature of sleep. It is one of nature's strangest evolutionary adaptations. After all, when you are asleep you cannot eat, socialize, mate, protect yourself, or safeguard your offspring.

Yet sleep is vital. Why? Because it contributes greatly to human health. Sleep supports a variety of functions, including the ability to learn, memorize, and make logical decisions. It strengthens your immune system, prevents infection, and helps ward off sickness. It regulates your appetite, lowers your blood pressure, and helps maintain a flourishing microbiome.

It is the single most effective thing we do each day to reset our brain and body health. Yet, according to the World Health Organization, more than two-thirds of adults in developed nations fail to obtain the organization's recommended eight hours of sleep a night.

The government agency even declared a sleep loss *epidemic* throughout the world's industrialized nations. *Epidemic* may sound extreme, but it won't after hearing out Dr. Matthew Walker, the director of UC Berkeley's Center for Human Sleep Science and the author of the national bestseller *Why We Sleep: Unlocking the Power of Sleep and Dreams*:

> *Routinely sleeping less than six or seven hours a night demolishes your immune system, more than doubling your risk of cancer. Insufficient sleep is a key lifestyle factor in determining whether you will develop Alzheimer's disease. Inadequate sleep — even moderate reductions for just one week — disrupts blood sugar levels so profoundly that you would be classified as pre-diabetic. Short sleeping increases the likelihood of your coronary arteries becoming blocked and brittle, setting you on a path toward cardiovascular disease, stroke and congestive heart failure.*

Sleep disruption also contributes to major psychiatric conditions, including depression, anxiety, and even suicidality. "I'll sleep when I'm dead," busy achievers often joke. But they may get that opportunity sooner than the rest of us. Multiple studies have concluded that the shorter your sleep, the shorter your life span.

Aside from ill health effects, sleeplessness creates other unwanted outcomes. Drowsy driving is responsible for hundreds of thousands of traffic accidents and fatalities each year. Car accidents caused by drowsy driving exceed those caused by alcohol and drugs *combined*.

In short, getting sufficient sleep is essential to living a longer, healthier life. How can you get more of it? In *Why We Sleep*, Dr. Scott Walker makes 12 recommendations:

- Stick to a sleep schedule. Try to go to bed and wake up at the same time each day.
- Exercise early in the day — or at least two to three hours before bedtime.
- Avoid caffeine and nicotine.
- Avoid alcohol before bedtime.
- Avoid large meals late at night.
- Avoid medicines that delay or disrupt your sleep. (If you're unsure, check with your doctor.)
- Don't take naps after 3 p.m.

- Relax before bed. Reading and listening to soothing music are helpful.
- Take a hot bath before bed.
- Keep your bedroom dark, cool, and free of electronic gadgetry.
- Have the right sunlight exposure. Daylight helps regulate sleep patterns. Try to get at least 30 minutes of natural sunlight each day.
- Don't lie awake. The anxiety of being unable to fall asleep only makes it harder. So get up and do something relaxing – like reading or listening to an online lecture – until you feel sleepy again.

Sleep is essential to human vitality. Even an extra 20 minutes of shut-eye a night can improve your mood, enhance your health, and lengthen your life. Sleep is preventive health care at its finest. And the cost of this host of benefits is zero.

The fourth and final component of a healthy life is close human relationships. You might wonder why some folks look back on their lives in old age and say they wouldn't change much . . . or anything. Is there a formula – some mix of love, work, habits, or attitudes – that offers the best chance of experiencing the good life?

Researchers at Harvard have examined this question for more than 80 years, following 268 men who entered college in the late 1930s through war, career, sickness, health, marriage, parenthood, grandparenthood, and old age.

Their discoveries about what constitutes a well-lived life will surprise you. Just listen to Dr. George Vaillant. Since 1966, the Harvard Medical School professor has dedicated his career to following the men of Harvard's Grant Study, named after its patron, the department store magnate W. T. Grant.

Vaillant's specialty is the longitudinal method of research, the comprehensive study of a small number of people over a long period of time. His subjects were never a representative sample of society. They were all young men, Harvard students, from relatively privileged backgrounds.

Yet Vaillant's findings offer profound insights into the human condition. They have universal applications. And they illuminate the one single factor that correlates most highly with a positive life assessment in old age.

From the beginning, the Grant Study was meant to be exhaustive. Harvard researchers assembled a team that included medical doctors, physiologists, psychologists, psychiatrists, social workers, anthropologists, and other specialists.

Over more than eight decades, participants were monitored, interviewed, and studied from every conceivable angle, including eating and drinking habits, exercise, mental and physical health, career changes, financial successes and setbacks, marital history, parenthood, grandparenthood, and old age. They were subjected to general aptitude tests and personality inventories and were required to provide regular letters and documentation.

Many of the Grant Study men achieved dramatic success. Some became captains of industry. One was a bestselling author. Four members ran for the US Senate. One served in a presidential cabinet. And one – John F. Kennedy (we now know) – was president. (His files are sealed until 2040.)

Some of the subjects were disappointments, too. Case number 47, for example, literally fell down drunk and died. (Not quite what the study had in mind.)

Most of the participants remain anonymous. Although a few, like Ben Bradlee, the longtime editor of the *Washington Post*, publicly identified themselves.

Over the last several decades, the lives of the Grant men were Vaillant's personal and professional obsession. And his analysis enabled him to reach some broad conclusions.

He found seven major factors that predict healthy aging, both physically and psychologically: education, stable marriage, healthy weight, some exercise, not smoking, not abusing alcohol, and "employing mature adaptations."

Vaillant believes social skills and coping methods are crucial in determining overall life satisfaction. However, his most important finding was revealed in an interview in 2008 when he was asked, "What have you learned from the Grant Study men?" Vaillant's response: "That the only thing that really matters in life are your relationships to other people."

The Grant Study confirms that a successful life is not about the grim determination to get or have more. Nor is it about low cholesterol levels or intellectual brilliance or career accomplishments.

It's about human connections: parents, siblings, spouses, children, friends, neighbors, and mentors. Without them, life quickly loses its flavor whatever material successes we enjoy. Lasting satisfaction is rare outside of meaningful, human relationships. Look back at your life and you'll almost certainly find that the most significant moments were births, deaths, weddings, and celebrations.

Your most profound moments? When you touched others... or they touched you. In times of suffering – loss, sickness, death – it is not prescriptions, formulas, or advice we seek, but the healing presence of another. When we forget this – when we think only of ourselves – we choke the source of our development.

Real meaning comes from taking care of those you love, letting them know how you feel. Fortunately, we have countless opportunities to give a bit of ourselves each day through a thoughtful act, a word of appreciation, or a sense of understanding. As Dr. Vaillant concluded, the greatest success – a life well lived – "is more about *us* than me."

In short, a healthy diet, regular exercise, sufficient sleep, and human connections are the four pillars of a healthy, happy life.

Most of us take practical steps to maintain good health. We promise to eat less sugar and fewer refined carbs, and more leafy greens and antioxidant-filled fruits. We resist binge-watching that new Netflix series to spend time outside or in the gym. We try to stop smoking, use alcohol in moderation (or not at all), and put on sunscreen before we head to the beach.

But if you truly want to do even more to protect your health, let me recommend one more thing you should do: turn down the risk in your portfolio.

According to a study in the *Journal of the American Medical Association* (*JAMA*), losing a significant percentage of your wealth isn't just an unfortunate development. It's as bad for your life expectancy as being broke.

Social scientists have recognized for years that rich people in this country live longer than poor people. In fact, a study coauthored by two MIT researchers found that the richest 1% of men live 14.6 years longer than the poorest 1% of men. (Among women, the difference is 10.1 years on average.)

There are several reasons for this. Poor people live in more dangerous neighborhoods. They are less likely to get preventive medical care. And their diets are far less healthy.

Indeed, people on government-subsidized food programs – 56% of the population – have the worst health, including higher risk for obesity, diabetes, inflammation, and high cholesterol. (The no. 1 item purchased by food stamp recipients is soda.)

Yet taking a serious hit to your investment portfolio can negate all the advantages of a richer, healthier lifestyle. According to *JAMA*, you're 50% more likely to die within 20 years of losing most of your assets. That's about as large a mortality effect as a diagnosis of heart disease. And it holds true even when existing health problems are factored in.

It didn't even matter whether people were affluent before and after the downturn. It was simply that they experienced a significant loss. (And the grief that comes with it.) Moreover, the study found that a full quarter of Americans 51 and older experienced what they called a "negative wealth shock."

If that number seems high, think back to the Great Recession. It came on the heels of everyday folks flipping preconstruction condos, buying subprime mortgage securities, and trading stocks on margin. We all know individuals who lost a significant chunk of their retirement savings or even filed personal bankruptcy.

You don't want to become one of those statistics, and you don't have to. There is plenty you can do about it today. There are far too many folks trading options, futures, penny stocks, and crypto. They are investing in things with flimsy fundamentals. They are thinking solely about upside potential and not about downside risk.

Fortunately, there is a simple cure for this. It's called a *portfolio pre-mortem*. Imagine that a devastating bear market has just hit and you work backward to determine what you could have done to minimize the damage.

If you're in retirement or close to it, take a few minutes to visualize this scenario and let it sink in. Recognize that what's at risk is real money that was probably attained over a period of many years and at great sacrifice. Realize too that a severe bear market early in your retirement can wreak havoc on your long-term investment plans if you must sell assets at depressed prices.

Think about just how you'd feel if this happened to you. Then take these six critical steps:

1. Adjust your asset allocation so that you have a good balance between equities and fixed income investments.
2. If you own individual equities, tweak your portfolio so you have fewer low-quality stocks and more high-quality ones. (High-quality stocks have earnings and pay dividends.)
3. Emphasize large-cap companies over small-cap ones. (History shows that large caps hold up far better in market downturns.)
4. Overweight value stocks relative to growth stocks. (Value stocks are less volatile because they trade at lower multiples to sales, earnings, and book value.)
5. Run a trailing stop behind your trading positions. This will protect both your principal and your profits.
6. Favor high-grade bonds over high-yield bonds. (There's a reason they're called "junk bonds.")

Of course, if you invest in one of Vanguard's Target Date Retirement Funds, you don't have to worry about these things. Vanguard has already taken care of it. I don't call it the world's simplest portfolio for nothing.

However, if you have a more aggressive portfolio and are close to or in retirement, consider dialing back your risk. Do it now – today – and then take a deep breath. After all, you haven't just safeguarded the nest egg it took you a lifetime to accumulate. You've protected something more valuable: your health.

CHAPTER 21

Paying the American Dream Forward

How wonderful it is that nobody need wait a single moment before starting to improve the world.

—Diarist Anne Frank

Many Americans – especially older ones – will see their own story in what I've written in these pages. They have worked hard, persisted during tough times, made tough financial choices, taken smart risks, and safeguarded their health. As a result, they have attained their version of the American Dream.

But to truly embody that feeling of *earned success*, there is still one more essential step: pay it forward. (I prefer this phrase to the more commonly heard phrase "give back." You can only give back what you took that wasn't yours. And I'll bet that doesn't describe your personal journey.)

Paying it forward is a powerful philosophy rooted in kindness and gratitude. If you've been successful in your life, you've no doubt made good decisions. But – if you're honest with yourself – you'll also admit that you've been incredibly fortunate.

You were born in the West in our prosperous and (mostly) peaceful modern era. You may have been born with a higher-than-average IQ. You probably had one or more parents who nurtured you and provided a positive role model. No doubt you received some favorable breaks along the way, as well.

These things alone don't explain your success. After all, millions of people had these advantages and still struggled. Many of them never made it. You should be grateful if you did.

It's probably too late to properly thank or repay all the people who helped you early in your lifelong adventure. However, you can still foster a culture of goodwill and interconnectedness by passing your knowledge and worldly experience on to others.

This probably starts with your kids and grandkids. They probably know about your greatest triumphs. But they may not know the obstacles you faced or how you struggled to get where you are. It would be a shame if your story, your beliefs, your values, and your experiences were taken with you to the grave. Why not share them with your children and grandchildren while you still can?

Let me provide a springboard for your discussion. If I were to interview you about the experiences that mattered most in your life and the causes you championed, here is what I would ask:

- Who has been the most important person in your life and why?
- What are the most meaningful life lessons you've learned?
- What are your favorite memories?
- How has your life turned out different than you imagined?
- What are you proudest of?
- What was your biggest break?
- What is your greatest regret?
- What words of wisdom would you like to pass on?
- What are your hopes and dreams for the future . . . and for your family's future?
- How would you like to be remembered?

Sharing your own experiences – both good and bad – can spark others to achieve their dreams. That extends beyond your immediate family to the local community. I'm sure there are plenty of people in your neighborhood, town, or city who would benefit from your time, experience, or money.

One of the greatest rewards of success is being able to share it within your community. Giving to others adds meaning to your life and offers you an opportunity to shape the way the world remembers you. You can lead by example, donate, volunteer, or do all the above.

Something surprising happens when you offer your time and talent to a nonprofit. Getting involved in their events energizes your giving strategy as you see firsthand the needs of the community. To maximize your impact, consider using a site like VolunteerMatch.org to find a nonprofit in search of your particular skill set.

Or you may want to become a mentor. Chances are someone helped you get where you are. You can be that lifeline for someone else. If you're a business owner, you can help budding entrepreneurs through SCORE or the Network for Teaching Entrepreneurship. Or mentor.org will match you with a child who needs a caring role model.

Perhaps you are in a better position to give money than time. That's fine. But be careful. Charitable donations can be reactive and therefore less targeted. And last-minute, year-end giving doesn't always thoughtfully further your purpose.

Your goal should be to become a more effective donor. That not only means identifying the people and organizations that best match your values but also using certain financial strategies to maximize the impact of your charitable dollars and potentially mitigate some of your tax liabilities.

Here's a basic example. Rather than giving cash to a nonprofit, it's often advantageous to donate a stock, bond, or fund where you have an unrealized capital gain. That's a win-win-win. Win 1: you contribute to a worthy cause that promotes your values. Win 2: you avoid paying a capital gains tax on the gain. Win 3: you may get a tax deduction for the full value of your donation.

Some will choose to give even more effectively by building an enduring philanthropic legacy. That generally entails intentional planning, strategic giving, and a commitment to having a lasting impact.

Here are some key steps to establishing a meaningful legacy that resonates across generations:

1. **Define your vision and values.** Ask yourself what you want the country – or the world – to look like because of your giving. Ideally, you'll identify causes that align with your passions and beliefs and will help create the transformative changes that you hope to achieve.
2. **Engage in strategic planning.** This means focusing on long-term solutions rather than one-off donations. Consider using tools like donor-advised funds, charitable trusts, or private foundations to ensure that your giving is systematic, impactful, and tax-advantaged.
3. **Involve family members.** Engage those closest to you in discussions about charitable priorities, involve them in decision-making, and create traditions around giving. For example, families can volunteer together or establish rituals such as holiday donations to shared causes.
4. **Measure your impact.** Regularly assess your philanthropic efforts to ensure they are achieving your desired outcomes. Set clear goals and metrics for success and adjust strategies as necessary. Celebrating achievements can also inspire continued engagement from family members and friends.
5. **Incorporate nonfinancial contributions.** In addition to donations, volunteer time and expertise. Sharing knowledge or mentoring nonprofit leaders can amplify the impact of your contributions while fostering a deeper connection with the causes that you support.

I've spilled a lot of ink over the past few decades showing readers effective ways to save, invest, and compound their money. More recently, I've also addressed a different but no less important topic: how to donate money in a way that promotes – rather than undermines – your highest values.

For example, I've suggested that readers might earmark some of the money they've been giving to their alma maters to a nonprofit that is more representative of their highest values.

That may seem like an odd request at first blush. Most university graduates have fond memories of their time in college. You still root for the football and basketball teams. You recognize the supreme importance of education and want to help pave the way for future generations.

There's only one problem. But it's a big one. Your university – with a few exceptions – is almost certainly not the institution it once was. Across the nation, millions of alumni are learning the disturbing truth.

On many of today's campuses, facts have been replaced with feelings. Moral complexity has been replaced with moral certainty. Debate has been replaced by de-platforming. Diversity of thought has been replaced by homogeneity of thought. Persuasion has been replaced by public shaming. Education has been replaced by indoctrination. And – while the pendulum has finally begun to swing the other way – this misguided ideology migrated into business and popular culture as well.

A recent *New York Times*/Siena College poll found that 84% of Americans say being afraid to exercise freedom of speech is a serious problem. And yet – out of a sense of tradition or loyalty – many still donate to educational institutions that are openly hostile to the principles that made them successful in their business and personal lives.

That's why I give not to my alma mater – guilty of everything charged above – but to Students For Liberty. The nonprofit is a global movement of young individuals committed to promoting the ideas of liberty, free markets, and limited government. It firmly believes that a society that respects individual rights and fosters economic and personal freedom leads to prosperity, innovation, and the overall well-being of its citizens. Its chapters are aimed at fostering a deeper understanding of these principles among students on campus and within the broader community.

As of 2024, 72% of the world's population lives under autocratic regimes. (That's up from 49% in 2004.) And our liberties are under assault here at home, too, with increased government surveillance, restrictions on press freedoms, and growing concerns about digital privacy.

Through seminars, workshops, guest lectures, and community outreach programs, the folks at Students For Liberty empower young minds to think critically, engage in constructive discussions, and develop a strong foundation of knowledge about the principles that shape our world – or should. To continue its impactful work, the organization relies on the support of generous individuals who share its vision for a freer and more prosperous future.

My donations to Students For Liberty – where I hold a board seat – reflect my dedication to empowering the next generation of leaders and thinkers, the people who will shape the future. I've become part of a movement that is creating lasting change and fostering a society rooted in liberty and individual rights.

I'm proud to give my time and money to this organization. (You might even visit StudentsForLiberty.org and do the same.) Donations, no matter the size, are put to effective use in promoting the ideas that have made freedom-loving countries the most peaceful and prosperous in the world. It's a shame that many universities are not actively working to promote the ideals that help societies flourish. But Students For Liberty *is*.

If you become a board member at a nonprofit, you will quickly learn that what most are interested in is the five Ws: willingness, work, wealth, wisdom, and wallop.

Willingness means you *want to* be there. You attend the meetings. You volunteer. You enthusiastically participate. Good intentions aren't enough. The organization needs you to *show up*.

Work has two parts. First, board meetings require a quorum, so being there is essential. However, if you can contribute in some other way – by sharing, say, business acumen, legal advice, or marketing expertise – that's important, too.

Wisdom is crucial. Knowledge about the mission and how the charitable community works can be invaluable to the organization. Those who share their understanding and guidance freely help make sure that things get done.

Wealth is easy to understand and to measure. But it's not just about stroking that annual check (or donating those appreciated securities). Sometimes there are unexpected expenses that need to be met. And volunteers can also write thank-you notes, make calls, or send emails to show appreciation to other donors – and encourage them to keep contributing.

Wallop means influence, which comes down to reputation and associations. Successful people often have not just good "connections" but entire networks of affluent and influential people. A good board member participates in fundraising and encourages others to give. Friends and business associates often want to be on the same team and are happy to participate in a shared mission.

Whatever suits your personal situation best – whether it's volunteering, donating, mentoring, sitting on a board, or starting a foundation – there are few pleasures in life better than the feeling of extending a helping hand to others.

When you've lived the American Dream, a worthy goal is helping others live it, too.

CHAPTER 22

Developing an Attitude of Gratitude

Gratitude is not only the greatest of virtues, but the parent of all the others.

—Roman philosopher Cicero

The fastest way to become wealthier isn't to pay closer attention to your bank statement, your brokerage account, or your real estate holdings. It's to expand your gratitude.

That may sound counterintuitive coming from someone who has spent four decades as a financial analyst and investment advisor. But it happens to be true. And acknowledging this can transform your life.

Study after study confirms what the ancients knew: gratitude is a force multiplier. It lowers anxiety and depression. It boosts optimism. It strengthens your immune system, improves your sleep, deepens relationships, and helps you savor life rather than simply survive it.

There are two main ways to foster a sense of gratitude. The first is to practice thankfulness for the life you've been given. The other is to deliberately notice what's right with your life, rather than dwelling on what's missing.

When we take a moment to feel grateful, most of us tell ourselves something like, "I have decent health, a loving family, good friends, and a comfortable home." But that hardly scratches the surface.

You won the ovarian lottery just by being born in the West in the modern era. Most of human history was pre-agricultural. For hundreds of thousands of years, people lived lives that were – in Thomas Hobbes's famous phrase "nasty, brutish, and short" – battling the elements, avoiding predators, and hunting and scavenging to survive.

Two hundred years ago, most of the world's population experienced the present standard of living of Bangladesh. Yet Americans today live in the world's richest, most prosperous country, one that offers unlimited opportunities.

Compared to everyone in the past – and billions around the world today – you enjoy an unprecedented standard of living. This is true even if you are struggling financially.

A hundred years ago, you could not have walked into a supermarket that offers the smorgasbord of foods and drinks available today. You would not have been able to decide on a whim between scores of nearby bistros, or Italian, Chinese, Thai, or Mexican restaurants, each waiting to serve you at a moment's notice. (Or – if you don't feel like going out – a service will be happy to deliver your order to your door.) In previous generations, most households could not afford to have someone else prepare their meals.

A hundred years ago, you would not have had instant power at the flick of a switch – or a safe, reliable, and comfortable vehicle to take you around town or across the country. You could not have bought a ticket from a budget airline to fly to hundreds of destinations. You would not have been able to browse the internet and instantly order from a limitless range of excellent, affordable clothes or tools or gadgets.

You would not have had a supercomputer in your pocket, one far more powerful than the computers that guided the Apollo astronauts. It's not just that you can call, text, or videoconference at minimal cost. You have instant access to a camera, video recorder, GPS, television, library, music studio, health tracker, personal assistant, and a gateway to all human knowledge. That means you can work, study, or collaborate from anywhere. Your way of life is made easy by markets, machines, and other people.

For millennia, the world was rife with despotism, slavery, hierarchy, class privilege, and literally no increase in the standard of living. The Enlightenment changed that – and ushered in a new world based on reason, science, and belief in progress and freedom. The American founding – the ideals of political and economic freedom – led to human rights, property rights, free trade, religious toleration, peace, human flourishing, and the right to pursue happiness.

That brought about what economist Dierdre McCloskey calls the Great Fact of human history: the tremendous, unprecedented growth in living standards starting about 1800. These ideas started in the West and then spread to the rest of the world.

Yes, humanity stumbled in the 20th century, enduring World War I, trade wars, the Great Depression, World War II, and rising violence and poverty. Some countries endured the horrors of communism or national socialism. And in some places today these problems still exist. But they are rarer – and in decline globally.

In my lifetime, we have experienced Jim Crow laws, military conscription, wage and price controls, indecency laws, and 90% marginal income tax rates. These have all ended.

And many wonderful things have sprung up during this period, including pacemakers; in vitro fertilization; oral contraceptives; heart, liver, kidney, and lung transplants; ultrasounds; coronary bypass surgery; vaccines for measles, rubella, mumps, hepatitis B, and COVID-19; cochlear implants; magnetic resonance imagining; the insulin pump; the first successful jet airliner; integrated circuits; lasers; industrial robots; microprocessors; personal computers; the internet; cell phones and smartphones; social media; Wi-Fi; obesity drugs; artificial intelligence; and quantum computing. to name just a few.

Along the way, we sent satellites into space, walked on the Moon, and won the Cold War without firing a shot. The rule of law spread, and democratic governments increased. Property rights and market institutions also expanded, lifting over a billion people around the globe out of extreme poverty.

We have more freedom and progress than ever before. As a result, we have more abundance, more social harmony, more human dignity, and more human flourishing.

And we have much to look forward to — even though we can't imagine all the advancements ahead of us. We now combine ideas recursively — have thoughts about our thoughts — and share ideas immediately and globally.

That means we're not just getting better. We're getting better faster. The people of Mesopotamia, for example, learned how to smelt copper 7,000 years ago. But it took another 4,000 years before the process was independently discovered in the Americas.

Today — thanks to global interconnectivity — discoveries spread instantaneously. And as we use increasingly powerful tools to expand our knowledge, we will have faster communications, safer homes, new lifesaving medical treatments, and much more.

Even if you understand this, your gratitude should be much deeper still. For example, the fact that you arrived on the scene at all defies the oddsmakers.

Physicist Ali Binazir provided a famous estimate of the improbability of any specific person being born. He factored in the odds of your parents meeting, the odds of them staying together and reproducing, the odds of the right sperm and egg meeting, and the survival of the embryo and baby.

This had to happen not just with both your parents, but with your 4 grandparents, your 8 great-grandparents, your 16 great-great-grandparents, and so on back for countless generations and millions of years.

The sex of a child is established randomly at conception, depending on whether the successful sperm carries an X or Y chromosome. If any one of your ancestors in the countless trillions of boxes back to the beginning of multicellular life had been of the opposite sex, then that individual could not occupy that box, and you would not exist. The odds of you ever being born are far longer than the odds of winning the Powerball jackpot, which is a mere 1 in 292.2 million.

Life was far more dangerous for our ancestors in the distant past. It's not just a mathematical miracle that we arrived, but a harrowing drama as well. Author Bill Bryson described nature's ruthless game of chance– almost poetically – in *A Brief History of Nearly Everything*:

> *You have been extremely – make that miraculously – fortunate in your personal ancestry. Consider the fact that for 3.8 billion years, a period of time older than the Earth's mountains and rivers and oceans, every one of your forebears on both sides has been attractive enough to find a mate, healthy enough to reproduce, and sufficiently blessed by fate and circumstances to live long enough to do so. Not one of your pertinent ancestors was squashed, devoured, drowned, starved, stranded, stuck fast, untimely wounded, or otherwise deflected from its life's quest of delivering a tiny charge of genetic material to the right partner at the right moment in order to perpetuate the only possible sequence of hereditary combinations that could result – eventually, astoundingly, and all too briefly – in you.*

Meditate on this for a moment. And recognize that the odds against you being here are practically incalculable. Yet Binazir and Bryson are still vastly *understating* the probability of your existence.

Let's step back even further and look at the *really* big picture . . .

The odds that the fundamental constants of the universe are precisely tuned to allow life to form and evolve are vanishingly small. If gravity were slightly stronger or weaker, stars might not form or burn in a stable way, making life impossible. If the electromagnetic force, which governs atomic bonding, were even slightly different, atoms and molecules essential for life wouldn't form. If the strong nuclear force were slightly weaker, atomic nuclei wouldn't hold together, preventing the formation of elements like carbon and oxygen. A small change in the weak nuclear force would have altered nuclear fusion in stars, preventing the formation of elements needed for life. If the initial expansion rate of the universe at the Big Bang had been slightly higher, no stars would have formed. (And without stars there would be no complex chemistry and, therefore, no life.) If it had been slightly lower, the universe would have quickly collapsed soon after the Big Bang.

Physicists and cosmologists describe the odds of these constants being precisely aligned to allow life on Earth as inconceivably small. Some estimates suggest the chance of a life-permitting universe is as tiny as 1 in 10 to the power of 120. To put this in perspective, the number of atoms in the observable universe is estimated at 10 to the power of 80.

In other words, a life-permitting universe is not just wildly improbable. It's *miraculous*.

Many scientists believe we live in a *multiverse*, that our universe is just one among many. They don't believe this due to observational evidence. (There isn't any.) They believe it because it seems preposterous that we live in a universe that is so precisely fine-tuned to allow life to arise.

Some, of course, will wave off this improbability by drawing theological conclusions. However, our specialness diminishes when you consider that we are inhabitants of a single planet, orbiting a rather ordinary star in an almost limitless universe. There are trillions of galaxies, each containing hundreds of billions of stars, and, likely, even more planets. The distances between these celestial bodies is so vast that light traveling 186,000 miles per second takes years, centuries, or even millennia to bridge the gaps. Our planet – and human beings – are insignificant on this scale.

The faithful must also contend with the concept of deep time. Deep time refers to the vast geological timescale that spans billions of years, far beyond human comprehension.

For example, the Earth formed about 4.5 billion years ago. Life on Earth arose approximately 3.7 billion to 4.1 billion years ago. And our species has been around for approximately 300,000 years.

Astronomer Carl Sagan helped us understand the immensity of deep time with his Cosmic Calendar, a visualization tool that compresses the 13.7-billion-year history of the universe into a single calendar year. Each day on this calendar represents about 38 million years, and every second represents about 438 years. Here are some of the highlights:

- Midnight on January 1 marks the Big Bang, the origin of the universe.
- The formation of the Milky Way Galaxy occurs about March 15.

- Our solar system and the planet Earth form on September 9.
- Life on Earth begins in late September, with simple organisms like bacteria appearing first.
- December 13: the first multicellular life appears.
- December 25: dinosaurs dominate the planet
- December 30: the dinosaurs go extinct, probably due to an asteroid impact.
- December 31, 10:24 pm: early humans appear.
- December 31: 11:59:46 pm: all recorded human history – agriculture, the rise of civilizations, scientific discoveries, and modern technologies – fits into the last 14 seconds of the last minute of the last hour of the last day of the year.

Sagan's Cosmic Calendar powerfully demonstrates that, in the context of the universe's history, everything humans have ever done occurs in the blink of an eye just before the stroke of midnight at the end of the cosmic year.

In sum, the chances of your ever being born are incalculably slim. The odds against arriving in the modern era are also staggering. Billions alive today were born into wrenching poverty in China, India, sub-Saharan Africa, or some miserable failed state. You could easily be living in a society without modern infrastructure, communications, or a reliable power supply. You might have no government that recognizes your rights, no court system to protect you, and no free market system to incentivize you. For all these reasons – and more – you should be grateful.

Some Americans concede that we are living longer, healthier, safer, richer, freer lives than ever before. And that we beat unimaginable odds to have ever been born at all. But they will still lament that – despite our many blessings – there is a great *moral decline* in the country and the world.

This is not true. I've already touched on some of the reasons. However, my friend Michael Shermer, publisher of *Skeptic* magazine, gave an excellent summary in his superb book *The Moral Arc*:

> *Improvements in the domain of morality are evident in many areas of life:* governance *(the rise of liberal democracies and the decline of theocracies and autocracies),* economics *(broader property rights and the freedom to trade goods and services with others without oppressive restrictions);* rights

(to life, liberty, property, marriage, reproduction, voting, speech, worship, assembly, protest, autonomy, and the pursuit of happiness), prosperity *(the explosion of wealth and increasing affluence for more people in more places; and the decline of poverty worldwide in which a smaller percentage of the world's people are impoverished than any time in history)*; health and longevity *(more people in more places more of the time live longer, healthier lives than at any time in the past)*; war *(a smaller percentage of people die as a result of violent conflict today than at any time since our species began)*; slavery *(outlawed everywhere in the world and practiced in only a few places in the form of sexual slavery and slave labor that are now being targeted for total abolition)*; homicide *(rates have fallen precipitously from over 100 murders per 100,000 in the Middle Ages to less than one per 100,000 today in the industrial West, and the chances of an individual dying violently is the lowest it has ever been in history)*; rape and sexual assault *(trending downward and while still too prevalent, it is outlawed by all Western states and increasingly prosecuted)*; judicial equality *(citizens of different nations are treated more equally under the law than at any time in the past)*, and civility *(people are kinder, more civilized, and less violent to one another than ever before)*. *In short, we are living in the most moral period in our species' history.*

It's a safe bet that most Americans don't know this, even the ones who consider themselves well-read, well-traveled, and highly educated. The conventional wisdom is that any informed person should feel the world is falling apart economically, politically, culturally, and morally. If you don't think everything is awful, you clearly aren't paying attention!

We can all recite a litany of what is wrong in the world. But we should also pay heed to what is going right – because we are astoundingly fortunate. This is not just a matter of opinion.

As Steven Pinker writes in *Enlightenment Now*,

> *The story of human progress is truly heroic. It is glorious. It is uplifting . . . We live longer, suffer less, learn more, get smarter, and enjoy more small pleasures and rich experiences . . . This heroic story is not just a myth. Myths are fictions, but this one is true. . . It requires only the convictions that life is better than death, health is better than sickness, abundance is better than want, freedom is better than coercion, happiness is better than suffering, and knowledge is better than superstition and ignorance.*

Understanding this is essential because it puts things in perspective, revealing how well we live compared to others around the world today and almost everyone in the past. It also makes it easier to invest, stay invested, and strive to get ahead when you realize that most long-term trends are positive.

Another good reason to cultivate gratitude: psychologists say it is impossible to feel grateful and unhappy at the same time.

Recognize your indebtedness to millions of others. They sacrificed and struggled so that we could enjoy the lives we live today. I'm talking about explorers, pioneers, inventors, artists, writers, activists, leaders, and everyday workers. (Not to mention parents and grandparents.) Their legacy is our inheritance.

Give thanks for the many men and women who have risked their lives – or laid down their lives – to uphold the many freedoms we enjoy today. Members of the armed forces mainly, but also police officers, rescue workers, and crisis volunteers. Many suffered through privation, fought the battles that made our lives free, physically built much of what we rely on for our prosperity, and shaped the ideals of liberty.

We live in the kind of nation they would have wished for us – in many ways, a better place than they dared imagine. It's not a perfect world. Just the best one humanity has ever known. For us not to feel grateful is not just short-sighted. It's ignorant.

Ingratitude breeds envy and resentment. It leaves you with a chronic sense of lack. You're always looking for something else . . . something more. Gratitude, by contrast, grounds you. It softens your struggles. It amplifies your joys. It reminds you – even in difficulty – that you are surrounded by abundance.

So, express your appreciation. Tell your coworkers that you value them. Show your friends that they matter. Let your family know they are loved.

In short, realize your immense good fortune. Put your gratitude into action. And live the American Dream.

ACKNOWLEDGMENTS

I'd like to thank some of the people who helped me live the American Dream – and inspired me to write this book.

That starts with my parents, Braxton and Judith Green, who are 95 and 96 and still living independently – enthusiastically even – just a few miles from my home.

My parents gave my three brothers and me very little advice and instruction growing up, even in the fraught teenage years. Yet they always modeled their version of the best way to live, with integrity and love centered on good people, good times, and good food.

They didn't tell us. They *showed* us what a life well lived is all about.

The most important decision most of us make is with whom we spend our lives. Fortunately, I chose well when I married Karen Passilla. We have two adult children – the ultimate oxymoron – Hannah and David. Raising them, and seeing them grow to happy adulthood has been the most rewarding part of our lives.

I'd also like to thank the cast of characters who wrote the blurbs on the back cover. We all graduated in the Class of 1976 from Robert E. Lee High School in Staunton, Virginia. And – trust me – you would not have pegged us back then as potential high achievers. None of us came from particularly auspicious circumstances.

Jimmy was raised in a modest household. His father was a foreman at a local power plant. But Jimmy worked for a professional services firm for 35 years and retired a millionaire many times over at the ripe old age of 56. He still serves as an executive on many nonprofit boards and is the founding sponsor of the Center for Civic Impact at Morven Park.

Bob and I went to kindergarten together, where he insists that I tormented him. We were best friends in high school but went to different colleges. After drifting unsuccessfully from job to job in his early 20s, he discovered his true calling: real estate development. He founded and still runs a Florida-based development firm that has developed over 20,000 lots and has had an economic impact of over $3.5 billion.

Scott grew up in a single-parent home. His father died in a hunting accident when he was 13. The fear of poverty drove him to start working at 14, taking jobs washing dishes, waiting tables, and later selling medical supplies. However, a successful career as a money manager enabled him to live comfortably and ultimately retire in style.

Rodney grew up "with no money," as he puts it. Both of his parents had serious disabilities. (His dad was the janitor at our junior high school.) He started working at age 6 – I thought there were laws against that – and worked 48 hours a week while attending college. (That could be why it took him so many years to graduate.) Today he is a successful entrepreneur who lives in a beautiful home overlooking Choctawhatchee Bay near Ft. Walton Beach, Florida.

Billy and I grew up two doors apart. He wasn't a great student but still holds our high school's records in long-distance track events. He struggled in various jobs after school but eventually got into the brokerage business and became a top producer and branch manager. A long battle with pneumonia and a cancer diagnosis forced him into early retirement, but he was already financially independent. Today Billy volunteers and contributes to Meals on Wheels, Vector Industries Foundation, Trinity Endowment, the local YMCA, and many more charitable causes.

Then there is John Reed. John grew up in simple circumstances but was the valedictorian of our high school class. He is currently executive vice president of Johnson & Johnson (J&J). Before joining J&J, John served as executive vice president and global head of research and development at Sanofi, global head of pharmaceutical research and early development at Roche, and CEO of the Sanford-Burnham Medical Research Institute (now Sanford Burnham Prebys), where he established several research centers focused on therapeutic areas and platform technologies.

John is among the world's most highly cited physician scientists, with over 900 scientific publications and more than 130 patents. He was recognized as one of the top 10 most cited researchers in life sciences and medicine for a decade and continues to be listed in the world's top 100 most highly cited scientists.

John remains a good friend and supplied a beautiful blurb for the book. Unfortunately, Johnson & Johnson's legal department – knowing nothing about me or the contents of the book – would not approve it.

Anyway, these six guys were my closest friends 50 years ago. And they remain six of my closest friends today. All of us have lived some version of the American Dream.

And while John has an IQ that ranks up there with Isaac Newton, no one would have bet on the rest of us knuckleheads a half-century ago. You would have been less surprised to see us in a police lineup than as role models. Yet somehow we made it.

If you want to live a great life, having the right parents helps. And so does having the right romantic partner. But having the right bunch of friends goes a long way, too.

While I'm on the subject, I want to mention Rob Fix, a great friend to whom I dedicated this book.

When I first met Rob at work four decades ago, I had two overwhelming impressions. One, he talked too much and, two, he was a bit of a kook. For the first several weeks that I knew him, I avoided him like he was the IRS.

But as I got to know him better, I realized that my first impressions were totally off base. Rob was not a guy who talked too much and was a bit of a kook. He was a guy who never stopped talking and is the biggest kook I've ever known. He is, in fact, the world's most lovable kook. Perhaps that's why he was the best man at my wedding.

Rob was the first person to really "show me" New York City, and for that I am eternally grateful. He introduced me to Broadway, Carnegie Hall and the Village Vanguard. He got me into astronomy and backyard telescopes the size of furniture. He introduced me to high-end audio. (But I forgave him.) We played golf and tennis together, attended concerts together, and laughed ourselves silly. We read the same books, listened to the same music, and drank the same overpriced wines. No single friend has shared so many interests with me. And I've only scratched the surface here.

In the past year, Rob has done something else. He has provided an inspiring example of grace and courage. A few months ago, he was diagnosed with an aggressive form of ALS (Lou Gehrig's disease).

I was shocked when he told me and demanded to know why he hadn't shared his diagnosis with me sooner. His answer? "You were celebrating your 30th wedding anniversary in the islands and I didn't want to bum you out."

That's Rob – more concerned about ruining my good time than sharing his health issues. In the months leading up to the diagnosis, Rob's speech began to slur. (His doctor initially thought he'd had a stroke.) Then he lost his speech altogether, a real handicap for one of the world's best and most incessant talkers.

I live on the East Coast and Rob lives in Dallas. But he still texts and emails me every day. Every communication is chock-full of his trademark enthusiasm and humor. You could read them and never imagine his health challenges. There is not a whiff of sadness or self-pity. Except on my side, since Rob is made of sterner stuff, and I am slowly losing a great friend.

Every life contains suffering and loss, either now or in the future. That's why it's so important to appreciate the people around us each day. Life is a dream – a fleeting, surreal experience. And I'm grateful to all the friends, colleagues, and family members who shared theirs with me. They made my own life worth living.

INDEX

A

Abundance denial (disconnect reason), 216
Actively managed funds, investment, 178–180
Affluence, achievement, 112
Affordability, measurement, 38
African Americans, impact/life changes, 85–86
Agnew, Spiro, 73
Agus, David B., 236
America. *See* United States
American Dream
　achievement, 6–7, 162, 201
　belief, 2, 7, 162
　collapse, Chomsky perception, 99
　contemporary view, 3
　death, Trump statement, 104
　existence, proof, 15
　fade, belief, 30
　faith, loss, 4
　influencers/enemies, 91–92
　reaching, 5, 10
　roadblocks, 50
　traditional view, 3
　truth, 49
　unattainability, perception, 1–2, 9
　vitality, 3
　Wall Street Journal definition, 8
American family, vision (narrowness), 36
American ingenuity/technology/ capital markets, impact, 28
American stock market, returns, 29
Anger, justification (problem), 130
Annual expenses, surrender amount (determination), 183
Annual taxes, payment amount, 183
Annuities, usage (caution), 226
Artificial intelligence (AI)
　advent, 142
　impact, 56–60, 136, 212
Asian households, median net worth, 86
Asset allocation
　adjustment, 244
　determination/decision, 182, 186
Atomic habits, 143
Atomic Habits (Clear), 142, 195

B

Babson, Roger, 166
Bailey, Ronald, 208
Balzac, Honoré de, 216
Barry, Dave, 72
Bear markets, impact, 173, 191–192

267

Beginning of Infinity: Explanations That Transform the World (Deutsch), 55, 56
Benioff, Marc, 56–57
Bernstein, William, 190, 191
Better Angels of Our Nature: Why Violence Has Declined (Pinker), 32
Beyond Wealth (Green), 5
Bezos, Jeff, 73, 75, 128
Bid/ask spreads, thinness, 114
Binazir, Ali, 256
Black Americans, 86–88
  American Dream belief, 4
  households, median net worth, 86
Black poverty, disproportion, 86
Blaming, unhappiness (correlation), 131
Bogle, John, 180, 183
Boudreaux, Donald J., 45, 70
Brief History of Nearly Everything, A (Bryson), 257
Brooks, Arthur, 167
Bryson, Bill, 257
Buffett, Warren, 71, 82, 119–120, 128, 179, 206, 211, 234
Bush, George H.W. (election phrase), 103
Business
  starting, 144
  visionary, fortunes (attachment), 144

C
Cable news, consumption (limitation), 121
Cancer, impact, 235
Capital
  access, 82
  flight, investment decline (relationship), 77

Capital gains tax, avoidance, 154
Capitalism
  benefits/effects, 53, 174
  disparagement, 100
  profit/loss system, 124
  promise, 112
Carnegie, D., 136
Celebrity, wealth conversion, 144
Change, power, 2
Character, focus, 120
Chatbot, answers (examples), 140–141
ChatGPT, usage (example), 137–140
Chief Executive Officer (CEO), becoming, 144
Children, marriage priority (milestone), 128
Chomsky, Noam, 98–100
Chronic diseases, prevention, 232
Churchill, Winston, 124, 160
Civil Rights Act of 1964, 85
Clark, Gregory, 18–20, 50, 195
Clear, James, 142
Climate change, 16
Collapse anxiety (disconnect reason), 216–217
Common stocks, investment, 176–177
Companies, success (process), 213–214
Compounding, 170, 220
Conflict resolution, 32
Consumer Price Index (CPI)
  increase, 43
  measurement limitations, 37–38
Contract for deed (land contract), usage, 154–155
Coolidge, Jr., Calvin (death), 58
Cosmic Calendar (Sagan), 258–259

Covey, S., 136
COVID-19 pandemic, 204
Creative destruction, impact, 124
Creative financing, usage, 155
Credit score
  building (chatbot question example), 141
  checking, 155
Cryptocurrencies/bitcoins, losses, 164–165
Cultural narrative, impact, 71
Cuomo, Mario (American Dream remark), 104

D
Data, creation, 59
da Vinci, Leonardo, 164
Death, leading causes, 232, 234, 235
Deaton, Angus, 45
Debt
  American Dream roadblock, 50
  management, 155
Declaration of Independence
  importance, 5, 25, 62
  signing/perception, 70
Deep risk (reduction), international diversification (impact), 195
Delayed/deferred
  gratification, 84, 167
  Stanford study, 65
Democrats, pessimism, 4
De-platforming, problem, 249
Deutsch, David, 55, 56
Diamandis, Peter, 57
Diet, control, 230–235, 242
Die with Zero (Perkins), 221
Digitization, Deception, Disruption, Demonetization, Dematerialization, Democratization (six Ds), 57
Dignity, money (impact), 10

Dimon, Jamie, 28
Disbelievers, American Dream (relationship), 5
Diversified portfolio, investment return, 172, 192
Diversity, equity, and inclusion (DEI), 125
Dividends, reinvestment, 207
Dollar cost averaging (DCA), 147, 195
Domestic violence, decline, 52
Double taxation, problem, 77
Down payment, money (saving), 155
Dream Achievers, American Dream (relationship), 5

E
Early, John, 20
Earned income, factors, 81
Earned success, concept, 167, 245
Easterbrook, Gregg, 208
Economic damage, 77
Economic expansion, growth, 57
Economic inequality, 87
  Buffett comment, 82
  exaggeration, 79
  irrelevance, 70
Economic mobility, quality, 20
Economic prosperity, happiness (relationship), 62
Economic security, achievement, 7
Educational resources, access, 72–73
Ehrlich, Paul, 97–98, 100
Eisner v. Macomber, 76
Ekelund, Robert, 20
Ellison, Larry, 71
Embarrassment of Riches, An (Green), 5
Emergency fund, building, 155

Index **269**

Emotional Intelligence: Why It Can Matter More Than IQ (Goleman), 218
Emotions, control, 189–190, 218
Energy, importance, 54
Enlightenment Now (Pinker), 51, 52, 54, 208, 260
Enlightenment, principles (impact), 51, 255
Entitlement (American Dream roadblock), 50
Environmental, social, and governance (ESG), 125
Epistemic humility, 212
Everyday Millionaires (Hogan), 114
Exchange-traded funds (ETFs), usage, 164–165
Exercise, importance, 230, 232, 234–238, 242
Experiences
  ranking, 246
  sharing, 247
Exponential growth, six Ds, 57
Exponential mindset, cultivation, 60
Exponential technologies, 58–59

F
Factfulness (Rosling), 208, 215
Facts
  ignorance (disconnect reason), 215
  replacement, feelings (usage), 249
Fair Housing Act (1968), 85
Fairness, obsession, 113
False impression, creation, 31
Family members, involvement, 248
Financial data, examination, 175
Financial education, absence, 10
Financial freedom, 191, 199
  stages, 227
Financial illiteracy, 93, 128
Financial impact, measurement, 248
Financial independence
  absence, mistakes, 81
  assistance, 143
  attainment, 166–167
  blocking, 196
  number, calculation, 188–199
Financial literacy
  Health and Retirement Survey, 160
  SEC report, 159–160
Financial security, 169
  difficulty, perception, 129
Financial welfare, accountability, 161
Financial well-being, behavior (impact), 84–85
Fisher, Ken, 144–146, 173
Fixed-mortgage rates, housing costs (relationship), 151
Flash Crash, 204
Food supply, increase, 45
Founding Fathers
  characteristics, 63
  mistakes/vilification, 24–25
Four Pillars of Investing, The (Bernstein), 190
Franklin, Benjamin, 199
Freedom, Americans (choice), 70
Free market system, benefits, 125
Frugality (virtue), 66, 146
Frustrated Dreamers, American Dream (relationship), 5
Full-time job (milestone), 128

G
gamification trend, 163
Gates, Bill, 52, 71, 120, 205, 2344
Gini coefficient, inequality measurement, 79

Global diversification, usage, 194–195
Globalization/automation, impact, 18
global wealth, increase (UBS Global Wealth Report), 19
Goals, dreams (connection), 187
Gods/services, availability (increase), 46
Go-go years (retirement division), 224
Golden Verses of Pythagoras, 63
Golden years, enjoyment, 221
Goleman, Daniel, 218
Gone Fishin' Portfolio: Get Wise, Get Wealthy. . .and Get On with Your Life (Green), 6, 193
Graham, Benjamin, 172, 190, 206
Gramm, Phil, 20, 70
Grant Study (Harvard), 240–241
Gratitude, expansion/sense, 253–254, 261
Great Depression, 255
Great Enrichment, 44
Great Fact, 255
Great Recession, aftermath, 2, 204
Greed, perception, 111–112
Greger, Michael, 231–235
Grocott, Bruce, 83
Gross Domestic Product (GDP), growth, 74
Growth, opportunities, 213

H
Habits, lagging indicator, 142
Habituation (disconnect reason), 215
Happiness
earned success, impact, 167
meaning, 62–63
money, relationship, 167
negative emotions, impact, 130–131
pursuit, 64–65
Harris, Kamala
American Dream statement, 129
populist issues, 104
Health
decline/problems, 229–230
fundamental four, 230
Hedonic treadmill (disconnect reason), 216
High-grade bonds, preference, 244
High school, completion (milestone), 128
Hill, N., 136
History, education process, 93
Hobbes, Thomas, 254
Hogan, Chris, 114–116
Home (housing)
affordability, problems, 150
annual property taxes, payment, 150
equity, usage, 225
expense/affordability, perception, 40–41
ownership, 149–150
prices, increase, 150
purchase, 152–153
sellers, involvement, 153–154
Homicides, decline, 17
How Not to Die: Discover the Foods Scientifically Proven to Prevent and Reverse Disease (Greger), 231, 235
How to Win Friends and Influence People (Carnegie), 136
Human connections, importance, 230, 233, 240–242

I
Ideas, importance, 105
Imperialism, 99

Income
  decision, 188
  maximization, 145
  streams, multiplicity
      (possibility), 34
  wealth, contrast, 9
Income inequality
  overstatement, 70
  repair, 80
Income/wealth distribution,
    inequality, 70–71
Index funds, investment,
    178–180
Industrial Revolution, impact,
    53, 55, 120
Inequality indicators, level, 79
Inflation-adjusted incomes,
    increase, 9
Ingraham, Christopher, 74–75
Ingratitude, impact, 261
Innovation
  American Dream, relationship, 2
  businesses, impact, 120
  opportunities, 213
Institutional checks, goals, 64
Interest rates, short-term
    increases, 41
Intergeneration income
    correlation, data, 19
Interracial marriage rates,
    increase, 27, 86
Investment
  automation, 189
  buy-and-hold strategy, 194
  compounding, time allotment
      (determination), 181–182
  deregulation, impact, 114
  discipline, 186
  long-term strategy, 192
  opportunities, 56
  patience, 127–128
  portfolio, long-term value
      (factors), 181–183, 186
  procrastination, impact, 190–191
  risk, 169–170
  success, emotions
      (control), 189–190
  system, 185
  value, decline (reaction), 170
Investors
  facts, grounding (necessity), 206
  hurdles, 203–205
  media consumption, problem, 207
  It's Better Than It Looks
      (Easterbrook), 208

J
Jensen, Michael (mutual fund
    manager evaluation), 179
Jobs, Steve, 75
Jordan, Michael, 30–31

K
Keynes, John Maynard, 98
King, Jr., Martin Luther, 85
Knowledge, 250
  expansion, impact, 43, 56
  wealth, relationship, 55
Krugman, Paul, 98, 100
Kurzweil, Ray, 60

L
Large cap companies, emphasis, 244
Law of accelerating returns
    (Kurzweil), 60
Lawyer, becoming, 145
Learning, opportunities, 213
Legacy, establishment, 248
Leverage, 151
Life
  decumulation phase, 221
  maximization, 223

outcomes, habits (lagging indicator), 142
safety, increase, 52
Lifestyle
 decision, 188
 relapse, 189
Liquidity, increase, 114
Little Book of Common Sense Investing, The (Bogle), 183
Lomborg, Bjorn, 16
Long-term bonds, investment, 172
Long-term financial success/goals, 199, 217
Long-term gains, maximization, 125–126
Long-term growth money, investment, 184
Lower-income Americans, American Dream faith (loss), 4
Lump-sum fallacy, incorrectness, 74
Lynch, Peter, 179, 211

M
MacDonald, Heather, 16
Mackey, John, 231
Mainstream media
 American Dream enemy, 94–95
 grievance, amplification, 73
 meta-narrative, problems, 27, 202
 negativity, 31–32, 94
Maladaptive mindset, development, 10
Maltz, M., 136
Market
 corrections, losses (perception), 192
 declines, survival, 191–192
 distortion, illiquidity (relationship), 77
 failures, inevitability, 124
 timing, elimination, 147
Marry for money, 145
Material wants/needs, decline, 223
Maull, Fleet, 129–130
McCloskey, Deirdre, 44, 255
Media negativity (disconnect reason), 216
Memory dividend, 223
Mentoring, value, 247
Meritocracy, attack, 98
Middle class
 past, perception, 34
 shrinkage, belief, 18
 taxes, mechanisms, 78
Millionaire Next Door, The (Stanley), 80, 133
Millionaires
 attributes, 116
 characteristics, 114–117, 133–134
 facts, 110–111
 goal orientation, 116–117
 intentionality, practice, 116
 numbers (analysis), 19, 109–110
Minor, Lloyd, 58
Money
 independence, equivalence, 9
 management, 145, 185–186
 saving, 83–84
 time, equivalence, 43
Moral Arc, The (Shermer), 259
Moral complexity, moral uncertainty (contrast), 249
Mortality effect, 243
Mortgage
 preapproval, 155
 rates, increase, 152
Multiverse, existence, 258
Musk, Elon, 73, 75

Mutual funds, advantages, 177–178
Myth of American Inequality, The (Gramm/Ekelund/Early), 20

N
National media, negativity, 31
Negative emotions, impact, 130–131
Negative mindset, consequences, 7–8, 120
Nest eggs, building/keeping/enjoying, 227
Newcomb, Simon, 98
Next Millionaire Next Door, The (Stanley/Stanley Fallaw), 80
Nightingale, E., 136
No-go years, 224
Nonfinancial contributions, usage, 248
Novogratz, Jacqueline, 120

O
Obama, Barack (UN address), 103
Obesity
  avoidance, 232, 235–236
  rate, increase, 230
Obstacles, overcoming, 214
Occam's razor (William of Occam), 179–180
On margin purchases, 163
Opportunities, following, 123
Oppressors/oppressed, world division (Chomsky), 99–100
Optimism
  power, 211
  sense, 162
Option contracts, usage, 163–164
Overpopulation, claims, 46–47

P
Partisan propaganda, consumption (limitation), 121
Paying forward, power, 246
Perkins, Bill, 221, 223–224
Personal Finance Index (2023), 87
Personal industry (virtue), 66
Personal policy, impact, 105
Personal responsibility, importance, 127
Perspective, absence (disconnect reason), 215
Pessimism (American Dream roadblock), 50, 53
Pinker, Steven, 32, 51–52, 54, 208, 260
Plutarch's Lives (Plutarch), 63
Political campaigns
  negative impact, 102
  opposition, defining, 103
Political messages, negativity, 103
Political polarization, 62, 103
Politicians, American Dream enemy, 101–105
Politics
  discussion/anger, 101
  power, relationship, 102
Pooley, Gale L., 38, 44, 208
Population Bomb, The (Ehrlich), 97
Portfolio
  adjustment, 244
  annual return, determination, 182
  diversification, benefit (questions), 160–161
  earnings, estimation, 222
  risk, reduction, 195
Poverty
  default condition, 17
  global escape, 31

Price changes, 39f
 comparison/contrast,
  40–42
Problem-solving mindset,
 adoption, 214
Procrastination (American Dream
 roadblock), 50,
 190–191
Productivity, acceleration, 59
Progress
 continuation, 214
 imagining, impossibility, 56
 negative perception, 52
Prosperity Paradox, The
 (Easterbrook), 208
Psycho-Cybernetics (Maltz), 136
Public intellectuals, American
 Dream enemy, 97–101
Purchasing power, improvement, 31

Q
Quantitative Analysis of Investment
 Behavior (Dalbar report), 202

R
Racism, existence, 86
Radical responsibility,
 embracing, 129–132
Rationalization (self-
  deception), 130
Rational optimism, 212, 215
Rational Optimist, The (Ridley),
  46–47, 208
Reagan, Ronald (election TV
 commercial), 103
Real estate wealth,
 monetization, 145
Reality, distortion, 16
Real median earnings, decline, 8

Reciprocal tariffs (Trump
 announcement), 205
Renters, earned returns
 (relationship), 151
Republicans, optimism, 4
Republic, vigilance/virtue/wisdom
 (requirement), 64
Requiem for the American Dream
 (Chomsky), 98
Research assistance program,
 homeowner usage, 155
Resilience, American Dream
 (impact), 2
Resource abundance, growth, 46
Retirement
 amount, adequacy, 222
 cost, news avoidance (Bankrate
  survey), 162
 income, Vanguard fund
  (selection), 197–198
 portfolio, usage, 189
 years, division, 224
Return, increase, 222
Revenue stream, invention, 145
Ridley, Matt, 46, 208
Risk, reality, 217
Risk reduction, 212
 diversification, usage, 67
Risk-taking, 67, 82
 American Dream, impact, 2
Rosling, Hans, 208, 215

S
Sagan, Carl, 258–259
Same-sex marriage, support, 27
Sanders, Bernie, 84
Sarcopenia, 237
Satisfied expectations, revolution
 (disconnect reason), 216

Savings, 157, 186
  account, examination, 165–166
  amount, determination, 181
  investment, 127
  long-term security,
    relationship, 161–162
Scientific Revolution,
  impact, 53, 55
Secret of Shelter Island, the (Green), 5
Seed/venture capital, availability, 29
Self-employed viewpoint,
  benefit, 132
Self-esteem, low level
  (problem), 131
Self-gratification, focus
  (problem), 65
Self-help, impact, 136–137
September 11, 2001 (attacks), 203
Service
  trilemma, 59
  value, 123
Serving others, 65–66
Seven Habits of Highly Successful People, The (Covey), 136
Share price
  earnings, relationship, 171–172
  fluctuations, 171
Shellenberger, Michael, 16
Shermer, Michael, 259
Shopping, addiction, 158
Short Guide to a Long Life, A (Agus), 236
Short-term stock trading, 184
Siegel, Jeremy, 172, 175
Skepticism, sense, 207
Skills, absence (American Dream roadblock), 50
Sleep
  disruption, 239
  importance, 230, 238–240, 242
  loss, epidemic, 238

Slow-go years (retirement
  division), 224
Smoking, deaths, 230–231
Socialism
  problems, 123
  promotion, 100
Social media
  advantages, 159
  American Dream enemy, 95–96
  consumption, limitation, 121
  influence, 158
  negative news articles, sharing
    frequency (increase), 95–96
Social mobility, contrasts, 20
Social problems, systemic
  explanations (focus), 100
Social Security, income source, 161
Sowell, Thomas, 16–17, 97, 100
Spending, control (absence), 158
Spiritual significance, absence
  (disconnect reason), 216
Standard of living, long-term
  improvement, 43–44
Standard & Poor's 500 (S&P 500)
  investment, 175
  losses/gains, 205
  tech bubble decline, 203
Stanley Fallaw, Sarah, 80
Stanley, Thomas, 80, 133
Status anxiety (disconnect
  reason), 216
Stock market, crash (1987), 203
Stocks
  long-term returns, 170–171, 175
  performance, 170–177
  stability/safety, 175–176
Stocks for the Long Run: The Definitive Guide to Financial Market Returns & Long Term Investment Strategies (Siegel), 172, 191

Stoic wisdom, 64
Strategic planning, engagement, 248
Students for Liberty, donations, 249–250
Success
  commitment/personal responsibility, impact, 199
  habit, 135
  meaning, 122–123
  negative emotions, impact, 130–131
  sequence, 128
Superabundance (Tupy/Pooley), 38–39, 45, 208

T
Taxes
  annual taxes, payment amount, 183
  base broadening, impact, 78
  bracket creep, impact, 78
  double taxation, 77
  examination, 76–79
  payment, 76
  rate normalization, 78
  retroactivity, 77
  valuation, process, 76–77
Temperance (virtue), 67
Templeton, John, 211
Ten Global Trends Every Smart Person Should Know (Bailey/Tupy), 208
Ten Roads to Riches, The (Fisher), 146
Think and Grow Rich (Hill), 136
Time price
  comparison/contrast, 40–42
  decline, 39
  measurement, advantage, 45
  ratio, 38
Tracy, Brian, 131
Trailing stop, usage, 244

Treasury bills (T-bills), investment, 170, 172, 175
Tribalism, 103
Trump, Donald (American Dream)
  death statement, 104
  return promise, 129
Tupy, Marian L., 38, 44, 208
Tusculan Disputations (Cicero), 63

U
Ultra-processed foods, avoidance, 230–231
United States (America)
  country faith, loss, 23–24
  improvements, 34–36
  knowledge-based society, 124
  Land of Opportunity, 28
  millionaires, numbers (record), 109
  productivity rate, 28–29
  statistics, 25–26
Universe, history, 258–259
Unrealized gains, income (contrast), 76
Upward comparison, problems, 73
Upward mobility, absence (perception), 8
US Constitution, importance, 5
U.S. public education, American Dream enemy, 92–93
U.S. Treasury debt, downgrade, 205
US violent crime, decline (FBI Uniform Crime Reporting data), 17

V
Vaillant, George, 240
Values, promotion, 247
Value stocks, overweighting, 244
Vanguard
  annual expense ratio, 198
  investments, 180, 193–194

Vanguard (*continued*)
  stock/bond index funds, selection, 194
  Target Date Retirement Funds, 194–196, 244
Variable annuity, avoidance, 225–226
Vision/values, defining, 248
Volatility, 174
  reduction, 212
Volunteering, value, 247
Voting Rights Act of 1965, 85

W
Wade, Joel, 236
Walker, Matthew, 238, 239
Walton, Sam, 75
Wealth
  compounding, 7
  creation, knowledge (impact), 55
  equalizer, 9
  Oxfam perception, 79–80
  pathways, 144
  understanding/measurement, 250

Wealth accumulation, 82–85
  factors, 88–89
  taxable income, redefinition (problems), 76–77
Wealth-building habits, 146
Wealth Survey (Schwab), 159
Wealth tax, perception, 76
Wealthy, myths, 114–115
Why We Sleep: Unlocking the Power of Sleep and Dreams (Walker), 238–239
Winfrey, Oprah (life change), 75
Wisdom, importance, 250
Women, optimism, 4
Work, time consumption, 83
World Happiness Report (2025), 62

Y
Young Americans, American Dream faith (loss), 4

Z
Zero-dated options, usage, 163–164
Zero-sum capitalism, 50–51
Ziglar, Z., 136